Discover Delphi

INTERNATIONAL COMPUTER SCIENCE SERIES

Consulting Editor **A D McGettrick** *University of Strathclyde*

SELECTED TITLES IN THE SERIES

Discover Delphi

Programming principles explained

Shirley Williams
Sue Walmsley
The University of Reading

ADDISON WESLEY

Harlow, England ● Reading, Massachusetts ● Menlo Park, California
New York ● Don Mills, Ontario ● Amsterdam ● Bonn ● Sydney ● Singapore
Tokyo ● Madrid ● San Juan ● Milan ● Mexico City ● Seoul ● Taipei

Addison Wesley Longman Limited
Edinburgh Gate
Harlow
Essex CM20 2JE
England

and Associated Companies throughout the World.

Cover designed by Senate
and printed by The Riverside Printing Co. (Reading) Ltd.
Line illustrations by Margaret Macknelly, Tadley, UK
Typeset by 34
Printed and bound in Great Britain by Biddles Ltd, Guildford and King's Lynn.

First printed 1998

ISBN 0-201-34286-3
6|2|99

British Library Cataloguing-in-Publication Data
A catalogue record for this book is available from the British Library

Library of Congress Cataloging-in-Publication Data
Williams, Shirley A.
    Discover Delphi: programming principles explained / Shirley
Williams, Sue Walmsley.
        p.   cm. – (International computer science series)
    Includes bibliographical references and index.
    ISBN 0-201-34286-3 (softback)
    1. Delphi (Computer file)   2. Computer software – Development.
I. Walmsley, Sue, 1943– . II. Title. III. Series.
    QA76.76.D47W535   1998
    005.26'8 – dc21   98-29593
                                                       CIP

To our families

Contents

Trademark notice

Borland, C++ Builder, Delphi, J Builder, and TurboPascal are trademarks or registered trademarks of Borland International Inc.

Java, Modula-2, and SUN are trademarks of Sun Microsystems Inc.

Microsoft Internet Explorer, Microsoft Paint, Microsoft Word, Visual Basic C++, Windows, Windows 3.1, Windows 95, and Windows NT are trademarks or registered trademarks of Microsoft Corporation.

UNIX is a trademark, licensed through X/Open Company Ltd

Preface

....

Delphi is a prize-winning language product. It is an easy to use tool for event-driven object-oriented Windows programming. The underlying language of Delphi is Object Pascal.

The Delphi environment is exciting because it is event driven. The very first programs within this book respond to actions from the user. In our experience this results not only in the programmers being pleased with their products but in their peers being impressed too. This has been very noticeable in our teaching of Delphi.

This book aims to develop the skills required by a professional programmer. On completion of this book you should be able to:

- program proficiently within the Delphi environment
- participate as a team member in large software engineering projects
- produce rapid prototypes
- learn further programming languages with ease.

These skills are taught within the Delphi environment, allowing the reader the fun of producing attractive Graphical User Interfaces (GUIs – gooeys), while learning the fundamentals of programming, which will be transferable to other imperative and object-based languages.

This book is aimed at people with limited or no programming experience – typically a self-taught BASIC programmer, a student with an initial programming qualification ('A' level, Further Education or a single university module), or a person who has not done any programming.

We intend this book to be a *guide* to Delphi – it is not meant to be encyclopaedic. Nor is it aimed at professional programmers with several years' experience. In much the same way, a tourist to Greece would want a guide to the main sites of the city of Delphi and a potted history of the Oracle and her ambiguous ways, whereas a Greek scholar would seek a different set of texts.

Delphi 1, 2, 3, 4

This book is equally applicable to all the main releases of Delphi that are currently available (see Section 1.3). Where there are differences we will explain them.

We expect new versions of both Delphi and the Windows operating system to be released. We are confident that the material in this book will still be applicable.

The Delphi environment's online help is extensive and provides the user with information that is orthogonal to that covered in the book.

Programming style

We assume familiarity with the use of a PC and the appropriate Windows operating system. The Glossary in Appendix B provides help with technical terms.

Within our programs we have aimed to produce readable code, by careful choice of identifiers and layout. Programmers should include comments to help the reader understand what the code does. Indeed, many software producers have a house style; it is not uncommon to find that 50% of a professional listing is comments, depending on the extent of other documentation available.

In many of our listings, the surrounding text explains in detail what the code does; in these cases we have not included extensive comments. To ease the cross-referencing of lines of code we include line numbers in most listings. We have used the style offered by Delphi when listings are printed. The programmer must not type the line numbers when entering the code. Our line numbers may not be exactly reflected in the programs you type, depending on various factors.

Object Pascal is not case sensitive: NUMBER means the same as number, Number and nUMBER. For common words we have followed the standard used in the online Delphi help systems. For reserved words we have used bold font, for example **begin**, the default for the Delphi editor.

We have run the code included in this book under all releases and versions of Delphi and on a variety of computers. The astute reader will be able to spot examples of screen shots taken from different versions of Delphi.

How this book is organized

We introduce appropriate components chapter by chapter alongside basic programming concepts. From the start the programmer is using components, which themselves are objects, but we postpone detailed discussion of object-oriented techniques in favour of emphasizing the event-driven strengths.

Here are brief descriptions of the 15 chapters and the appendices:

- Chapter 1 presents a brief overview of Delphi and develops a first program.
- Chapter 2 discusses the Delphi programming environment in greater detail. We will develop a program that allows the user to select and display an image from the file store.
- Chapter 3 introduces arithmetic in Object Pascal; the Delphi edit component is used for inputting and outputting data. This Edit component uses simple strings which we will discuss briefly.
- Chapter 4 introduces conditional statements, that change the order of code execution, and message boxes that show what is happening. The chapter concludes with the prototype of a guessing game.

C-based products (such as Visual C++ and Java). BASIC (Beginner's All-purpose Symbolic Instruction Code) is easy to learn. However, most BASIC code is interpreted. An interpreter works source line by source line at run time and so there is no opportunity for optimizing across the program. So interpreted BASIC applications run much slower than the Delphi compiled equivalent. A compiler parses the whole program one or more times and as a result generates efficient code to be executed. C is a powerful language, with many of the advantages of programming in assembler. It is weakly typed, allowing programmers to manipulate all types of data and operations. Unfortunately the many features available in C make it more difficult to use, and inadvertent manipulation can lead to errors that are difficult to find.

1.3 Delphi versions

There are currently four releases of Delphi available:

- **Delphi 1** – the 16-bit release running under Windows 3.1 and Windows 95, sometimes called Delphi 16.
- **Delphi 2** – the 32-bit release running under Windows 95 and NT, sometimes called Delphi 32.
- **Delphi 3** – as Delphi 2, with enhancements allowing the easy creation and management of DLLs (Dynamic Linked Libraries), including those that can be downloaded across the Internet and viewed in a Web browser.
- **Delphi 4** – as Delphi 3, designed to create large-scale 'enterprise class' applications in heterogeneous environments.

There are variations within the releases. Delphi 3 and 4 offer three versions:

- **Standard** – the entry level version.
- **Professional** – offering additional components and providing the source code for the Delphi component library.
- **Client-Server** – the most expensive and extensive, including many database facilities and tools for group working.

In this text we cover the essentials of Delphi, the majority of which are equally applicable to all versions. Where there are differences these are highlighted.

The version of Windows used will also have some minimal effect on the appearance of Delphi. For example, the appearance of a window border under Windows 3.1 (on the left of Figure 1.1) is different from that of Windows 95 (on the right), even when running the same release of Delphi.

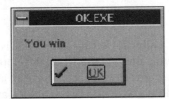
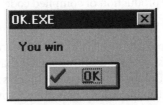

Figure 1.1   The same box displayed in Windows 3.1 and Windows 95.

Chapter 1

Introduction to Delphi

1.1 Introduction

In this chapter we will present a brief overview of Delphi and develop a program that illustrates how readily a Delphi programmer can produce a professional looking application. Detailed explanation of the constituent parts of the Delphi environment is postponed until the following chapter.

1.2 Programming in Delphi

Programming in Delphi is fun. It is an easy to use tool for event-driven object-oriented Windows programming. The underlying language of Delphi is Object Pascal. Pascal gained popularity as a programming language because of:

- its support for structured programming
- the production of compiled code
- the ease of writing correct code.

Delphi adds to Pascal the power of Graphical User Interfaces (GUIs, pronounced gooeys). Delphi itself has a GUI that programmers use when developing programs using Delphi. Professional Windows programs almost always have an attractive GUI. Delphi enables all programmers to produce a GUI with the right look and feel.

Alternatives to Delphi are BASIC-based products (such as Visual BASIC) and

1

At the end of each chapter there is a quiz and exercises. Three answers are offered for each quiz question; *one or more* may be right. The answers are in Appendix D.

Acknowledgements

Delphi was developed by Borland (Inprise) and we are grateful to them for producing a superior product.

We have taught Delphi to many groups, ranging from school children and undergraduates to postgraduates, colleagues and industrialists. We are grateful to all of them for their comments.

The University of Reading has supported our move to Delphi as the language through which students are first introduced to programming. We are particularly grateful to our colleagues in Computer Science and Cybernetics for their encouragement in this exciting development. We also wish to thank the staff at Addison Wesley Longman for their support in producing this book.

Finally we would like thank our families for their help and encouragement. They have read and corrected many drafts of this book, tested many programs, and provided drawings. Any remaining mistakes are our own.

Shirley Williams and Sue Walmsley
Reading, June 1998

- Chapter 5 uses basic iteration techniques and illustrates their use with graphics. As an advanced topic we use a timer component.

- Chapter 6 introduces further non-deterministic iteration techniques and extends our use of graphics. We describe the use of files for data handling. We will also discuss the running of older-style Pascal programs within the Delphi environment.

- Chapter 7 describes the array data structure, which can associate a single name with a collection of data values. A number of Delphi's components echo the array concept and we will use the StringGrid and DrawGrid components. We will present a deeper discussion of strings; the string facilities vary according to the version of Delphi that is in use.

- Chapter 8 introduces the concept of scope and records; these are illustrated by the use of single and multiple forms.

- Chapter 9 tells the programmer how to write recursive and non-recursive functions and procedures, comparing these with event handlers. We use the ListBox component to illustrate the use of procedures. A ListBox displays a list of items which the programmer can manipulate.

- Chapter 10 describes the anatomy of objects and demonstrates their use. We will discuss how to manage the memory allocated to objects.

- Chapter 11 explains how Delphi and the programmer can use exceptions to trap run time errors. We demonstrate exception handling in a program that allows the user to *drag and drop* shapes around a form.

- Chapter 12 introduces the related topics of enumerated types and sets. We illustrate their use with the Delphi check boxes and radio buttons.

- Chapter 13 demonstrates how units are used to provide libraries of objects and operations.

- Chapter 14 examines the idea and simple uses of pointers, before discussing linked list structures that are built using pointers.

- Chapter 15 indicates briefly some of the ways in which the programmer may wish to extend the skills developed so far.

- Appendix A describes the use of the integrated debugger.

- Appendix B is a glossary of technical terms.

- Appendix C lists suggested reading and books we have found useful.

- Appendix D contains answers to quizzes.

- Appendix E contains a summary of the main Object Pascal constructs.

In some chapters advanced material is included, which the reader can omit at the first reading, as indicated by the asterisk appended to the section heading. Subsequent chapters may, however, reference this material. For instance, main menus are introduced at the end of Chapter 2. They help produce professional looking programs but some programmers find implementing them tricky. Later in the book other programs will require them.

(1.4) Starting Delphi

Delphi has to be installed in a computer to run. It will not work directly from the CD on which it is provided. If it is not installed, the CD will help you do this.

Having started the PC, find the Delphi window. With the left mouse button double click (i.e. click twice in rapid succession) one of the Delphi program icons (which look like Greek temples, see Figure 1.2) to start the Delphi environment. Delphi can also be started using the File Manager or Explorer, or the Start button.

Figure 1.2 The Delphi 3 icon.

Starting Delphi 3 should produce a screen similar to that shown in Figure 1.3. Delphi 1 and 2 will look slightly different, as will other variants of Delphi 3, but the essentials will be the same.

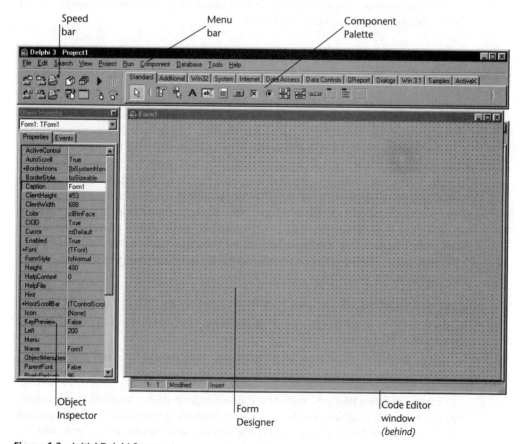

Figure 1.3 Initial Delphi 3 screen.

When using a small screen there may not be room to show all of the options and so a scroll bar will appear to give access to distant options.

With a pre-installed version of Delphi there may be some differences from what is shown here. Previous users may have customized the setting to what they like. Alternatively system managers may have provided different initial screens. At the very least there will be the menu bar with a list of options. The programmer can expose whatever is missing by selecting View from the menu.

The visible parts are normally:

- The menu bar, along the top of the screen containing the list of options File, Edit, etc.
- The speed bar attached to the menu bar (the set of 14 buttons on the left)
- The Component Palette also attached to the menu bar (the tabbed list on the right)
- The Object Inspector (on the left-hand side)
- The Form Designer window and, behind that, the Code Editor window.

These constitute the major part of the Delphi Interactive Development Environment (IDE). Chapter 2 describes their roles in detail.

1.5 Saving projects

For any one project Delphi creates a number of files. For ease of working it is wise to create a directory for each project and then store all the files associated with it in the one place.

The default name for a Delphi project is `Project1.dpr` and the `.dpr` extension is essential so that the file is recognized as a Delphi project. The name should be chosen to indicate what the project is about. Windows 3.1 limits names to eight characters whereas newer versions of Windows allow longer names. Each unit in a project contains Object Pascal code; the default name for the first unit is `Unit1.pas`. This should be stored with a unique name. Every form has an associated unit. The form file will be stored under the same name as the unit but with a `.dfm` extension (Delphi Form). To create a backup of a current project it is essential to copy all of the following:

1. The project file, with the `.dpr` extension.
2. All the unit files, with the `.pas` extension; there may be more than one of these in advanced projects.
3. All the form files, with the `.dfm` extension; there should be a matching unit file with the same name for each form.

A variety of other files are created containing information about the environment options set and backup copies of the previous versions of code files. Compiling a unit creates a compiled file. The compiled file has the same name as the unit and the extension `.dcu`. Linking the project joins the compiled units together with other project information to create an executable file with the name of the project and the extension .exe.

This executable file is all that is needed to distribute an application (so others can run it). No other files are needed for this .exe file to execute, nor is the Delphi environment needed. More ambitious projects may use Dynamic Linked Libraries (DLLs), which can also be generated with Delphi, and these DLLs will be in files with the extension .dll, which must be distributed with the executable file.

1.6 Exiting Delphi

The Exit option for Delphi is selected from the File menu of the main Delphi window. Options like Exit are conventionally written as File|Exit. As with most Windows applications this can be selected using the mouse or by pressing Alt+F and then X, where Alt is the key normally to the left of the space bar on the keyboard. If there have been any changes to the current project Delphi will ask if these changes should be saved. It is tempting to answer these questions mechanically but it is much wiser to consider the options carefully. If the use of Delphi was experimental, it may not be necessary to save each experiment. If changes to a project have not had the desired effect, it may be best to revert to the previous version rather than save the changes. In general (as with other computer work) it is wise to save any computer work every few minutes. An error may occur necessitating rebooting of the computer and any unsaved work will be lost. Important work should be backed up onto multiple floppy or zip discs, a tape streamer or a central file server over several generations. These should be stored in different places, preferably in a fireproof safe.

1.7 The traditional first program

In this project the programmer will only need to enter two lines of code and set some properties in the Object Inspector. The completed program will allow the user to click a button and then display a message saying *Hello World!*. A Quit button will be provided to exit when finished.

A program that says *Hello World!* is a traditional first example program. In most programming languages this would merely display the words as plain text on the screen. In this Delphi version a Graphical User Interface will be created and used to display this time-honoured message on the press of the appropriate button.

1. Create a new directory for storing this project and start Delphi.

2. Use the Object Inspector to change the Caption property on the form to say Hello. To do this, with the form selected, choose the properties page of the Object Inspector, scroll to the Caption option and click on it. Replace the text Form1 to the right of Caption with Hello (see Figure 1.4).

3. Put a button on the form, by clicking on the button icon on the Standard page of the Component Palette (see Figure 1.5) and then clicking on the form (double clicking on the button icon has the same effect).

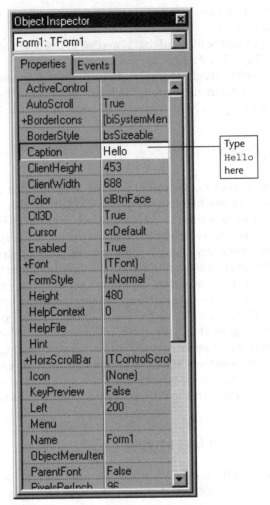

Figure 1.4   Set the caption property of the form.

4. If necessary, reposition the button by dragging with the mouse.

5. Change the Caption on the button to say Press me. If the button is not selected within the Object Inspector window, use the pull down menu immediately below the Object Inspector bar to select the button, called Button1 (see Figure 1.6). The Name of the button could be changed using the Object Inspector, but in this example Button1 is an acceptable Name but not a helpful Caption.

6. Add a second button, position it in the bottom right corner and change its Caption to Quit.

7. Add a label: the position of the label component on the Component Palette is shown in Figure 1.7. Position the label in the middle of the screen below the Press me button. Change the Caption of the label to Hello World!.

First click the
button on the
Component Palette

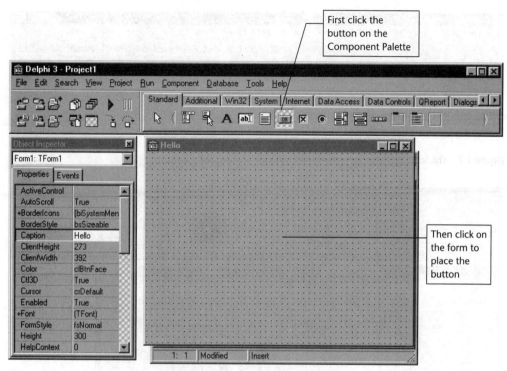

Then click on
the form to
place the
button

Figure 1.5   Adding a button to a form.

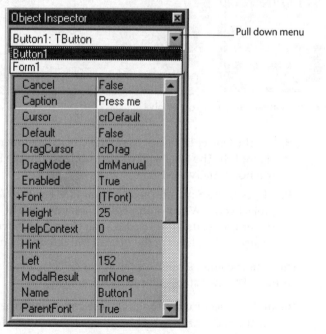

Pull down menu

Figure 1.6   Selecting an object with the Object Inspector.

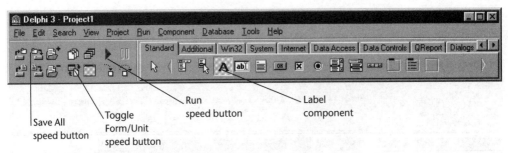

Figure 1.7 The label component and speed buttons.

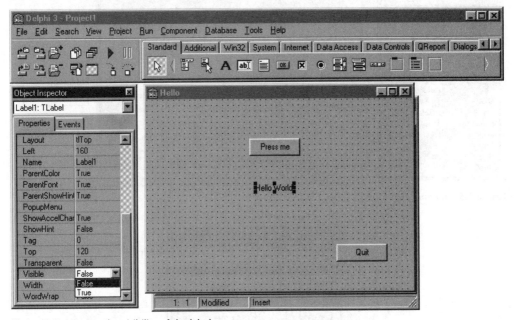

Figure 1.8 Setting the visibility of the label.

8. Use the Object Inspector to set the `Visible` property of the label to `False` (see Figure 1.8). The label will remain visible within the Form Designer; at run time it will not initially be visible.

9. Click on the Save All speed button (see Figure 1.7) to save the unit code and project code. When prompted for a name call the unit code `UHello.pas` and the project code `PHello.dpr`. Make sure you have selected the directory you created earlier. Later in the text we will discuss the naming of units and projects.

The project could be run now but it has no functionality, that is to say it would do nothing. The next steps will add functionality.

10. In the Object Inspector select the Events page for `Button2`. Double click opposite the `OnClick` event. This will open the Unit Code Editor window as shown in Figure 1.9.

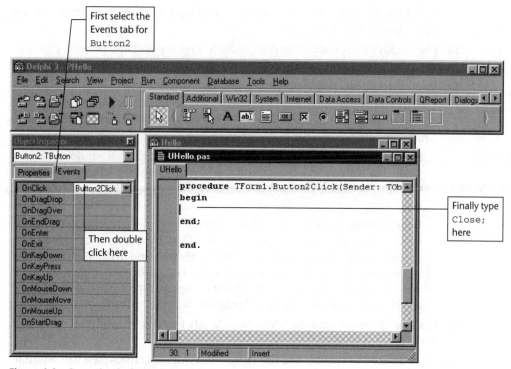

Figure 1.9 Open the Code window.

11. Between the words **begin** and **end** type the word Close followed by a semi-colon (see Figure 1.9).

12. Bring the Form Designer in front of the Code Editor window by pressing the Toggle Form/Unit speed button; the button is labelled in Figure 1.7. Avoid closing the code editor box by using the Windows close facility. If this is done by mistake Delphi will prompt for the unit code to be saved (see Figure 1.10). At this point the programmer can cancel the close.

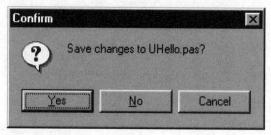

Figure 1.10 Delphi prompt.

13. In the Object Inspector select the Events page for Button1. Double click opposite the OnClick event. This will open the Code Editor window at the event

handler `Button1Click`. Now between the **begin** and **end** type the following line: `Label1.Visible:= True;`

14. Use the Save All speed button once again to save the unit and project. This time it will not prompt for names, but will use those provided on the first save.

15. Select the Run speed button (see Figure 1.7 for its position).

16. This should display the Hello form with the two buttons visible, but the label does not show. If this does not happen, there must be a mistake somewhere which needs to be found and corrected.

   ● If the program fails to compile, stopping in the Code Editor window, it is very likely that the code has been mistyped. Check carefully with the above – particularly check that a 1 (one) has not been entered as an l (*el*) – and make the correction.

   ● If the program starts to execute but when the form is displayed it looks wrong, close it and check the properties. If the Quit button is not working, the running Delphi form can be closed using the close icon in the Window box or by pressing Alt+F4. A common error is to change the visibility of an object other than the label to `False`. Use the Object Inspector to check for and correct such errors. The corrected program can now be run.

17. Click on 'Press me' and the 'Hello World!' label should be displayed (see Figure 1.11).

18. Click on the Quit button and the application will close: the screen will return to the design form.

19. Exit Delphi by choosing File|Exit from the Delphi menu.

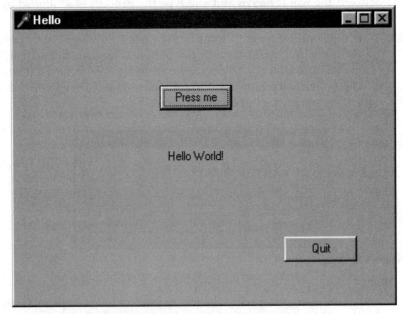

Figure 1.11   The running program.

(1.8) Summary

In this chapter we have presented an overview of Delphi. We have developed a program that displays a simple greeting. Using a conventional programming language, producing a program that displayed an interface like this would have involved an expert programmer in producing hundreds of lines of code. With Delphi the programmer had to set a few properties and enter two lines of code.

Quiz

1. Which was the first release of Delphi?
    (a) Delphi 1
    (b) Delphi 2
    (c) Delphi 4

2. What does GUI stand for?
    (a) Good User Interface
    (b) Graphical User Interface
    (c) Graphical Unit Interface

3. Delphi produces executable code by:
    (a) executing
    (b) interpreting
    (c) compiling

4. Which of the following are true?
    (a) Forms produced under different operating systems may look different.
    (b) Forms are identical whichever operating system is used.
    (c) Delphi 3 will not work with Windows 3.1.

5. What is the extension of a project file?
    (a) `.dfm`
    (b) `.dpr`
    (c) `.pas`

6. How often should a program be saved?
    (a) once a week
    (b) at the end of development
    (c) every few minutes

7. Which speed button should be pressed to change the top window from the Form Designer to the Code Editor, or vice versa?
    (a) Run
    (b) Toggle Form/Unit
    (c) Save All

8. How should a Delphi session be terminated?
    (a) Choosing File from the menu and selecting Exit.
    (b) Turning the computer off.
    (c) It should not be terminated; Delphi should be left running.

9. The Delphi icon looks like which of the following?
    (a) a Greek temple
    (b) a triangle
    (c) a capital D

10. Why may you need a backup copy of your program files?
    (a) To allow working on another computer.
    (b) In case your computer crashes and loses all your work.
    (c) In case you decide that the changes you have made to a program should be abandoned.

Exercises

1. Adapt the program in Section 1.7 so that the message it displays contains your name.

2. Add a third button, with the Caption 'or me', that has the following code in its OnClick event:

    ```
    Label1.Visible:= False;
    ```

    Run this program and watch the label appear and disappear as the buttons 'Press me' and 'or me' are clicked.

3. Write a program with five square buttons running diagonally across the form. Use the Object Inspector to change their captions to the five single words:

    ```
    Press, Me, I, go, Quit
    ```

    For each button open the OnClick event handler and add code so that when the user clicks that button it disappears. The Quit button closes the form.

Chapter 2

The Delphi programming environment

2.1 Introduction

In this chapter we will describe the Delphi programming environment and illustrate its use by designing programs. We will select predefined components from the Component Palette and place them on a prototype form. The Object Inspector will be used to set properties for these components and to associate events with the components. The code for the events will be entered in the Code Editor window.

One of the programs developed allows the user to select an image from the file store and display it. The second, more advanced example will introduce menus and show how they can be incorporated into programs.

2.2 Objects and events

Objects are a fundamental building block for software development with Delphi. Later in this book we will develop our own objects, but initially we will use pre-existing objects known as components. Essentially an object is data and associated operations. In the first chapter we placed a button on a form. The button is an object. The data associated with the button is represented by its properties, including its position and caption. The operations associated with an object are called *methods*; these include events. An event is something that may happen at run time; for example, the event OnClick for a button refers to whenever the user clicks on the button with the mouse. There may be other methods, not associated with events, that are part of an object.

Almost all programming with Delphi uses objects and so it is sometimes called object-oriented programming. Most of the applications which are written respond to events occurring to objects at run time and so Delphi programs can be called event driven.

2.3 The Object Inspector

The Object Inspector is displayed on the left-hand side of the Delphi screen. It works together with the Form Designer. The programmer can use the Object Inspector to examine and change *published properties* and *events* of objects, including the form and components placed on it. The component designer will have decided which properties and events should be published, and as such are accessible via the Object Inspector. There may be other properties and events that are not published. The programmer can use the Delphi help facility to get a full list for each component; this will include details of methods that are not events. Help can be accessed from the Delphi tool bar or by pressing the function key F1, as with most other Windows applications.

The Object Inspector is a two-page grid. The two pages are labelled *Properties* and *Events*. Programmers can use the tabs to flick from one page to the other. Clicking with the left mouse button on the Events tab will cause the Events page to be displayed, while clicking on the Properties tab will cause the Properties page to be displayed. With Delphi 1 the tabs are at the bottom of the Object Inspector's window, whereas with later releases they are at the top (see Figure 2.1), but apart from this they do the same job.

The current object in Figure 2.1 is Form1 of the class TForm1, as shown at the top of the Object Inspector. The left-hand column lists all possible properties that can be set via the Object Inspector. The list on the right contains the values corresponding to the properties on the left. Most properties in Figure 2.1 contain default values. For example, the Caption contains the string Form1. At design time the programmer can change this string in the Object Inspector to any appropriate string, by clicking on the row labelled Caption and then replacing the existing Form1 with the required string.

It is possible for the programmer to set all of the properties in the Object Inspector at design time, but also code can be used to change the values of properties at run time. The effect of individual changes can be tested by making the change and then selecting the Run speed button (or choosing Run|Run from the menu bar or pressing F9). The run can be terminated by pressing the Alt key and F4 (Alt+F4) or by clicking

Current object ——

Drop down menu of
other available objects

Properties ——

Current value of
properties
(default or as set by
programmer)

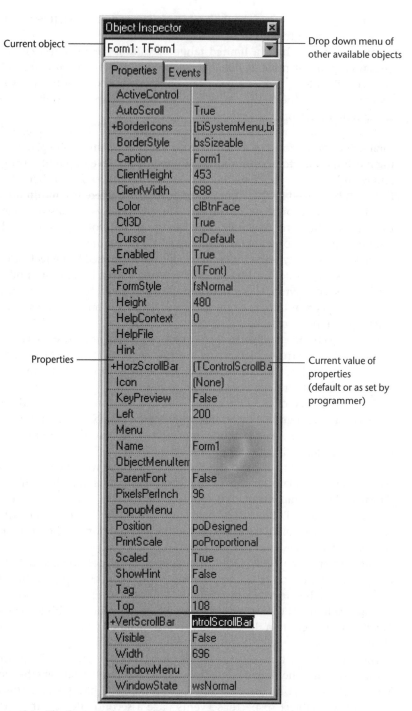

Figure 2.1   The Properties page of the Object Inspector.

the close icon at the top of the form (the small bar on the top left with Windows 3.1, the X in the top right with other versions of Windows).

Some properties have a limited range of values. For instance, choosing Color displays a pull down list of possible colours and the programmer can choose one; alternatively a long numeric code can be entered according to RGB values. Some properties can just be True or False; for example, Enabled is only True if the form can accept input from the keyboard.

Other properties may require a number to be entered. For example, Height is the total height of the form in screen pixels; in Figure 2.1 this is 480 pixels. When resizing it is important to bear in mind that screens can have different settings and sizes and what looks acceptable on one screen may not be so on another. The prototype form can be resized in the Form Designer window. There is a minimum size below which a form cannot be shrunk further. The programmer can also change the size of the form in the Form Designer, by clicking on the prototype form and using the mouse to drag the corner of the form to make it bigger or smaller.

The Name property is the logical name for the form used by Object Pascal. As such, it must obey the rules for identifiers of starting with a letter or an underscore, not including special symbols or spaces. On the other hand, the Caption property is the text that appears at the top of the form and this may contain spaces or special characters such as punctuation.

Most objects have properties, so when changing properties it is important to ensure that the correct object name is displayed at the top of the Object Inspector; clicking on the form in the Form Designer will ensure that the form itself is the current object rather than a component placed on it.

The Events page of the Object Inspector for the form offers a series of possible events that the program may act upon (see Figure 2.2). Notice that the events do not have default values, so the programmer must provide the actions to take on all events to be handled.

Double clicking on an event in the Object Inspector will open up the Code Editor window at a template for that event. The programmer can then enter the Object Pascal code for that event. For example, by double clicking next to the event OnClick the Code Editor will open as shown in Figure 2.3. The Code window holds the code for the unit associated with the current form. The Form Designer is described in detail later in this section.

Once actions for an event exist, the name of the procedure associated with those actions will appear on the right-hand side of the Object Inspector. In this example FormClick is the procedure associated with the OnClick event and so will appear in the right column of the Object Inspector. Procedures such as this are known as *event handlers* as they contain the code that will be executed when the events occur at run time.

The programmer can control whether the Form Designer or Code window is in front by pressing the Toggle Form/Unit speed button (alternatively the menu option View|Toggle Form/Unit can be selected, or pressing F12 has the same effect).

Within the Object Inspector's Events page a second click on the OnClick will cause the Code Editor to open again at the same procedure.

If the programmer finds the code entered for an event is wrong, it is tempting to

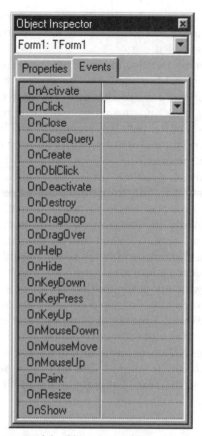

Figure 2.2   The Events page of the Object Inspector.

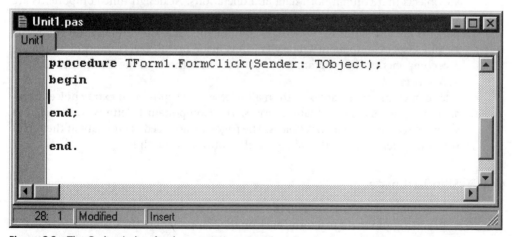

Figure 2.3   The Code window for the OnClick event.

delete the whole of the event handler. This is unwise and may lead to problems. A safer approach is first to disconnect the event handler and then to delete the parts of code the programmer added.

The event handler can be disconnected from the event by deleting its name from the appropriate event field in the Object Inspector; the program will need to be recompiled (not just run) for this change to be registered. The event handler will remain in the unit code and the programmer can reconnect it via the Object Inspector. To the right of the `OnClick` event there will be a pull down arrow giving access to all valid procedures; for instance, by choosing `FormClick` the actions will be reconnected with the event.

If the event handler is definitely no longer required it still should not be fully deleted by the programmer; only the parts that have been added by the programmer should be deleted. This is because Delphi adds information about the event to other parts of the code and may enter an error state if the procedure of an event disappears while the other parts remain. When all the programmer-added information is deleted the procedure becomes empty. On saving the unit, empty procedures are discarded along with related information.

The general rule with any of the code is that the programmer should not change any of the parts provided by the Delphi environment as doing so will often lead to compile or run time errors. For example, the programmer can change the unit name by going to the top of the unit code and typing over the existing name, but this does not change the other references to this unit or the file name. So there will be a compiler error: *module header is incorrect*. The unit name should only be changed by saving it as a new unit. This can be done by selecting File|Save As, which will update all references.

2.4) The Component Palette

Components can be considered as the building blocks of Delphi applications. These are objects that contain both data and operations. At design time components are visual objects that can be manipulated by the programmer. Many, but not all, components are also controls, which are components that are visible at run time. The Delphi Visual Component Library (VCL) is made up of objects, most of which are also components; the programmer usually accesses these via the Component Palette – see Figure 2.4.

Similar components are offered in all releases of Delphi, with extra choices available in some versions and later releases. The Component Palette is constructed as several pages of component choices. The pages are accessed via the tabs at the top of the Component Palette (the tabs are at the bottom with Delphi 1).

2.4.1   Standard page

The components represented on the Standard page are described in Table 2.1.

To add a component to a form, click on the component in the Component Palette: this will cause its icon to be depressed and the arrow icon on the palette will no

Table 2.1   Standard page.

Description	Normal purpose
MainMenu	Designs ordinary menus, that go along the top of a form
PopupMenu	Designs pop up menus, that can be linked to controls and then will appear when the user presses the right-hand mouse button, over that control
Label	Labels other components or displays one line of text that does not usually change
Edit	Displays an area in which the user and program can enter a single line of text
MemoBox	Allows the user to enter multiple lines of text or the program to display a number of lines
Button	Creates a simple command button
CheckBox	Creates options where there are only two choices
RadioButton	Used to create a group of mutually exclusive options
ListBox	Displays a list of choices
ComboBox	A combination of an edit and list box, allowing the user to choose from an existing list or enter a choice
ScrollBar	Allows movement through a range of choices
GroupBox	Groups items so they behave as an entity
RadioGroup	A group box designed for radio buttons
Panel	A general box for grouping other components

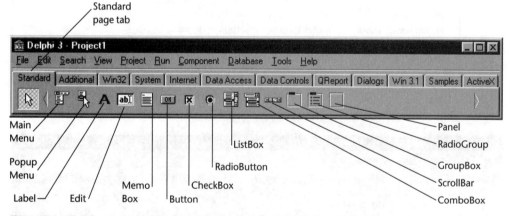

Figure 2.4   The Component Palette for Delphi 3 Professional Edition.

longer be depressed. Subsequently clicking on the form will cause the component to be placed on the form. If it has a visual representation, that will appear, otherwise an appropriate icon will be shown. Visual components can be resized when selected by dragging one of the corners using the mouse. If the component is in the wrong place it can be dragged to the required position.

2.4.2   Dialogs page

The Dialogs page allows access to components that can interact with the operating system, allowing the programmer to introduce dialog boxes for actions such as opening files. The Dialogs page of the Component Palette is accessed by clicking on the Dialogs tab: see Figure 2.5.

Each component on this page enables the application to use the appropriate Windows common dialog box. Some of the common dialog boxes differ in format between versions of Windows; where this is the case Delphi 1 offers the Windows 3.1 dialog box.

The components represented in Figure 2.5 are described in Table 2.2.

When a dialog component is placed on the form at design time, that component's icon appears – see Figure 2.6. The component does not appear on the form at run time.

Table 2.2   Dialogs page.

Description	Purpose
OpenDialog	Creates the open file dialog box
SaveDialog	Creates the save file dialog box
OpenPictureDialog	As OpenDialog, with an image preview window (only available with later versions)
SavePictureDialog	As SaveDialog, with an image preview window (only available with later versions)
FontDialog	Creates a dialog box for choosing fonts
ColorDialog	Creates a dialog box for choosing colours
PrintDialog	Creates the print dialog box
PrinterSetupDialog	Creates the printer setup dialog box
FindDialog	Creates a dialog box for entering text to be found
ReplaceDialog	Creates a dialog box for entering two texts: one to be found and one to replace it

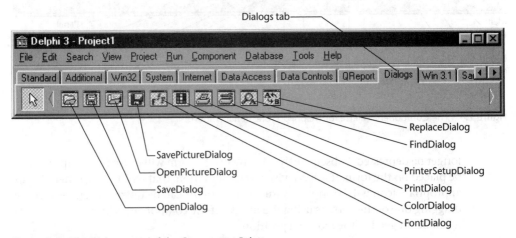

Figure 2.5   The Dialogs page of the Component Palette.

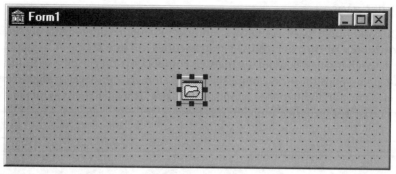

Figure 2.6 An OpenDialog component on a form.

To open the dialog box at run time the component's `Execute` method has to be called from code. The `Execute` method is part of a dialog component that displays the appropriate Windows box at run time. For instance the programmer could add a button to the form in Figure 2.6, open its `OnClick` event and add the single line of code `OpenDialog1.Execute` as shown in Listing 2.1. Delphi has automatically generated the lines labelled 1, 2 and 4, while the programmer entered line 3.

Listing 2.1   The `OnClick` event for Button1

```
1: procedure TForm1.Button1Click(Sender: TObject);
2: begin
3:   OpenDialog1.Execute;
4: end;
```

When the program is run and the user clicks the button a dialog box similar to the one shown in Figure 2.7 will be displayed.

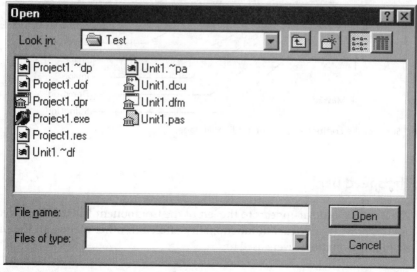

Figure 2.7 Execution of an open dialog.

2.4.3   Other pages

The Additional page contains a number of useful components including those specifically labelled in Figure 2.8 and described in Table 2.3.

The other pages contain a variety of components that will be useful in a diverse range of applications. Accomplished programmers can develop their own components and add them to the Component Palette. Third-party components can also be incorporated into the Component Palette.

Table 2.3   Additional page.

Description	Purpose
BitButton	Creates a button component that can display a bitmap, including some predefined options
SpeedButton	Creates a button that can display a glyph (a bitmap or picture) but not a caption
MaskEdit	Creates an edit box that can use a mask to allow only valid input, for instance to allow only an alphabetic character to be entered
StringGrid	Creates a grid in which textual data can be represented in rows and columns
DrawGrid	Creates a grid in which data can be represented in rows and columns
Image	Displays an image (bitmap, icon or metafile)
Shape	Draws a limited number of geometric shapes
CheckListBox	A combination of a list box and check boxes, available with later versions

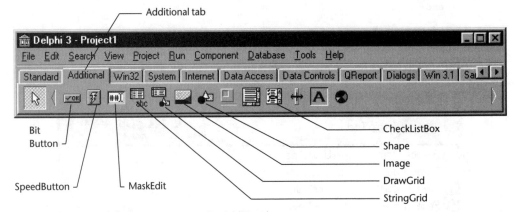

Figure 2.8   Some of the components on the Additional page.

2.5   The speed bar

The Delphi speed bar appears to the left of the Component Palette. The speed bar is used to provide shortcuts to functionality offered in other menus. In the previous chapter speed buttons were used to:

- save all
- toggle form/unit
- run.

These will be the speed buttons most often used in early program development. The Delphi Help system provides details of the other buttons.

Programmers can reconfigure the speed bar by clicking right on the speed bar and using the Speed Bar Editor; there is also an option to return to the defaults.

2.6 Interacting with the operating system

We will now develop a program to allow the user to browse a list of the bitmaps stored in the Windows file store, choose one and display it. In many programming languages this would be considered to be a very advanced piece of work, but by using existing Delphi components and setting properties in the Object Inspector we can achieve this with just three lines of Object Pascal code.

1. Create a new directory for this project and start Delphi.

2. Create a prototype form as shown in Figure 2.9. The form's Caption has been changed to Viewing. The components placed on the form are:

   - A button, from the Standard page of the Component Palette. The button's Caption is altered to be Press to change.

   - A bit button, selected from the Additional page of the Component Palette. There are a number of different kinds of bit buttons, with existing pictures and messages. Here a predefined button with Close on it will be used; this is chosen via the Object Inspector. Select the bit button on the form, then, in the Properties page of the Object Inspector, click opposite Kind and select bkClose, as shown in Figure 2.10. The alternative kinds of bit buttons have different words and pictures, or these can be set by the programmer.

   - An image component, from the Additional page of the Component Palette. The image component can be considered to be a place holder without any specific contents. When initially placed on the form it appears only as the outline of a box; see Figure 2.9.

   - An OpenDialog component, selected from the Dialogs page of the Component Palette. An OpenDialog is a non-visual component and will not be seen at run time, so the position on the form of non-visual components is not important.

3. Change the colour of the form, by ensuring that the form is selected in the Object Inspector and then selecting the Color property and setting it to a chosen colour. In this example clWhite is chosen.

4. Set the initial image to a chosen picture or graphic. This is achieved by selecting the image in the Object Inspector and then Picture on the Properties page. When Picture is selected the entry opposite Picture will initially be [None],

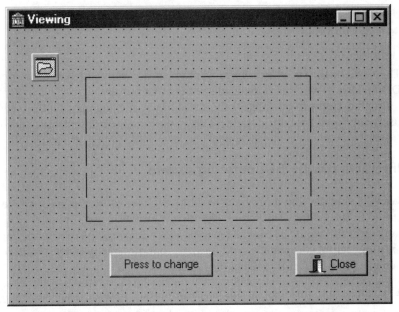

Figure 2.9   The prototype form.

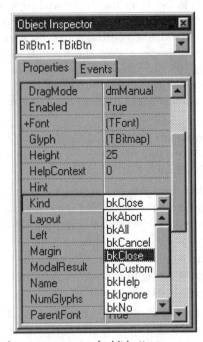

Figure 2.10   Setting the Kind property of a bit button.

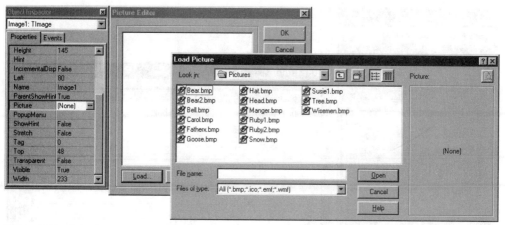

Figure 2.11   Selecting an initial image.

but an ellipsis (three dots) will appear to the side of [None]. Click on the ellipsis to load the Picture Editor, select Load from here to give access to the file store and find an appropriate image. See Figure 2.11 for the Delphi 3 version; with different operating systems or releases of Delphi the appearance will vary, but the techniques are the same. If there are no personal images available then one can be selected from the Delphi Images directory or the Windows directory. Having selected a suitable image, click Open in the Load Picture window, and OK in the Picture Editor window.

5. The OpenDialog component will give access to all of the directories in the file store, and by setting the Filter property in the Object Inspector, only certain types of files can be found, as shown in Figure 2.12. The Filter Editor is accessed in a similar manner to the Image's Picture Editor. The Name of the Filter can be any text that will help the user when displayed, but the Filter itself must give the specific format. In this example *.bmp means display only those files that end with .bmp. The character * is known as a wildcard and is used to represent any combination of characters other than full stop. The Filter *.* would be used if it were required to display all files.

6. Now we add the small amount of code needed to make the program work. In the Object Inspector select the event page for BitBtn1. Double click opposite the OnClick event. This will open the Unit Code window at the event handler BitBtn1Click and between the **begin** and **end** type Close as shown in Listing 2.2.

Listing 2.2   Close

```
1: procedure TForm1.BitBtn1Click(Sender: TObject);
2: begin
3:   Close;
4: end;
```

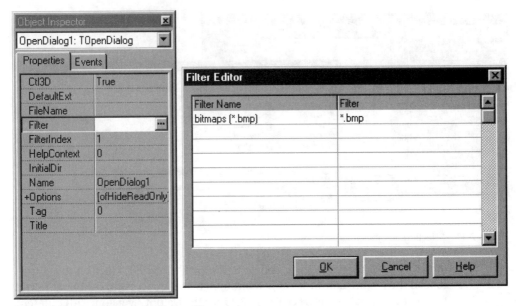

Figure 2.12   Setting the OpenDialog `Filter` property.

In Listing 2.2:

● Lines 1, 2 and 4 are automatically generated by the Delphi system.

● Line 3 is entered by the programmer.

There is a shortcut to the Code window for the `OnClick` events of buttons. In the Form Designer, double click on the `Button1` and the Code Editor window will automatically open at the `Button1Click` event handler. This saves having to manipulate the Object Inspector, and the two lines of code labelled 3 and 4 in Listing 2.3 can now be entered.

Listing 2.3   Loading the image

```
1: procedure TForm1.Button1Click(Sender: TObject);
2: begin
3:   OpenDialog1.Execute;
4:   Image1.Picture.LoadFromFile(OpenDialog1.FileName);
5: end;
```

In Listing 2.3:

● Lines 1, 2 and 5 are automatically generated.

● Line 3 will cause the display of a dialog box that allows the user to choose a file from those available.

● Line 4 then uses that filename to load the picture into `Image1`.

● Object Pascal is not case sensitive; upper and lower case letters can be used interchangeably. The use of capital letters in lines 3 and 4 is to help readability.

7. Use the save all speed button to save the unit and project code in the directory created, as UView.pas and PView.dpr respectively.

8. The project is now ready to run. If on selecting run the project fails to compile, check the lines of code entered. Delphi has generated a large amount of additional code that surrounds the three lines entered by the programmer; the complete unit code is given in Listing 2.4.

Listing 2.4 The unit for the viewer program

```
 1: unit UView;
 2:
 3: interface
 4:
 5: uses
 6:   Windows, Messages, SysUtils, Classes, Graphics, Controls,
 7:   Forms, Dialogs, ExtCtrls, StdCtrls, Buttons;
 8:
 9: type
10:   TForm1 = class(TForm)
11:     BitBtn1: TBitBtn;
12:     Button1: TButton;
13:     Image1: TImage;
14:     OpenDialog1: TOpenDialog;
15:     procedure BitBtn1Click(Sender: TObject);
16:     procedure Button1Click(Sender: TObject);
17:   private
18:     { Private declarations }
19:   public
20:     { Public declarations }
21:   end;
22:
23: var
24:   Form1: TForm1;
25:
26: implementation
27:
28: {$R *.DFM}
29:
30: procedure TForm1.BitBtn1Click(Sender: TObject);
31: begin
32:   Close;
33: end;
34:
35: procedure TForm1.Button1Click(Sender: TObject);
36: begin
```

```
37:     OpenDialog1.Execute;
38:     Image1.Picture.LoadFromFile(OpenDialog1.FileName);
39: end;
40:
41: end.
```

In Listing 2.4:

- The **uses** statement in lines 5 to 7 indicates which library units will be used in this program. With Delphi 1 the two units WinTypes and WinProcs would appear in the place of Windows.

- The **type** definition in lines 9 to 21 reflects the components and events on the form (more details are stored in the corresponding .dfm file). The sections labelled **public** and **private** can be used by the programmer and will be explained in Chapter 10.

- At line 28 {$R *.DFM} is a compiler directive and should not be deleted. It ensures the form is shown.

- Lines 32, 37 and 38 are the lines added by the programmer.

9. When the program is running, clicking the 'Press to change' button will display a typical Windows file selection window which allows access up and down the file store. The user selects an appropriate file and then presses Open in that window; the image displayed will change. This process can be repeated indefinitely. Clicking the bit button Close will stop the program.

   If the program does not work in the expected manner, it is probably because the properties have been set incorrectly, or have been set for the wrong object, so check all the stages above, using the Object Inspector.

The program is now complete. A useful program has been created, though it is not resilient and an error can easily be raised by a user providing an incorrect file.

2.7 Menus*

Professionally produced programs usually have a menu bar along the top offering various options. Likewise most applications also offer pop up menus that the user accesses by right clicking on the mouse. Buttons such as Quit are often better replaced with a menu option. Delphi offers two menu components, main menu and pop up menu, that allow programmers to incorporate menus into their programs.

In this section we will present an example that will outline how to use the menu components. The example will use pop up menus to change the colour of the form and a panel. A main menu will allow the colours to be reset to their original state and the application to exit.

1. Using a new directory, start Delphi. Create a prototype form with the following components: a main menu, a panel and two pop up menus – see Figure 2.13.

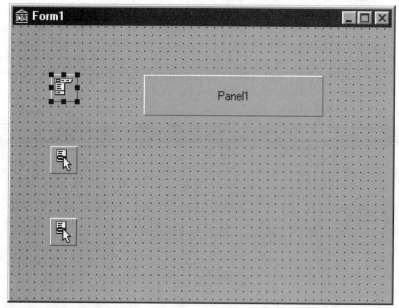

Figure 2.13   The prototype form.

2. In the Object Inspector select the Items property of MainMenu1, then click on the ellipsis to produce the menu design window – see Figure 2.14.

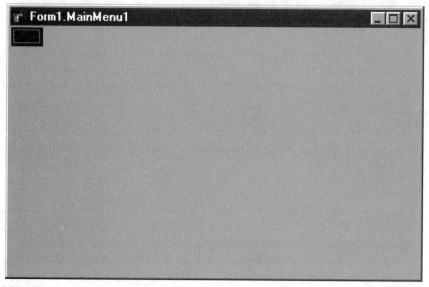

Figure 2.14   The main menu design window.

3. Set the Caption property of this first (unnamed) item to &File (the role of the &
    is explained below). The item is automatically named File1 to match the
    caption, though it could be manually named. Click on the menu design window
    to enter the pull down list associated with the File item. In this pull down list set
    the Caption of the first item to &New. The next item will have as its caption a –
    (dash), which will create a bar across the menu list. The final item will given the
    Caption E&xit. Figure 2.15 shows the completed list in the menu designer. If
    the main menu were to offer choices other than File these would be accessed by
    clicking the dotted rectangle to the right of File.

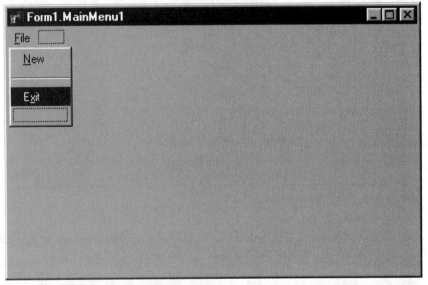

Figure 2.15   Setting the main menu items.

4. In the Object Inspector, select Exit1 as the current component. There is only
    one event, OnClick, associated with this. Double click opposite this to open the
    Code window and add the statement Close as shown at line 3 of Listing 2.5.

Listing 2.5

```
1: procedure TForm1.Exit1Click(Sender: TObject);
2: begin
3:   Close;
4: end;
```

5. Now select New1 in the Object Inspector and open the Code window for its
    OnClick event and add the code at lines 3 and 4 in Listing 2.6. These two lines
    set the colour of the form and the panel to their original values. Lines 1, 2 and 5
    were automatically generated by Delphi.

Listing 2.6

```
1: procedure TForm1.New1Click(Sender: TObject);
2: begin
3:     Form1.Color:= clBtnFace;
4:     Panel1.Color:= clBtnFace;
5: end;
```

6. The unit and project can now be saved in the directory created; the default names of Unit1.pas and Project1.dpr can be used. The code can then be run. Its functionality is extremely limited, though the main menu will work. The option New appears to do nothing as it sets the colours to the values they already have. The Exit option works and will terminate the program.

   The ampersand (&) in front of certain letters in the menu options causes that letter to be underlined in the design and run mode. At run time this enables the use of shortcuts, which can be tested at this stage. The File option can be chosen by pressing Alt+F. Once the menu is displayed, pressing N chooses New and X chooses Exit. The X of Exit is chosen to match most other Windows-based programs, including Delphi.

7. Pop up menus work in much the same way as the main menu. They allow the user to click right on a particular component and then choose from the menu options. As there can be many pop up menus it is necessary to link the correct menu to the correct component via the Object Inspector.

   Double click on the PopUpMenu component to open the PopUpMenu designer for PopUpMenu1. Set the first item's Caption for PopupMenu1 to be Red and the second to be Blue. Then open the PopUpMenu designer for PopUpMenu2 and set the items to be White and Lime.

8. Use the Object Inspector to select the Events page for the red option – see Figure 2.16. Double click opposite its OnClick event and enter a line of code:

   ```
   Panel1.Color:= clRed;
   ```

   Similarly select the OnClick event associated with the blue option and add:

   ```
   Panel1.Color:= clBlue;
   ```

9. The white and lime options are going to be used to change the colour of the form, so set their respective OnClick events to:

   ```
   Form1.Color:= clWhite;
   ```

   and

   ```
   Form1.Color:= clLime;
   ```

   The pop up menus now have to be linked to the part of the form they will be displayed with. PopupMenu1 is to be associated with the panel. In the Object Inspector select the panel's Properties page. From the pull down menu opposite PopUpMenu choose PopupMenu1 – see Figure 2.17. PopupMenu2 can similarly be linked to Form1.

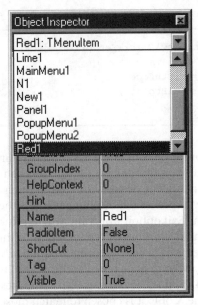

Figure 2.16   Selecting the red option.

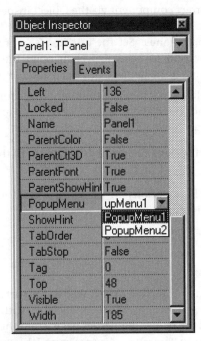

Figure 2.17   Linking pop up menu to Panel1.

10. Save the unit and run the project. Clicking right on the panel should give the option of changing the colour to red or blue, with the appropriate effect when one is selected. Clicking right on the remainder of the form displays the pull down menu offering the choice of the colour lime or white. Choosing File|New sets the form and panel back to their original colours, while File|Exit terminates the execution of the program.

2.8   Summary

In this chapter we introduced the programming environment of Delphi and some prototype forms were designed. We discussed the roles of the individual parts of the environment, including the Object Inspector, Component Palette, speed bar, Form Designer window and Code window. The use of tabs to access different pages of both the Object Inspector and the Component Palette was demonstrated.

A number of components were used, including buttons, images, labels and dialogs. Properties and events were set for components allowing effective programs to be created, using only a few lines of code supplied by the programmer. Here a program was developed that allows a user to display any images found in the file store. Finally we showed how menus could be introduced into programs.

Quiz

1. What is a unit?
   (a) The window displayed at run time.
   (b) The Object Pascal code associated with a form.
   (c) A collection of files that make up a Delphi application.

2. What are the two pages available in the Object Inspector?
   (a) Properties and Events
   (b) Standard and Additional
   (c) File and Edit

3. What is the Component Palette used for?
   (a) Setting the colour of the form.
   (b) Running the application.
   (c) Placing components on the form at design time.

4. For what purpose may the OpenDialog component be used?
   (a) To open an existing project at design time.
   (b) To create an open file dialog box at run time.
   (c) To create a new unit.

5. Why is the speed bar useful?
   (a) It provides shortcuts to other menus.
   (b) It makes the code run faster.
   (c) It shortens compilation time.

6.   Clicking a button on a running Delphi form causes:
(a) an event
(b) a property
(c) an error

7.   By default Delphi units contain this line:

```
{$R *.DFM}
```

What is its purpose?
(a) It is a compiler directive and ensures the form is shown.
(b) It serves no purpose and can be deleted.
(c) It turns checking on.

8.   How is a main menu component displayed at run time?
(a) The component looks the same as at design time.
(b) As a band along the top of the form.
(c) The main menu is not displayed until the right mouse button is clicked.

9.   What property needs to be changed to alter the wording of a label?
(a) `Caption`
(b) `Text`
(c) `Visible`

10.   When can the properties displayed in the Object Inspector be changed?
(a) Only at design time.
(b) Only within the code.
(c) At design time or within the code.

Exercises

1.   Develop a program that will show two overlapping images, both of which can be changed by the user.

2.   Use the ColorDialog component to develop a program that allows the user to change the colour of the form, to the colour selected when ColorDialog is executed.

3.   Write a program that enlarges a label when the user clicks it.

4.   Kim's game is a test of memory. A tray of objects is shown to the players, then it is hidden. The players try to remember as many objects as possible. Write a program to play the game by loading pictures which are hidden initially, showing them on the click of a button, and then hiding them on the click of a second button.

5.   **Delphi 3 and 4 programmers only**. In the 'Interacting with the Operating System' program, replace the OpenDialog component with an OpenPictureDialog.

Chapter 3

Arithmetic and simple strings

3.1 Introduction

The essence of most computation is arithmetic. An engineer must evaluate formulae to find the stress on a bridge or the resistance of some equipment. The calculations must be correct, otherwise the bridge may fall, or the equipment may develop a critical fault. The earliest high-level languages incorporated arithmetic operations for addition, subtraction, multiplication and division. Object Pascal has sophisticated arithmetic operators for different types of operand. Before doing arithmetic, the programmer must ensure that values of the operands have been set, and for flexibility those values should be read in from an input stream.

Delphi provides the edit component (edit box) to allow the input of text strings, and functions to convert those strings to numeric form. Taken together, the edit boxes and type conversion routines allow the programmer to provide neat and reasonably foolproof input facilities.

Both arithmetic and edit boxes demonstrate the strong typing that is a feature of Pascal-like languages. Strong typing makes for code which 'works' with minimal effort by the programmer, because the programmer must indicate conversion from one type of value to another explicitly. Inexperienced programmers sometimes prefer weakly typed languages because they compile with greater ease, but unfortunately the programs do not always perform predictably. Bugs can be extremely difficult to track down in a weakly typed language.

3.2 Identifiers and variables

In earlier chapters we used the default identifiers supplied by the Delphi environment, such as `Label1` and `Button1`. Programmers can change these to their choice of identifiers, within limitations, by use of the Object Inspector.

Another example of an identifier is the name of the project itself: if the programmer has chosen to save a project in a file called

```
Mine.dpr
```

then `Mine` is the name or identifier of the project, and will appear on the first line of the project source code (the programmer can see it by choosing View|Project Source). This program identifier is rather special, in that one should not edit the code to change it, but should always use the save project facility that updates the identifier itself (except in special circumstances). A typical program requires many such identifiers, and many will be introduced explicitly by the programmer.

An identifier, or name, must begin with a letter or underscore; after that it may contain any series of letters or digits or underscores (the Delphi compiler distinguishes the first 63 characters). Delphi does not allow blanks in identifiers.

Each variable used by Pascal has both an identifier and a specific type. Variables get both in the variable declaration. It begins with the reserved word **var**, then each identifier is listed along with its type. Looking back at Listing 2.4, immediately above the reserved word **implementation** are the lines

```
var
Form1: TForm1;
```

which declare `Form1` to be of type `TForm1`, or in object-oriented terminology, declare `Form1` to be an instance of the class `TForm1`. In fact, `TForm1` is a special class which is not declared by the programmer, but programmers can declare any number of other variables. They are listed in the statement starting **var** (var statement). Variables of different types are separated by semicolons. For example

```
var Total, Sum, TotalSoFar, ThisOne, LastOne: Integer; Average: Double;
```

The above line warns the compiler to reserve space for five memory locations suitable to hold one integer each and one memory location to hold a floating-point number of type double. The space reserved depends on the type specified, which in turn may depend on the version of Delphi in use. Figures 3.1 and 3.2 show diagrams of the store of the computer resulting from this variable declaration. The contents of the memory locations are unknown.

The assignment operator (`:=`) changes the value of a variable within the program, either to give it an initial value or to change that value. The symbol `:=` does not

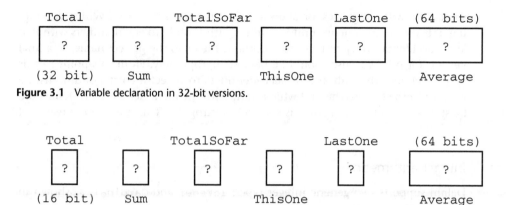

Figure 3.1 Variable declaration in 32-bit versions.

Figure 3.2 Variable declaration in Delphi 1.

mean 'equals' but 'takes the value of'. The expression on the right of : = is evaluated, and the result is stored in the variable on the left-hand side. A semicolon (;) ends each line except the last. Semicolons separate Pascal statements, rather than line breaks as in some other languages. This free format lets the programmer break long lines of code, and there are many examples of statements spanning several lines later in this text.

Programmers should not assume that variables are zero initially, even though generous compilers sometimes do initialize to zero, and indeed Delphi does so in some cases. Delphi initializes global variables, that is, those declared outside procedures, to zero; on the other hand it does not zero local (procedure) variables. In Chapter 8, which deals with scope, we discuss global and local variables in detail. Assuming that a compiler initializes variables is very bad practice. Subtle bugs may arise, notably on porting the code to another platform. It is best practice to assume that all variables must be initialized by the program.

Examples of the use of the assignment operator are as follows:

```
1:  Total:= 0;
2:  Sum:= 7+5;
3:  TotalSoFar:= TotalSoFar+1;
4:  ThisOne:= LastOne;
```

- In line 1 the value of the variable with identifier Total is set to zero.
- In line 2 two integer literals are added together, and the result is assigned to Sum.
- In line 3 the value of the variable with identifier TotalSoFar is accessed, and 1 is added to it. The result is then assigned to TotalSoFar, thus overwriting the previous value.
- In line 4 ThisOne is changed, but LastOne remains as it was.

The choice of identifiers is important. Meaningful identifiers are the first step to producing readable and reusable code, which should be the aim of every programmer. A typical programmer might call such a unit ULang to indicate that it did something with languages, or URun to reflect the form Caption. Whilst developing, it is wise to commence unit identifiers with U and project identifiers with P to avoid accidental overwriting. The executable file takes the project name, so a final version for others to use should be named appropriately. From this point in this text we choose the unit and project identifiers to reflect a corresponding listing number in the text, so the unit which starts with the identifier U3_1 , which would be stored in the file U3_1.pas, is shown in Listing 3.1. This is to aid the reader of this book.

3.2.1   Integer arithmetic

Delphi supports two generic integer types: Integer and Cardinal, as shown in Table 3.1. Delphi 4 supports 64-bit integers.

It is normally preferable to use these for optimal performance, but there are also fundamental integer types available (ShortInt, SmallInt, LongInt, Byte and Word). The fundamental types can be useful for advanced programming if the range or the method of storage is important, because their range does not vary from one version to another. For the present, most programmers can ignore fundamental types, then find details in online help when needed.

The integer operators are listed in Table 3.2.

● Multiplication and division are performed before addition or subtraction, so in the statement

```
Area:= 2*Height*Length+Width+Ceiling;
```

the expression 2*Height*Length will be evaluated before any addition is done.

Table 3.1   Integer types.

	Type	Range	Internal format
32-bit versions	Integer	−2,147,483,648 to 2,147,483,647	Signed 32 bit (4 bytes)
	Cardinal	0 to 2,147,483,647	Unsigned 32 bit (4 bytes)
Delphi 1	Integer	−32,768 to 32,767	Signed 16 bit (2 bytes)
	Cardinal	0 to 65,535	Unsigned 16 bit (2 bytes)

Table 3.2   Integer operators.

Operator	Action	Example
+	addition	TotalSoFar + 1
−	subtraction	TotalSoFar − 1
*	multiplication	Result * Scale
div	'whole number' division	11 **div** 3 (giving 3)
mod	'remainder' on division	11 **mod** 3 (giving 2)

- There is *no* operator to raise an operand to a power, unlike in BASIC.
- Multiplication must be explicit – the * must appear, in common with practice in other programming languages and spreadsheet packages.
- The programmer can change the precedence by using round brackets as in ordinary mathematics. Hence the result of executing the statement

```
Area:= 2*Height*(Length+Width)+Ceiling;
```

will be to perform the addition

```
Length+Width
```

before doing any multiplication. The addition

```
+ Ceiling
```

is done last of all, and the final result is assigned to `Area`.

(3.3) Edit boxes

In Chapter 1 we used a label to display text. Another way of displaying a single line of text is to use an edit box, which the programmer can also use to provide input or output. The programmer can change various properties of an edit component, either initially by the Object Inspector or during execution by the Object Pascal code. A few of the most useful properties are shown in Table 3.3.

Provided `ReadOnly` is `False`, which is the default, the user has the facilities not only to edit text but also to overwrite, insert and delete it.

Frequently programs require numerical input and output. An edit component is an elegant way of providing this. Notice, however, that edit boxes handle text, or more precisely, variables of type string. Hence Delphi provides a considerable number of routines to convert numbers to and from strings. The most useful are listed below, and online help will give details of others:

```
StrToInt, IntToStr, FloatToStr, StrToFloat
```

To illustrate the use of edit boxes and simple calculations, we describe a project which initially shows the word 'Pascal' in an edit box. When the user clicks on the form, 'Pascal' will change to 'Delphi', and the version number of Delphi in a separate edit box will be incremented. Like the forms from previous projects, this one has a Quit button. The prototype form is shown in Figure 3.3. Notice that Figure 3.3 shows a form patterned with dots; this indicates that the program is not running but is in design mode.

Table 3.3 Some edit component properties.

MaxLength	Maximum number of characters that the user may enter
PasswordChar	May be set to a non-null character to mask input
ReadOnly	May be set to `True` to prevent the user from entering data
Text	Determines what is displayed

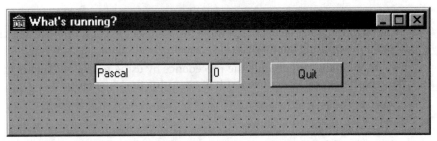

Figure 3.3   Prototype form for the 'What's running?' project.

To create the project, do as follows:

1. If necessary, create a suitable directory to hold the various files which make up this project.

2. Open Delphi and save the unit file and the project in that directory: we will call them U3_1.pas and P3_1.dpr.

3. Use the Object Inspector to change the Caption at the top of the form. This is done by first selecting the Properties tab of the Object Inspector if necessary, then typing in the new Caption:

   What's running?

   in the right-hand column opposite Caption.

4. Edit boxes are on the Standard page of the Component Palette. Insert an edit component, by clicking first on the edit icon, then on the form. Now use the Object Inspector in the manner described above to change the initial contents of the field Text to Pascal.

5. Insert a second edit component, and use the Object Inspector in the manner described above to change the initial contents of the field Text to zero. Position the component and resize it in the normal manner as shown on the prototype.

6. Add a Quit button.

7. The form itself is now complete. The dots show it is in design mode. Now add the functional code as follows.

8. Double click on the Quit button. This opens the code skeleton of the attached unit at procedure TForm1.Button1Click. This procedure is the event handler that will be executed when the user clicks the Quit button. Between the **begin** and **end**, type

   Close;

   which when executed will close the form and will exit this program.

9. Go to the Object Inspector and select Form1 from the window at the top, then select the Events tab, and double click opposite OnClick to open another skeleton event handler, TForm1.FormClick

10. Between **begin** and **end** type these two statements:

```
Edit1.text:= 'Delphi';
Edit2.text:= IntToStr(StrToInt(Edit2.Text) + 1);
```

The finished unit should look like Listing 3.1.

Listing 3.1) Changing the contents of an edit box

```
 1: unit U3_1;
 2:
 3: interface
 4:
 5: uses
 6:   Windows, Messages, SysUtils, Classes, Graphics, Controls,
 7:   Forms, Dialogs, StdCtrls;
 8:
 9: type
10:   TForm1 = class(TForm)
11:     Edit1: TEdit;
12:     Edit2: TEdit;
13:     Button1: TButton;
14:     procedure Button1Click(Sender: TObject);
15:     procedure FormClick(Sender: TObject);
16:   private
17:     { Private declarations }
18:   public
19:     { Public declarations }
20:   end;
21:
22: var
23:   Form1: TForm1;
24:
25: implementation
26:
27: {$R *.DFM}
28:
29: procedure TForm1.Button1Click(Sender: TObject);
30: begin
31:   Close;
32: end;
33:
34: procedure TForm1.FormClick(Sender: TObject);
35: {-----------------------------------------------------------}
36: {This is a comment; it will be ignored by compiler.         }
37: {Comments are useful to clarify code.                       }
38: {This code changes the contents of both edit boxes.         }
39: {-----------------------------------------------------------}
40: begin
41:   Edit1.Text:= 'Delphi';
42:   Edit2.Text:= IntToStr(StrToInt(Edit2.Text) + 1);
```

```
43: end;
44:
45: end.
```

In Listing 3.1:

- Line 41 copies a new string into the `Text` property of the appropriate edit box.

- Line 42 takes the value in the `Text` property of `Edit2`, converts it to an integer type (held in memory), then adds 1 to the result. That answer is then converted back to a `string` type, so it can finally be assigned to the `Text` property of `Edit1`. The net result is that the number in the box increases, and the type conversion functions `IntToStr` and `StrToInt` are necessary because of the strong typing of the language.

- The compiler ignores text between { and }, such as lines 35 to 39. This is a comment, or note to the human reader. Other comment delimiters are available, but they vary across versions, see online help. The exception is the compiler directive in line 27, which provides a link to the form.

Save the unit and project again before trying to run it. Press the Run button on the speed bar and the form will appear if there are no syntax errors. Clicking once anywhere on the form, apart from on the Quit button or edit box, changes Pascal to Delphi, and subsequent clicks increase the version number. See Figure 3.4.

It is advisable always to include a Quit button, or a menu with an equivalent option, on a form, so that your project is not left running. Clicking on the Quit button closes the program. If the project is left running, the form is plain as in Figure 3.4, and attempts to recompile will give an error message as in Figure 3.5.

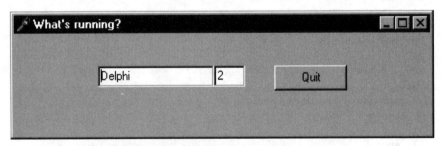

Figure 3.4   Execution of the 'What's running?' project.

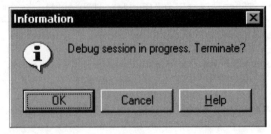

Figure 3.5   Information about a debug session.

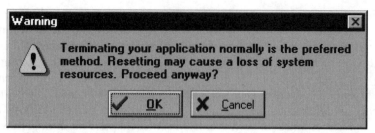

Figure 3.6 Warning message.

Replying OK in Delphi 1 may bring up a further message box as shown in Figure 3.6, and then replying OK again will stop the project execution.

The user can also close forms by using Alt+F4, as in most other Windows applications, or by using the close box on the window frame itself.

Windows users do expect a Quit option, and this also allows the programmer to do any necessary housekeeping. On closing, many commercial Windows applications, store the current state ready for the next use; for example a game may store a high-score table.

If there are syntax errors which are not obvious on comparison of your code with the text, the status line at the bottom of the window, or failing that the online help, should give a clue. For easy access to the online help select the error then press F1.

(3.4) Further integer arithmetic

The previous example used integer arithmetic, but without the introduction of integer variables. A further simple example will demonstrate the use of variables, which are essential for more complex event handlers. This project will double a given number at every click of one button, the other button just closing the form. The prototype form will look like Figure 3.7.

Within Delphi all objects, including components, have a set of possible events that can be handled. By default a component does not respond to any of its events. It

Illustrates variable use

Enter the starting number below

0

Double it!

Quit

Figure 3.7 Prototype form for the 'Double a number' project.

is the programmer's responsibility to write the code that represents the response to a specific event. For the code to be executed the event has to occur at run time. It is usually the user's responsibility to make an event happen, although the code may be written in such a way that an event is forced to happen. Normally a component will respond to only a few of the possible events – for example, if a component responds to the OnClick event it is unlikely also to respond to 'mouse down' – but if these events are offered by the component the programmer can choose to develop appropriate responses to both events. In earlier chapters we showed how the Object Inspector is used to add event handlers to the unit code a programmer is developing.

1. Start a new project and save the unit file and the project in a suitable directory. Suitable filenames could be UDouble and PDouble.

2. Use the Object Inspector to change the Caption of the form to

   ```
   Illustrates variable use
   ```

3. Insert one edit component, and use the Object Inspector to change the initial contents of the field Text to zero.

4. Add a label above it, and change its Caption to

   ```
   Enter the starting number below
   ```

5. Insert two buttons and change the captions to

   ```
   Double it!
   ```

   and

   ```
   Quit
   ```

   respectively.

6. Now to add the functionality of the Quit button, double click on the Quit button, to open the code for the event handler, and add

   ```
   Close;
   ```

   as before.

7. Double click on the 'Double it!' button to open the code for that event handler. Between the **begin** and **end** insert the following two lines of code:

   ```
   Twice:= 2*StrToInt(Edit1.Text);
   Edit1.Text:= IntToStr(Twice);
   ```

8. The project as it stands now will not even compile. The variable Twice must be declared before use. To do so, insert the line

   ```
   var Twice: Integer;
   ```

   between the lines starting

   ```
   procedure TForm1.Button1Click
   ```

   and

   ```
   begin
   ```

9. It is also good practice to add a comment at the start of each procedure stating what it does.

Listing 3.2 shows the two event handlers.

Listing 3.2) The 'Double a number' project

```
 1: procedure TForm1.Button1Click(Sender: TObject);
 2: {-----------------------------------------------------------}
 3: {This event handler doubles the contents of the edit box   }
 4: {- assuming the contents are a whole number                }
 5: {-----------------------------------------------------------}
 6: var Twice: Integer;
 7: begin
 8:    Twice:= 2*StrToInt(Edit1.Text);
 9:    Edit1.Text:= IntToStr(Twice);
10: end;
11:
12: procedure TForm1.Button2Click(Sender: TObject);
13: begin
14:    Close;
15: end;
```

In Listing 3.2:

- Line 8 picks up the value of the Text property of the edit box, which is of type **string**, converts it to an integer, and doubles that integer. That result is then assigned to the variable Twice, which is of type Integer.
- Line 9 converts the contents of Twice to type **string**, and then assigns that result to the Text property of Edit1.

If there is no executable file already, then choosing the Run button on the speed bar will compile and then run the project. When a program is first run Delphi automatically compiles both the project source and the unit and builds all the compiled files together to form an executable file (that is, the code that is run). Subsequently Delphi just recompiles code that it believes has been changed. Most of the time this works very well: the programmer makes some changes and selects Run, and Delphi automatically recompiles the code then builds the executable. Occasionally the Delphi system can be tricked into not recognizing changes, particularly when moving code between machines where the clocks are set to different times, or when the programmer has changed the environment and not the code. To ensure code is always compiled the programmer can select Project|Compile or Project|Build All. Most of the time this will be unnecessary.

Type 1 in the edit box, then click the 'Double it!' button time after time and watch the number in the edit box increase through powers of 2. If a 32-bit version of Delphi is being run, it reaches 1,073,741,824, which is 2^{30}, and one further click gives a negative number, $-2,147,483,648$. This is the smallest value of integer allowed in the 32-bit versions of Delphi, -2^{31}. The 16-bit integer range is $-32,768$ to 32,767 which can be stored in 15 bits, plus one for the sign. So doubling 16,384 would give a value outside the allowable range. Thus in Delphi 1, the switchover occurs between 2^{14} and 2^{-15} which equals $-32,768$. Further doubling will give an illegal answer.

3.5 Cardinals

Open the previous project, and save it and the associated unit with different names, say PDoubC and UDoubC. Now change the type of the variable Twice to Cardinal, so line 6 of Listing 3.2 reads

```
var Twice: Cardinal;
```

Run the project again, and initially it will give the same results as the earlier (integer) version. Notice that repeated clicks of the 'Double it!' button give numbers that rise above 32,767 even in Delphi 1. Cardinals have a larger positive range than integers in Delphi 1; this is possible because they do not require a sign bit. They were not available in the early versions of Pascal, but have been added to Object Pascal. Eventually, when the number calculated would exceed the maximum allowed for cardinals, the edit box shows zero – the minimum of the Cardinal range. Again, the switchover occurs at a much higher value in later releases.

Integer and Cardinal are both ordinal types. Given one value, you can determine the one immediately before or after it. Real is not ordinal, and because there are restrictions on where programmers may use real variables and literals (such as 3.142) in their code, execution of a real expression is generally slower than that of an equivalent Integer or Cardinal expression. However, actual things – the weight of an atom, the length of a road – are normally measured as fractions, not just whole numbers. Furthermore, calculations frequently lead to decimal fractions. Thus real types are very useful, but Integer and Cardinal types should be used when feasible, not only because there are restrictions on where reals can be used but also because using integers and cardinals will give efficient code.

3.6 Floating-point arithmetic

To express a very large or very small real number, Pascal uses *floating-point notation* in which E stands for 'times 10 to the power of', so a half can be expressed as 0.5, 5E$-$1 or even 0.005E2, but never just .5. All releases of Delphi offer a selection of floating-point types, which vary in accuracy and the space each occupies. The main ones are shown in Table 3.4.

Table 3.4 Some floating-point types.

Type	Range for positive and negative values	Accuracy	Internal format
Single	1.5×10^{-25} to 3.4×10^{38}	7–8 digits	4 bytes
Double	5.0×10^{-324} to 1.7×10^{308}	15–16 digits	8 bytes
Extended	3.4×10^{-4932} to 1.1×10^{4932}	19–20 digits	10 bytes
Comp	$-2^{63}-1$ to $2^{63}+1$ (approximately -10^{19} to 10^{19})	19–20 digits	8 bytes
Currency	Up to almost 10^{15}, with 4 decimal places (not available in Delphi 1)	19–20 digits	8 bytes

The Extended type affords more accuracy than the Double type, and so it is useful in calculations where accuracy is paramount. The results of certain calculations with Single and Double types are held as an Extended type too. The Comp type is for holding large integer values, rather than floating point. The largest integer that the processor can handle directly is the maximum value of the type LongInt, that is MaxLongInt. In 32-bit versions of Delphi the range of LongInt is the same as that of Integer. Delphi 1 is only 16-bit but LongInt offers the same range as the 32-bit versions. Certain applications require yet larger integers, and the Comp type gives this facility. Operations on values of type Comp, like operations on floating-point types, are handled by code generated by the compiler.

The Currency type is not available in Delphi 1, but is a useful addition in later versions. It is a fixed-point data type, stored with a precision of four decimal places, so it is suitable for monetary calculations in most major currencies and avoids troublesome rounding errors. It is compatible not only with the other floating-point types but also with database types representing money.

There is also a type Real that is included for compatibility with earlier versions of Pascal, but it is not native to the processor. Every operation requires conversions, so operations take longer than equivalent ones on either Single or Double types. Hence it is greatly preferable to use Single or Double type rather than Real.

The floating-point operators are shown in Table 3.5.

The programmer can mix various floating-point types within expressions: they are compatible. If an expression contains both floating-point types and integer types (or only floating-point types), then the result of evaluating it will be of Extended type, with an accuracy of 19–20 digits. The result of any expression that uses the floating-point division operator is also of Extended type, even if all variables in it are integers. Hence the three expressions

```
10/5
10.0/5
10.0/5.0
```

all give the same result, the Extended type value of 2, approximately. Note that the result may not be exactly 2 because calculations use only a limited number of bits.

Given the declarations

```
var IntNo: Integer; SingleReal: Single;
```

Table 3.5 Floating-point operators.

Operator	Action	Example
+	addition	Cost + VAT
−	subtraction	Profit − Loss
*	multiplication	32.87*6.5E-02
/	division	Annual/12

each expression can appear in statements such as

```
SingleReal:= 10/5;
SingleReal:= 10.0/5;
SingleReal:= 10.0/5.0;
```

However, any of the three statements

```
IntNo:= 10/5;
IntNo:= 10.0/5;
IntNo:= 10.0/5.0;
```

will cause a compilation error such as

```
incompatible types 'integer' and 'real'
```

This is because we are trying to assign an expression which gives a result of Extended type to an integer variable.

To summarize, each of the expressions

```
10/5
10.0/5
10.0/5.0
```

can be assigned to a floating-point variable, but none can be assigned to an integer type of variable. In other words a floating-point type is not assignment compatible with an integer type, whereas an integer type is assignment compatible with a floating-point type. For example:

```
SingleReal:= 10*5;
```

is allowed.

Note also that either of the expressions

```
10.0 div 5
```

or

```
10.0 div 5.0
```

will cause a compilation error such as 'Operator not applicable to this operator type', because div is an integer operator.

Hence the programmer needs mechanisms to convert a floating-point value to an integer value. These are as follows:

● Trunc(x) which returns the integer part of real x. Trunc(5.75) is 5 and Trunc(-5.75) is −5.

● Round(x) which returns the value of real x rounded to the nearest integer. Round(5.75) is 6 and Round(-5.75) is −6.

Both Trunc and Round are examples of functions, and their use is illustrated in Listing 3.3.

Listing 3.3) Use of `Trunc` and `Round`

```
1: var Bill,Tender,BillWhole: Single;
2:     Pounds,RoundPounds: Cardinal;
3: begin
4:    Bill:= 34.25;
5:    Tender:= 40.00;
6:    Pounds:= Trunc(Tender - Bill);
7:    RoundPounds:= Round(Tender - Bill);
```

The effect of line 6 is to retrieve the current values in `Tender` and `Bill` and then subtract them, giving 5.75 as an intermediate result. That intermediate result is fed into the function `Trunc`, which then returns the integer 5 which is assigned to the variable `Pounds` which is itself of integer type. In line 7 the function `Trunc` is replaced by `Round`, so then the integer 6 will be assigned to `RoundPounds`. In any case, the values in `Bill` and `Tender` are unchanged by lines 6 and 7.

There are also functions `Int` and `Frac` which return the integral (whole number) and fractional parts of a real number respectively as real values. If we add further lines to the end of Listing 3.3:

```
BillWhole:= Int(Bill);
Bill:= Frac(Tender - Bill);
```

this will assign 34.0 to `BillWhole` and 0.75 to `Bill`.

In later versions of Delphi there is a further type, called a `Variant` type, that we have not discussed. As its name implies, it can accommodate integers and floating-point numbers and even strings in the manner of variables in BASIC. Using the `Variant` type not only increases execution times, but bypasses the safeguards provided by strong typing, and hence it should not be used lightly.

3.7) A change calculator

We will illustrate the uses of real and integer arithmetic and some conversion functions in this section. The basic idea is to develop an application to calculate the change required for a given bill when a customer tenders a given sum, by analogy with tills in supermarkets. This application goes further than a typical till, in that it will also calculate the cash to be given in each type of coinage, starting with the largest denomination available. A suitable form might look like Figure 3.8.

1. Build the form as follows in the currency of Figure 3.8 or an alternative currency.

2. Place edit components on the form as shown, to hold bill total, cash tendered total and change total, then boxes for each denomination to be considered. In order to place a series of similar components on a form, hold down Shift before selecting the component, then click to place as required. To revert to the normal method of working, click the white pointer icon on the extreme left of the Component Palette.

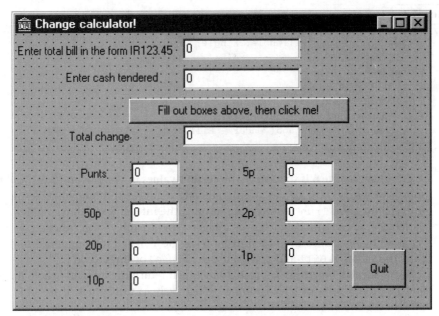

Figure 3.8   Prototype form for the currency conversion project.

3. Add two buttons, one to do the calculation and one to quit the project, and change their captions appropriately.

4. Now resize the edit boxes as required. This can be done by eye on the form, or if precise sizes are wanted the width and height can be measured in the Object Inspector.

5. Add labels as appropriate.

6. Select the top three edit boxes (for bill total, cash tendered total and change total) one at a time and use the Object Inspector to change the initial value of the Text property of each to zero.

7. Select the edit boxes for amounts of change one at a time, and use the Object Inspector to change the Text property to zero and then to set the ReadOnly property of each to True.

8. Change the Name properties of the edit components so they are meaningful. Double clicking on the buttons in turn will open the underlying unit at the appropriate point, and the functional code can be inserted so the event handlers are as shown in Listing 3.4. Alternatively the right-hand column of the Object Inspector can be double clicked opposite the OnClick event for those objects.

   ● Lines 15 and 16 utilize the StrToFloat function which works in an analogous manner to StrToInt.

   ● Line 18 uses the FloatToStrF library function. This takes a floating-point value, the first parameter, and returns the string equivalent. Parameters are supplied in parentheses following the identifier of a function, and they

Listing 3.4

```
 1: procedure TForm1.Button2Click(Sender: TObject);
 2: begin
 3:   Close;
 4: end;
 5:
 6: procedure TForm1.Button1Click(Sender: TObject);
 7: {---------------------------------------------------------}
 8: { Works out change from Irish punts tendered             }
 9: { Assumes top 2 edit boxes have been filled appropriately }
10: {---------------------------------------------------------}
11: var
12:   Bill,Tender : Single;
13:   CoinCount,Pounds, Rem: Cardinal;
14: begin
15:   Bill:= StrToFloat(Edit1.Text);
16:   Tender:= StrToFloat(Edit2.Text);
17:   {now find change, starting with biggest currency}
18:   Edit3.Text:= FloatToStrF(Tender - Bill,ffCurrency,7,2);
19:   Pounds:= Trunc(Tender - Bill);
20:   Editp.Text:=IntToStr(pounds);
21:   Rem:= Round(100*Frac(Tender-Bill));
22:   CoinCount:= Rem div 50;
23:   Edit50.Text:= IntToStr(CoinCount);
24:   Rem:= Rem mod 50;
25:   CoinCount:= Rem div 20;
26:   Edit20.Text:= IntToStr(CoinCount);
27:   Rem:= Rem mod 20;
28:   CoinCount:= Rem div 10;
29:   Edit10.Text:= IntToStr(CoinCount);
30:   Rem:= Rem mod 10;
31:   CoinCount:= Rem div 5;
32:   Edit05.Text:= IntToStr(CoinCount);
33:   Rem:= Rem mod 5;
34:   CoinCount:= Rem div 2;
35:   Edit02.Text:= IntToStr(CoinCount);
36:   Rem:= Rem mod 2;
37:   Edit01.Text:= IntToStr(Rem);
38: end;
```

provide input to that function. The number and type of parameters must be appropriate. The remaining parameters control the format of the string. The parameters given will ensure that the display looks like Irish punts. For further details see Chapter 9 and online help facilities (F1) within Delphi.

- Line 19 was discussed earlier in this section; it assigns the number of punt coins to be given in change to the variable Pounds, and line 20 displays the result in an edit box.

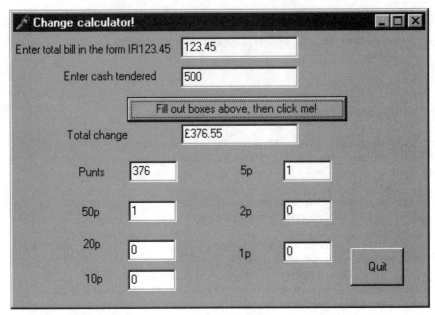

Figure 3.9 Currency converter.

- Line 21 uses the inbuilt function Frac, which was not available in earlier Pascal compilers, to find the change to be given apart from whole pounds.

- The rest of the unit works by successively using the **div** and **mod** operators. Line 22 performs integer division by 50 to find the number of 50 pence pieces to be given, displays that count in the appropriate edit box, then uses the **mod** operator in line 24 to ascertain the remainder of change still owing.

9. Save the unit and project and choose Run. If it does not compile first time, inspect the error messages at the base of the window and use F1 (help) if necessary.

Unless you are very lucky, the program will fail to compile because of a typing error. The Delphi system will take you into the Code window and highlight where it believes the error is. There will be a brief message at the bottom of the Code window indicating what the error is. If a newer version of Delphi is in use, then all the errors will be listed and the first will be highlighted. If this does not help, use the Delphi help system. The most common errors when copying in code are:

- missing semicolons

- mistyping some of the words

- typing = in place of : =

- not closing comments with the right brace

- not matching quotes to close a string or spreading a string over two lines.

The Delphi environment options can be used to add colours and font changes to the code that we find to help avoid or spot programming errors. For example, putting reserved words in bold makes it easy to see if a reserved word is incorrectly spelt. Highlighting comments in blue will turn a large proportion of the code blue if the closing brace is omitted. Highlighting strings in red will likewise make it simple to spot if the quotes do not match.

10. Correct the errors and try again. The result of one run is shown in Figure 3.9.

When the project runs it will be obvious that it is not as robust as one might like. Try entering a larger sum for the bill than for the amount of cash tendered, or type characters in place of numbers. Trapping faulty input such as this is vital in any useful application, and will be addressed in later chapters.

3.8 Mathematical functions*

The library functions `Trunc`, `Round` and `Frac` were discussed earlier. In addition Pascal has a selection of mathematical functions. Commonly used ones are shown in Table 3.6.

- `Abs(x)` and `Sqr(x)` return real or integer values according to whether x is real or integer.
- Trigonometric functions, `Sqrt`, `Ln` and `Exp` always return real results.
- a^r can be translated into Pascal as `Exp(r*(Ln(a)))`.
- `Pi` is a useful addition to standard Pascal.

The use of some of these functions will be illustrated with a project to calculate the length of the hypotenuse and the angles of a right-angled triangle from the lengths of the two sides adjacent to the right angle.

The finished form will look like Figure 3.10. The triangle is merely to indicate the data that is required, in particular which angle is which.

Use a drawing package to draw a labelled triangle similar to that in Figure 3.10 and save it as a bitmap file; you may omit the drawing if no suitable drawing package is available.

Open a new Delphi project, and place an image component on the form as described in Chapter 2.

Table 3.6 Mathematical functions.

`Abs(x)`	returns the absolute value of x
`ArcTan(x)`	returns, in radians, the inverse tangent of x
`Cos(x)`	returns the cosine of x, where x is in radians
`Sin(x)`	returns the sine of x, where x is in radians
`Exp(x)`	returns e^x
`Ln(x)`	returns the natural log of x ($x \geqslant 0$)
`Pi`	returns the value of π (to 19–20 digits, unless the software floating-point option has been set)
`Sqr(x)`	returns the square of x
`Sqrt(x)`	returns the square root of x

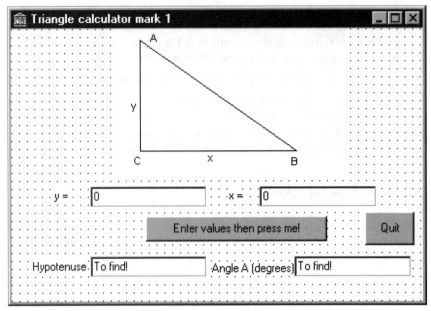

Figure 3.10   Prototype form for the triangle calculator.

1. Load into it the triangle drawing by using the Properties page and clicking on the ellipsis opposite the `Picture` property to load the Picture Editor.

2. Add two buttons to the form for 'Enter values …' and Quit. Resize and alter captions as required.

3. Add four edit components for the input and results and four corresponding labels.

4. Use the Object Inspector as before to change the initial values of the edit boxes to match Figure 3.10.

5. Change the `ReadOnly` property of the bottom two edit boxes to `True`.

6. Change the `Color` property of `Form1` itself to `clWhite`, and its `Caption` as shown.

7. Double click on the larger button and insert the code shown in Listing 3.5.

In Listing 3.5:

● Lines 9 and 10 pick up text from edit boxes and convert each to floating-point representation prior to assigning it to two real variables, x and y.

● Pythagoras' theorem states that the square on the hypotenuse equals the sum of the squares on the other two sides.

● Using standard trigonometry, the tangent of angle A equals BC divided by AC, or x/y.

● Hence angle A equals arctan (x/y) in radians. Line 12 calculates A and then converts it to degrees.

● Lines 13 and 14 display the results in the appropriate edit boxes.

Listing 3.5 Triangle calculator

```
 1: procedure TForm1.Button1Click(Sender: TObject);
 2: {-------------------------------------------------------}
 3: {Given length of 2 adjacent sides of right angle triangle, }
 4: {this procedure finds length of hypotenuse              }
 5: {plus angle opposite x in degrees                       }
 6: {-------------------------------------------------------}
 7: var x,y,z,AngleA: Single;
 8: begin
 9:    y:= StrToFloat(Edit1.Text);
10:    x:= StrToFloat(Edit2.Text);
11:    z:= Sqrt(Sqr(x)+Sqr(y));
12:    AngleA:= ArcTan(x/y)*180/Pi;
13:    Edit3.Text:= FloatToStr(z);
14:    Edit4.Text:= FloatToStr(AngleA);
15: end;
```

● The variables could be declared to be of type Double rather than Single for greater accuracy.

In common with the change calculator, this project does no checking for faulty input, and hence it is not 'user proof'. This can be rectified using skills discussed in later chapters, and further functionality can be added to redraw the triangle according to the side lengths entered.

3.9 Summary

In this chapter we introduced the basic numeric types, that is cardinal types, integer types and floating-point types. Also we used arithmetic operators and library functions to manipulate numeric types, including the two division operators and functions to convert from one type to another. The projects for doubling a number, calculating change and finding an angle of a triangle used edit boxes, which provide a neat method of obtaining input and displaying output in the Delphi environment.

Quiz

1. Which of these numbers could be of type cardinal?
   (a) 32
   (b) 0.5
   (c) −10

2. Which of these are valid identifiers?
   (a) My-variable
   (b) Four
   (c) 4Z

3. Which of the following has highest precedence when calculating an arithmetic expression?
   (a) unary minus
   (b) addition
   (c) multiplication

4. What is the **div** operator used for?
   (a) dividing floating point numbers
   (b) dividing integer numbers
   (c) dividing numbers represented as strings

5. On what page of the Component Palette is the edit component found?
   (a) Standard
   (b) Additional
   (c) Dialogs

6. If the programmer wanted to stop the user entering text in an edit box, what property should be altered?
   (a) `PasswordChar`
   (b) `ReadOnly`
   (c) `Text`

7. What, approximately, is the largest number that can be represented by the type `Single`?
   (a) 3.4×10^{38}
   (b) 1.7×10^{308}
   (c) 1.1×10^{4932}

8. What does the function `IntToStr` do?
   (a) Takes a string and returns an integer.
   (b) Takes an integer and returns a string.
   (c) Takes a real number and returns a string.

9. In the expression `Abs(X)` what type can `X` be?
   (a) It must be of type `Single`.
   (b) It must be of type `Cardinal`.
   (c) It can be of any integer or floating-point type.

10. Which of the following are legitimate notations for comments in your version of Delphi?
    (a) `{ a comment}`
    (b) `// a comment`
    (c) `(* a comment *)`

Exercises

1. Develop a rudimentary calculator which adds, subtracts, multiplies and divides. The user puts the operands into two edit boxes and clicks a button to indicate the operation wanted, then the result will be shown in a third edit box.

2. Write a program to move words round three visible edit boxes.

3. Write a program to convert various currencies. Use two edit boxes and a button to perform each conversion.

4. Write a program to reverse the order of the digits in a three-digit number, so if the user types 123 into one edit box, the program will put 321 into another box.

5. Write a program to find the roots of a quadratic equation from the standard formula: the roots of the equation $ax^2 + bx + c = 0$ are

$$\frac{-b + \sqrt{(b^2 - 4ac)}}{2a} \text{ and } \frac{-b - \sqrt{(b^2 - 4ac)}}{2a}$$

Chapter 4

Conditional statements

4.1 Introduction

Traditionally programs are executed one statement at a time. When the execution of one statement is completed, control passes to another statement. The statement to be executed next is dictated by the statement content and the order in which the statements are listed in the program source code. We will use message boxes to illustrate the execution order of conditional statements.

Delphi's Object Pascal allows program statements to be written that control the order of execution, but in addition Delphi allows event-driven programming which does not adhere strictly to rules of control flow. A programmer can create a number of event handlers for a variety of components on a form. Different sequences of program statements will be executed depending on which events occur. For example, if there is an event OnClick associated with a button, then the code statements for OnClick will be executed only if the button is clicked. If the button is clicked several times then the code is executed several times.

Within Pascal-based languages compound statements can always be substituted for a single statement. With Pascal a compound statement is a sequence of statements that are enclosed by a pair of **begin end** keywords. In this chapter we will give examples using both single and compound statements, showing how one can replace the other.

A statement in Pascal can be considered to be a complete *sentence*. In Delphi, statements are used mostly to calculate numeric expressions or to operate on Delphi objects, for instance to alter properties of objects. A statement generally occurs on a line of its own, but statements (such as the **if** statement described below) can spread over many lines. Some statements can themselves contain other statements; these inner statements are sometimes referred to as *clauses* of the encompassing statement. Statements are separated by semicolons. Pascal is a free-format language which means that line boundaries are not important; programmers can choose to lay out their work in any manner, one word per line if they want. Delphi has a maximum line length of 1024 (127 characters with Delphi 1). The most common practice is to line up **begin end** pairs and to slightly indent code between them (for example two spaces).

4.2   Simple **if** statements

The simplest form of an **if** statement is:

    if *something is true* **then** *do this*

For example:

    if Number < 0 **then** Number:= -Number;

is a simple statement that checks if the value of Number is less than zero and if so negates it. After execution of this statement the value of Number will always be positive or zero.

Listing 4.1   A simple **if** statement

```
1: Total:= 0;
2: Number:= -10;
3: if Number < 0 then
4:    Number:= -Number;
5: Total:= Total+Number;
```

Consider the sequence of statements in Listing 4.1:

- This sequence of statements would start when control passed to the assignment of 0 to Total in line 1.

- On completion of line 1 control passes to the statement on line 2.

- After line 2 is executed control passes to the **if** statement that spreads over lines 3 and 4. The expression

    Number < 0

    at line 3 is evaluated and because this is true execution passes to the statement associated with the **then** clause, at line 4.

- On completion of the `if` statement, control passes to the next statement which is at line 5. Control would have been passed here even if the expression at line 3 evaluated to false, but in this case the statement at line 4 would not have been executed.

The single statement:

```
Number:= -Number
```

can be replaced by a compound statement, which is any number of statements enclosed between the keywords **begin** and **end**.

(Listing 4.2)   A compound statement as the **then** clause

```
1: if Number < 0 then
2: begin
3:    Number:= -Number;
4:    NegativeTotal:= NegativeTotal + Number;
5:    Inc(NumberOfNegativeNumbers);
6: end;
```

In Listing 4.2 the statements between lines 2 and 6 will only be executed if Number is less than zero (for example if it is initialized to -10). Execution will result in:

- Number being negated
- NegativeTotal being increased by the absolute value of Number
- NumberOfNegativeNumbers being incremented by one, using the library function Inc

If Number is not less than zero, the statements between lines 2 and 6 will not be executed; control will pass to the first statement after line 6.

The semicolon in Pascal acts as a statement separator, so it is not necessary to have one between the Inc statement and the **end**; however, if one is included there will not be a compiler error, as the compiler accepts a null statement (a statement that does nothing) as a valid statement. Most programmers find it easier to put a semicolon at the end of every statement, except where Pascal specifically forbids it.

It is good programming practice to indent the statements that create part of a compound statement, so that the **begin** and **end** are at the same level of indentation as the **if** and the statements they enclose are further indented. With a compound statement we normally type the **begin end** pair first and then enter the indented statements between them. This ensures the **begin** and **end** are at the same level of indentation and avoids the possibility of omitting the matching **end**. The default Delphi editor will continue at the same level of indentation as the previous line, unless backspace is pressed. However, indentation is simply to improve readability; the program will execute the same whether indented or not.

4.3 Boolean types

The condition following the **if** must be either a variable of one of the Boolean types or an expression that evaluates to a Boolean type. All Boolean types have two just possible values: `True` or `False`.

The generic type `Boolean` is the preferred choice for logical variables, as it takes the least possible memory. The other Boolean types are size specific, for example `WordBool` is a word sized Boolean taking two bytes, but still only capable of representing the two values `True` or `False`. These types only become necessary when compatibility is required with low-level interfaces to Windows.

There are six relational operators in Pascal that can be used in Boolean expressions:

<	less than
<=	less than or equal to
>	greater than
>=	greater than or equal to
=	equal
<>	not equal

Conditions can be linked by the Boolean operations **and**, **xor** and **or**, or negated by the unary operator **not**.

The Boolean operations have a higher priority than the relational ones, so brackets may be needed to ensure correct evaluation, as in the expression below:

```
if (Number>=10) and (Number<100) then Inc(Tens);
```

Omitting the brackets would lead to an attempt to evaluate the expression:

```
10 and Number
```

and a compiler error would occur.

4.4 The **else** clause

The **then** clause described earlier allows a statement to be executed if a condition is true. When the condition is false that statement is not executed, but in the above example control just passes to the next statement in the program. The addition of an **else** clause allows the inclusion of a further statement, to be executed only if the condition is false: a two-way switch. The general form of the **if** statement is:

```
if something is true then do this else do that
```

An example of the use of a general **if** statement is shown in Listing 4.3. The example computes how many numbers lie in the range 0 to 100 and how many are outside it.

This will cause 1 to be added to `InRange` if the value of `Number` is between 0 and 100 inclusive. If it is not in this range, 1 will be added to `OutOfRange`. After any single execution of this **if** statement, either `InRange` or `OutOfRange` (but not both) will have been incremented.

Listing 4.3 An **else** clause

```
1: if (Number>=0) and (Number<=100) then
2:    Inc(InRange)
3: else
4:    Inc(OutOfRange);
```

Note that there must *not* be a semicolon between line 2 and the **else** on line 3. By putting a semicolon there the programmer would indicate that the **if** statement only has a **then** clause and that what occurs next is a new statement. An **else** on its own is not a legitimate start of a statement and so the compiler will raise an error.

The expression in line 1 of Listing 4.3 evaluates to true if the value of Number lies between 0 and 100. The logic of the expression could be reversed to give a condition that evaluates to true if the value of the number is not in the range 0 to 100: see Listing 4.4.

Listing 4.4 Alternative condition

```
if (Number<0) or (Number>100) then
   Inc(OutOfRange)
else
   Inc(InRange);
```

Normal programming practice is to put the most obvious case in the **then** clause of the **if** statement. Bugs often sneak into logical expressions. For example, mistakenly putting an **and** in the place of **or** in Listing 4.4 will give rise to a condition that will never be true, as Number cannot be both less than 0 and greater than 100. Running the program in the Interactive Development Environment (IDE), with the integrated debugger enabled, will often help to spot such bugs. See Appendix A for hints on debugging programs.

The **else** clause, like the **then** clause, may contain either a single statement or a compound statement.

Listing 4.5 A nested **if** statement

```
1: if Number>0 then
2:    Inc(PositiveCount)
3: else
4:    if Number<0 then
5:       Inc(NegativeCount)
6:    else
7:       Inc(ZeroCount);
8: Total:= Total+Number;
```

In Listing 4.5:

- The **if** statement that starts at line 1 continues down to include line 7.
- The **else** clause of this **if** is itself an **if** statement that starts at line 4 and continues to line 7.
- The effect of this code is to add 1 to PositiveCount if Number is greater than zero, or to add 1 to NegativeCount if Number is less than zero, or to add 1 to ZeroCount if Number is zero.
- Whatever the value of Number control will eventually pass to line 8 and the value of Number will be added to Total.

4.5 case statements

The previous section included a three-way switch; separate portions of code were executed according to whether Number was positive, negative or zero. Using multiple nested **if** statements for complicated switches can make code difficult to follow. In some instances a **case** statement can be used as an alternative to multiple nested **if** statements, resulting in more readable code. A simple **case** statement makes a selection based on the values of a variable. Possible values of the variable must be listed, along with the appropriate statements to be executed for each value. A catchall **else** clause can be included for any possible values not listed.

Note that in the **case** statement the possible values of the **case** selector are separated from the associated statements by a colon. This looks a little like the line numbering used in the printing of Delphi listings. Line numbers are included in our listings for convenient referencing; they are not entered by the programmer. With the **case** statement the possible values of the selector and their associated colons are part of the program and must be entered by the programmer when required.

In this example of a **case** statement:

```
case Number of
    10: Inc(TenCount);
    20: Inc(TwentyCount);
    30: Inc(ThirtyCount);
end;
```

execution would increment TenCount if the value of Number was 10, while if the value of Number was 20 then TwentyCount would be incremented, and if the value of Number was 30 then ThirtyCount would be incremented. If the value of Number was none of 10, 20 or 30, execution would immediately pass to the next statement.

The addition of an **else** clause will provide a set of statements to execute if Number does not take any of the values listed.

```
case Number of
    10: Inc(TenCount);
    20: Inc(TwentyCount);
    30: Inc(ThirtyCount);
```

```
    else
        Inc(OutOfRangeCount)
end;
```

A single statement associated with a possible value of `Number` can be replaced by a compound statement (which is several statements between a **begin end** pair). In what appears to be a contrary fashion, there is no need to put in a **begin** if several statements are associated with the **else** clause; the compiler 'knows' that a **case** statement must finish with the word **end** and so will readily accept several statements between the **else** and the **end**.

A selection part of a statement within a **case** may be made from a list of values or a range of values. Ranges are discussed in Section 7.2. In the following, `'J'..'N'` means all the letters from 'J' to 'N' inclusive.

Listing 4.6 A **case** statement

```
case Letter of
'a','e','i','o','u':
        begin
            Inc(VowelCount);
            Inc(LowerCaseVowelCount);
        end;
'A','E','I','O','U':
        begin
            Inc(VowelCount);
            Inc(UpperCaseVowelCount);
        end;
'B'..'D','F'..'H','J'..'N','P'..'T','V'..'Z':
{upper case consonants}
        Inc(UpperCaseCount);
'b'..'d','f'..'h','j'..'n','p'..'t','v'..'z':
{lower case consonants}
        Inc(LowerCaseCount);
else
    Inc(SomeOtherCount);
    if Letter='#' then Inc(HashCount);
end;
```

Consider Listing 4.6. The clauses are matched in the order presented. However, if duplicate constants appear in the range of values there will be a compile time error. So it is not possible to replace the list of ranges of consonants by the more succinct `'A'..'Z'`. This is different from earlier versions of Pascal which would allow repeated constants.

4.6 Message boxes

Delphi allows the programmer to use a number of special-purpose message boxes for displaying information. Such boxes are commonplace in Windows applications and users are accustomed to seeing boxes informing them they have just won a game or asking if they really want to quit. Delphi itself uses Windows message boxes; for instance, if a programmer attempts to exit Delphi without saving the current project, a box will be displayed seeking confirmation.

The message boxes displayed by Delphi belong to Windows and so will vary slightly depending on the version of Windows the program is running under. Because message boxes are not directly Delphi components the programmer cannot control them visually. They are not found amongst the Component Palette nor can they be viewed by the Object Inspector. However, they are easy to use and can give a very professional appearance to a piece of software.

The simplest way of displaying a message box is by using the ShowMessage procedure. For example,

```
ShowMessage('You win!');
```

will produce a box similar to that shown in Figure 4.1.

Figure 4.1   A message box.

The user has only the 'choice' of pressing the OK button. Like all message boxes this one is *modal*, which means it must be closed before the application can continue.

4.7 Dialog boxes*

The MessageDlg function provides a more general-purpose message box, which can allow the user a choice of answers. The syntax of the MessageDlg function and the parameters passed are quite complex, but by correctly using the call the programmer is able to present the user with the sorts of box that are used by professionally produced Windows packages. MessageDlg is called a *function* because it returns a value that the programmer can test to see what option the user has chosen.

This call,

```
MessageDlg('Do you really want to quit?',
        mtConfirmation, [mbYes,mbNo], 0);
```

creates a box that will look something like the one shown in Figure 4.2.

mtConfirmation is one possible type of message box. mbYes and mbNo are buttons that can appear in message boxes. The message box returns the values mrYes or mrNo according to which button is clicked.

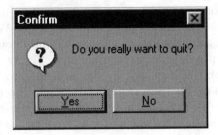

Figure 4.2   A dialog box.

Tables 4.1 and 4.2 summarize the boxes and buttons commonly used.

Displaying a message dialog box does not cause any changes to the flow of execution of a program. The programmer must test the value returned by the function and then use a conditional statement to ensure the correct action is taken. For example, using the above box:

```
if MessageDlg('Do you really want to quit?',
   mtConfirmation,[mbYes,mbNo],0) = mrYes then
      Application.Terminate;
```

will mean that if the user presses the Yes button `Application.Terminate` will be executed and the application will finish. If the other button is pressed the program continues to the next statement. This example is one that a user may well have seen

Table 4.1   Dialog box types.

Box name	Title	When displayed contains
mtConfirmation	Confirm	question mark
mtCustom	Name of the executable file	no picture
mtError	Error	stop sign
mtInformation	Information	an 'I'
mtWarning	Warning	exclamation mark

Table 4.2   Button types.

Button name	Word on face
mbAbort	Abort
mbAll	All
mbCancel	Cancel
mbHelp	Help
mbIgnore	Ignore
mbNo	No
mbOK	OK
mbRetry	Retry
mbYes	Yes

in other applications; however, because execution terminates it is not a good example of a conditional statement, where control normally passes to the next statement. A better example might be:

```
if MessageDlg('Do you want to increment number?',
  mtConfirmation,[mbYes,mbIgnore],0) = mrYes then
  Inc(Number);
{next statements}
```

This would increment the value of `Number` only if the Yes button was clicked. Whichever is clicked, control passes to the next statements.

The parameters to the `MessageDlg` function are:

const Msg:**string**	the string that will be displayed
AType:TMsgDlgType	the message box type to be displayed
AButtons:TMsgDlgButtons	a list of the value of buttons to be displayed, enclosed in square brackets
HelpCtx:LongInt	a link into the help system; in this case 0 means there is not one

A variant on the `MessageDlg` function is `MessageDlgPos`, which takes two extra integer parameters, indicating the *x* and *y* positions of the top left-hand corner of the dialog box relative to the top left-hand corner of the screen.

4.8 Input dialog box

An `InputBox` provides a simple way of eliciting information from a user. For example, the function:

```
InputBox('Who are you?','Please type your name','anon');
```

displays a box similar to the one shown in Figure 4.3.

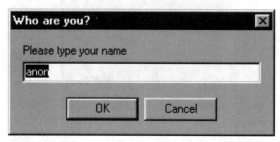

Figure 4.3 An input dialog box.

This box returns a string containing the characters typed in if the user presses OK, or 'anon' if the user presses Cancel. As with the message box, it is generated by Windows.

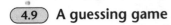

(4.9) A guessing game

In this section we will develop a Delphi program to allow the user to guess a number that the computer has chosen. The computer will tell the user if the guess is:

- too big
- too small
- correct.

1. Open Delphi and save the unit file and project in a suitable directory; here they are called U4_8.pas and P4_8.dpr respectively, to correspond to Listing 4.8 below, which contains the complete listing of the unit.

2. Create a prototype form as shown in Figure 4.4. Use the Object Inspector to set the properties as outlined below, and the Form Designer to size and position the components correctly.

   - The Caption on the form is set to Guessing Game.
   - The Text field of the edit box is cleared.
   - The captions of the labels are set to:

     ```
     I'm thinking of a number
     What do you think it is?
     ```
     respectively.

   - One button is given the Name property CompareButton and the Caption property Compare.
   - The other button is given the Name property QuitButton and the Caption property Quit.

Figure 4.4 The prototype form.

3. Use the Save All speed button to save the unit and project. The code that will do the work can now be added. The complete listing is shown below in Listing 4.8.

4. Using the Object Inspector in design mode, add the code that will close the form to the OnClick event of the QuitButton. This will require the programmer to type:

```
Close;
```

in the code template, as can be seen at line 36 in Listing 4.8.

5. The code will now be developed that allows the computer to choose a number at random. Use the Object Inspector to select the OnCreate event for the form; in the Code window this will open a template similar to this:

```
procedure TForm1.FormCreate(Sender: TObject);
begin

end;
```

Between the **begin** and **end** insert the following statements:

```
Randomize;
ComputerNumber := Random(MaxNumber);
```

See lines 44 and 45 of Listing 4.8.

The library function Random generates an integer random number that takes a value between 0 and MaxNumber (including 0 but not MaxNumber). Randomize is called as otherwise the computer would choose the same number every time the application was executed. The ability to repeat a series of random numbers is important in some applications, but not in this one. ComputerNumber is a variable, but it will need to be visible to other procedures in this unit, so it must be declared outside the procedure FormCreate. Likewise MaxNumber is a constant that may need to be visible to other procedures in this unit. Both are declared within the implementation section of the unit (reached by scrolling just above this procedure). The declarations are shown in lines 31 and 32 of Listing 4.8. The implementation section occurs after the keyword **implementation**. The role of the implementation section will be discussed in detail in Chapter 13.

Variables declared in the implementation section (such as ComputerNumber) are sometimes called *globals*. In fact such variables are only available within the unit where they are declared and so we will normally refer to them as *unit-wide* variables.

Assigning 100 to MaxNumber means the computer's choice of number will always be between 0 and 99 inclusive.

6. Finally the code for the OnClick event of the Compare button needs to be added. Use the Object Inspector to create the skeleton event handler:

```
procedure TForm1.CompareButtonClick(Sender: TObject);
begin

end;
```

This event handler will need to get the value of the user's guess, and it does this with the following statement:

```
UserNumber := StrToInt(Edit1.Text);
```

By the time this statement is executed the user should have already typed a number into the text field of the edit box. The number in the box is, in fact, a collection of characters, so the library function StrToInt is used to convert the string of characters into an integer number. The number can then be stored in a variable UserNumber. If the text in the edit box is not an integer Delphi will raise an exception. Exceptions are discussed in detail in Chapter 11 but for now they can be ignored.

The variable `UserNumber` must be declared. This is done by inserting the following declaration above the **begin** and below the procedure's header:

```
var UserNumber: Integer;
```

The variable `UserNumber` is only used locally within this procedure, so it is preferable that it is declared locally to this procedure, rather than made accessible throughout the unit like `ComputerNumber`.

The remaining code can now be added to the procedure, in the guise of a nested **if** statement, which compares `ComputerNumber` and `UserNumber`: see Listing 4.7.

Listing 4.7   Comparing the user's guess with the computer's number

```
if UserNumber<ComputerNumber then
  ShowMessage('Too small, try again')
else
  if UserNumber>ComputerNumber then
    ShowMessage('Too big, try again')
  else
  begin
    ShowMessage
      ('That''s Right. I''ll think up a new number');
    ComputerNumber:= Random(MaxNumber);
  end;{end of inner if}
{end outer if - for which the else clause is a single statement}
```

Different messages will be displayed using the procedure `ShowMessage`, depending on the relative values of `ComputerNumber` and `UserNumber`. The two consecutive single quotes appearing in `That''s` are so that a single quote will appear in the message. Single quotes are the usual delimiter for strings in Pascal and the use of two adjacent quotes is the mechanism for displaying a single one! Two single quotes need four quotes to be entered; alternatively the double quotes character can be used. When the right answer has been chosen the computer generates a new random number. The comments indicating the ends of the **if** statements are there for the programmer's convenience.

The final procedure is shown in lines 48 to 68 of Listing 4.8. The comment below the procedure header summarizes what the event handler does and will be useful to the programmer if subsequently this program has to be revised.

7. It is prudent at this point to save the whole project. It can then be run.

Listing 4.8   The complete unit for the guessing game

```
1: unit U4_8;
2:
3: interface
```

```
 4:
 5: uses
 6:    Windows, Messages, SysUtils, Classes, Graphics, Controls,
 7:    Forms, Dialogs, StdCtrls;
 8:
 9: type
10:    TForm1 = class(TForm)
11:       Edit1: TEdit;
12:       Label1: TLabel;
13:       Label2: TLabel;
14:       CompareButton: TButton;
15:       QuitButton: TButton;
16:       procedure QuitButtonClick(Sender: TObject);
17:       procedure FormCreate(Sender: TObject);
18:       procedure CompareButtonClick(Sender: TObject);
19:    private
20:       { Private declarations }
21:    public
22:       { Public declarations }
23:    end;
24:
25: var
26:    Form1: TForm1;
27:
28: implementation
29: {$R *.DFM}
30:
31: var ComputerNumber: Integer;
32: const MaxNumber= 100;
33:
34: procedure TForm1.QuitButtonClick(Sender: TObject);
35: begin
36:    Close;
37: end;
38:
39: procedure TForm1.FormCreate(Sender: TObject);
40: {----------------------------------------------------------}
41: { Make the computer choose an initial random number        }
42: {----------------------------------------------------------}
43: begin
44:    Randomize;
45:    ComputerNumber:= Random(MaxNumber);
46: end;
47:
48: procedure TForm1.CompareButtonClick(Sender: TObject);
49: {----------------------------------------------------------}
50: { Get the user's choice of number, compare with the        }
51: { computer's  number and display an appropriate message    }
52: {----------------------------------------------------------}
53: var UserNumber: Integer;
```

```
54: begin
55:   UserNumber:= StrToInt(Edit1.text);
56:   if UserNumber<ComputerNumber then
57:     ShowMessage('Too small, try again')
58:   else
59:     if UserNumber>ComputerNumber then
60:       ShowMessage('Too big, try again')
61:     else
62:     begin
63:       ShowMessage
64:         ('That''s Right. I''ll think up a new number');
65:       ComputerNumber:= Random(MaxNumber);
66:     end;{end of inner if}
67:   {end of outer if}
68: end;
69:
70: end.
```

8. Once the program correctly compiles it will run and the user can start to play the game of guessing the computer's number. When played the game will look similar to Figure 4.5.

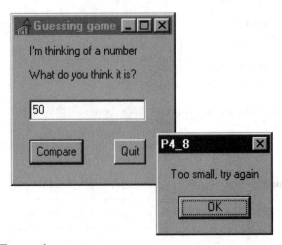

Figure 4.5 The guessing game.

As the game is played the user will create events and the program will respond to them.

- When the ShowMessage procedure displays a message, the OK button must be clicked before any other events can happen.
- When the Quit button is clicked the application will terminate.
- When characters are typed in the edit box they will be displayed. The characters in the edit box can be edited in the normal manner, by selection, deletion and typing.

● When the Compare button is clicked it will execute the code that compares the user's choice of number against the computer's and display an appropriate message box. This event will happen whether or not the user has changed the value in the edit box.

(4.10) Guessing game Mark 2*

When the guessing game above is compared with other Windows games a number of shortcomings will be noticed. In this section we will try to rectify most of these short-comings while not learning advanced issues that will be covered in later chapters.

We will amend the code so that the user's guess is accepted when the enter key is pressed, and so will no longer need the Compare button. Entry of non-digits will be ignored. A main menu will be added with a new option that will allow the user to change the maximum number the computer can guess. An Exit option on the main menu will replace the Quit button.

1. Within Delphi save the unit and project from the original guessing game using new names. We use U4_10.pas and P4_10.dpr to match the unit listing in Listing 4.10 below. It is best to do this via the Delphi environment: copying with the file manager will leave a mismatch between the file name and the names at the top of the unit and project which will give rise to errors.

2. With the Object Inspector select the event page of Edit1 and double click oppo-site the event OnKeyPress to open the Code Editor at the event handler for Edit1KeyPress. As part of this improved code it will be necessary to use unprintable characters. These obviously cannot be represented by characters in quotes. Instead a number of constants will be set to the ASCII code for the required characters. The # character is used to signify that the following integer is an ASCII code.

```
const BackSpace= #8; Null= #0; Enter= #13;
```

The declaration only needs to be local to the event handler, so it is placed between the procedure header and the **begin**, as can be seen in line 77 of Listing 4.10. Within the event handler different action will be taken depending on which key is pressed – see Listing 4.9.

In Listing 4.9:

● Key is the character that the user has just pressed on the keyboard.

● Line 2 selects whether a character between 0 and 9 has been pressed; backspace is also permitted for when the user wants to correct a guess.

● Line 3 is an empty statement as no action is required. The semicolon is essential.

● Line 4 indicates that the user has pressed Enter (sometimes called Return).

● Line 6 replaces the Enter key by Null so it is not processed as part of the number the user has guessed.

● Line 7 calls the event handler previously written for the Compare button. We will see in Chapter 9 how we can write our own procedures, but since

---

Listing 4.9 **case** statement for key pressed

```
 1: case Key of
 2:   '0'..'9',BackSpace:
 3:     ;
 4:   Enter:
 5:   begin
 6:     Key:= Null;
 7:     CompareButtonClick(Sender);
 8:     Edit1.SelectAll;
 9:   end
10:   else
11:     Key:= Null;
12: end;
```

CompareButtonClick already exists it is convenient to use it. The event handler needs a parameter; the role of Sender will be explained in Chapter 10, but briefly it tells the event handler who called it.

- Line 8 highlights the number in the edit box so the user can type over it with the next guess.
- The **else** clause at lines 10 and 11 replaces any other key presses by Null, that is they are ignored.

3. Add a main menu component to the prototype form, and remove the Compare and Quit buttons (as in Section 2.7). Using the menu editor give the menu the caption &File and two options: &New and E&xit, separated by a bar.

4. Use the Object Inspector to open the Code Editor at the template for the OnClick event of the Exit option and insert the Close command, see line 95 of Listing 4.10.

5. Use the Object Inspector to open the Code Editor at the template for the OnClick event of the new option: see lines 98 to 111 of Listing 4.10. Delphi automatically generates lines 98, 104 and 111. Add the comments (lines 99 to 102) and declaration of a local string at line 103. Now add the code to allow the user to reset the maximum and a new computer number to be generated: see lines 105 to 110 of Listing 4.10.

- Lines 105 to 108 are a single assignment statement, broken across four lines for ease of reading. The InputBox they generate is similar to the one shown in Figure 4.6.

Figure 4.6 An input box.

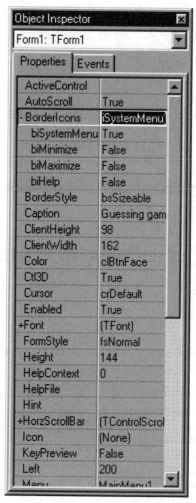

Figure 4.7   Border icons.

- The string the user enters is assigned to `TempStr`.
- Line 109 converts `TempStr` to an integer.
- Line 110 generates a new choice as the computer's number, as in line 65.

6. The original form had the default minimize and maximize icons at the top of the form. These are not very useful to the player of the guessing game and can be removed as follows. On the property page of the Object Inspector, with the form selected, click on the property `+BorderIcons`; this will reveal further choices as shown in Figure 4.7, and the plus sign will become a minus. Set both `biMinimize` and `biMaximize` to `False` (as shown).

7. The unit and project should now be saved and then run. When the game is played the form will look like Figure 4.8. The number in the input box is selected, so the

user can simply type a new number and press Enter to run the game, or can choose Exit from the File menu to quit.

Figure 4.8   The running form.

Listing 4.10   Complete unit code for Mark 2 of the guessing game

```
 1: unit U4_10;
 2:
 3: interface
 4:
 5: uses
 6:   Windows, Messages, SysUtils, Classes, Graphics, Controls,
 7:   Forms, Dialogs, StdCtrls, Menus;
 8:
 9: type
10:   TForm1 = class(TForm)
11:     Edit1: TEdit;
12:     Label1: TLabel;
13:     Label2: TLabel;
14:     MainMenu1: TMainMenu;
15:     File1: TMenuItem;
16:     New1: TMenuItem;
17:     N1: TMenuItem;
18:     Exit1: TMenuItem;
19:     procedure FormCreate(Sender: TObject);
20:     procedure CompareButtonClick(Sender: TObject);
21:     procedure Edit1KeyPress(Sender: TObject; var Key: Char);
22:     procedure Exit1Click(Sender: TObject);
23:     procedure New1Click(Sender: TObject);
24:   private
25:     { Private declarations }
26:   public
27:     { Public declarations }
28:   end;
29:
30: var
31:   Form1: TForm1;
32:
```

```
33: implementation
34: {$R *.DFM}
35:
36: var ComputerNumber: Integer;
37: const MaxNumber: Integer= 100;
38:
39: procedure TForm1.FormCreate(Sender: TObject);
40: {----------------------------------------------------------}
41: { Make the computer choose an initial random number        }
42: {----------------------------------------------------------}
43: begin
44:    Randomize;
45:    ComputerNumber:= Random(MaxNumber);
46: end;
47:
48: procedure TForm1.CompareButtonClick(Sender: TObject);
49: {----------------------------------------------------------}
50: { Get the user's choice of number, compare with the        }
51: { computer's  number and display an appropriate message    }
52: {----------------------------------------------------------}
53: var UserNumber: Integer;
54: begin
55:    UserNumber:= StrToInt(Edit1.text);
56:    if UserNumber<ComputerNumber then
57:      ShowMessage('Too small, try again')
58:    else
59:      if UserNumber>ComputerNumber then
60:        ShowMessage('Too big, try again')
61:      else
62:      begin
63:        ShowMessage
64:           ('That''s Right. I''ll think up a new number');
65:        ComputerNumber:= Random(MaxNumber);
66:      end;{end of inner if}
67:    {end of outer if}
68: end;
69:
70: procedure TForm1.Edit1KeyPress
71:           (Sender: TObject; var Key: Char);
72: {----------------------------------------------------------}
73: { Accept inputs of digits and backspace                    }
74: { Do comparison when Enter pressed                         }
75: { Ignore all other key presses                            }
76: {----------------------------------------------------------}
77: const BackSpace= #8; Null= #0; Enter= #13;
78: begin
79:    case Key of
80:    '0'..'9',BackSpace:
81:      ;{Key is a digit or backspace so no action necessary}
82:    Enter:
```

```
83:   begin
84:     Key:= Null; {don't include the Enter key with the number}
85:     CompareButtonClick(Sender);
86:     Edit1.SelectAll;
87:   end
88:   else
89:     Key:= Null;  {all other key presses replaced by null}
90:   end ;
91: end;
92:
93: procedure TForm1.Exit1Click(Sender: TObject);
94: begin
95:   Close;
96: end;
97:
98: procedure TForm1.New1Click(Sender: TObject);
99: {-----------------------------------------------------------}
100: { Allow the user to reset the maximum number              }
101: { Generate a new number for the computer's choice         }
102: {-----------------------------------------------------------}
103: var TempStr: string;
104: begin
105:   TempStr:= InputBox
106:                ('Reset Maximum Number',
107:                 'Type the new maximum',
108:                  IntToStr(MaxNumber));
109:   MaxNumber:= StrToInt(TempStr);
110:   ComputerNumber:= Random(MaxNumber);
111: end;
112:
113: end.
```

(4.11) Summary

In this chapter we introduced conditional execution of code using both program constructs and events.

The use of **if** statements with **then** clauses and optional **else** clauses was described. The role of **begin end** pairs to create compound statements was illustrated by replacing single statements within clauses by multiple statements enclosed by **begin end** pairs. The **case** statement was discussed as an alternative to multiple nested **if** statements.

Message boxes were used as a mechanism for the program to transmit information to the user and to receive simple information from the user. As message boxes are generated by Windows the Delphi programmer has limited control over their appearance. However, as illustrated in this chapter, their use can give a professional appearance to even the simplest programs. The role of events was discussed and examples given.

A game was prototyped and then developed into a program that is easier to use and resilient to user errors.

Quiz

1. What is a compound statement?
    (a)   a sequence of statements enclosed by a pair of **begin end** keywords
    (b)   an assignment
    (c)   a **case** statement

2. Consider this Boolean expression:

    ```
    (Y>10) and (Y<20)
    ```

    For which of the following values of Y will it be true?
    (a)   10
    (b)   16
    (c)   22

3. What is the role of a semicolon?
    (a)   Terminating declarations and separating statements.
    (b)   Marking the end of a line.
    (c)   Goes in front of an equals sign to represent assignment.

4. Which of the following is true?
    (a)   A **case** statement must always have an **else** clause.
    (b)   An **else** clause is always executed.
    (c)   An **else** clause is optional in an **if** statement.

5. Consider this fragment of a **case** statement:

    ```
    case X of
    ```

    What type can X be?
    (a)   any type
    (b)   any real type
    (c)   any ordinal type

6. Why do message boxes look different according to the version of Windows that is running?
    (a)   Delphi is using Windows' own message box.
    (b)   Different versions of Delphi run under different versions of Windows.
    (c)   There is an option that has not been set.

7. Consider the call:

    ```
    MessageDlg('That could fail',mtWarning,
                [mbIgnore,mbAbort],0);
    ```

    What does it do?
    (a)   Causes the program to fail.
    (b)   Displays a warning message box with two buttons.
    (c)   Displays an ignore/abort message box with no buttons.

8.   Consider this statement:

```
Number:= Random(10);
```

After executing this statement what value will be in `Number`?

(a)   10

(b)   an integer number between 0 and 9 inclusive

(c)   a real number between 0 and 10

9.   Consider the following statement:

```
ShowMessage('It''s me');
```

What will happen when it is included in a program?

(a)   The program will fail to compile.

(b)   At run time the program will raise an error at this line.

(c)   A message box will be displayed when this line is executed.

10.   Which of the following are ways of accessing the Delphi help system?

(a)   pressing F1

(b)   selecting Help from the Delphi main menu

(c)   typing the word Help

Exercises

1.   Adapt the program in Section 4.8 so that it displays messages 'very hot, just too big' or 'very hot, just too small' if the user's guess is close to the right answer.

2.   Write a program that allows the user to enter text in an edit box. Each time the key is pressed the program will display a message indicating something about the key, for example that it was:

   ⬤ a lower case letter

   ⬤ a capital

   ⬤ a number

   ⬤ a backspace

   ⬤ some other character.

3.   Write a program that increases the number in an edit box (initially 1) every time the form is clicked. If the number shown is a multiple of 3 or contains the digit 3, a message box appears with the word 'buzz'. If both are true the message is 'buzz buzz'.

4.   Write a program that increases the size of a button each time it is clicked, and displays a message saying whether it is bigger or smaller than another button.

5.   Write a program to specify whether a triangle is equilateral, isosceles (two sides equal), right angled or scalene (all the sides of different lengths). Note that some classifications are mutually exclusive; others are not. The user will be expected to supply coordinates via an input box.

Chapter 5

Counted loops

5.1 Introduction

One of the most compelling reasons for using a computer to perform a task is that it can be programmed to repeat a series of instructions, or *iterate*. There is little advantage in using a PC over using a calculator to evaluate a formula once, save for the record of operations performed. Usually, however, a scientist requires to evaluate the same formula many times, possibly with different values, and certainly a large employer must make a payroll calculation for many employees. The very early programming languages had instructions to jump to another point in the code, so that the programmer could cause iteration. High-level languages have incorporated constructs to make iteration easy and foolproof to perform. In fact modern high-level languages usually offer constructs for both *deterministic* loops, where the number of iterations is known before iteration commences, and for *non-deterministic* loops. In this chapter we will discuss deterministic loops.

PCs in homes today are used mainly for word processing and for games, not for calculations as such. The underlying software relies heavily on iteration and conditionals, and most obviously on graphics in the case of games. Iteration is useful both with and without graphics. As indicated in Chapter 2, and later in the current chapter, the Delphi programmer can use graphics without iteration. Frequently in Delphi and in more traditional programming environments the two concepts are used together to give the appearance of images moving. Computer graphics is a vast subject in itself, but this chapter will indicate how the Delphi environment allows drawing on a form, and how the programmer can incorporate simple animation.

5.2   Simple counted loops

We introduce deterministic loops by first demonstrating the action of the **for** construct. We will use the prototype form shown in Figure 5.1.

1. Open a new project, then place two buttons on the form.

2. Make one button a Quit button as in previous projects, by changing the Name property to Quit. This also changes the Caption property. Then insert

    ```
    Close;
    ```

    in the OnClick event handler for the Quit button.

    Note in passing that changing the Name property changes the Caption property too, but the converse is not so. Also, it is inadvisable to set the Name property equal to Close, because doing so will hide the event Close, leading to problems when closing the form!

3. Change the Name property of the other button to Iterate thus changing its Caption too. The code to be put in the OnClick event handler of the Iterate button will cause the same statement, to show a message box, to be executed several times.

4. Use the Object Inspector to change the Caption on the form to

    ```
    Experiments with the for construct
    ```

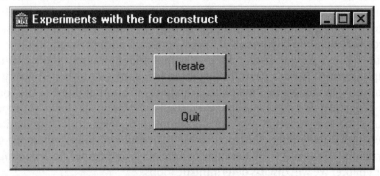

Figure 5.1 Prototype form to demonstrate loops.

5. In the Object Inspector, set the `ActiveControl` property of the form to `Iterate`. This ensures that the Iterate button will have the initial focus when project runs. This means that the Iterate button will be highlighted, and if the user presses Enter immediately then the `IterateClick` event handler will run. If the user selects the Quit button before pressing Enter, then the `QuitClick` event handler runs instead, but clicking the button will still work. The `ActiveControl` property can also be used in code; for details see online help. The form should now look like Figure 5.1.

6. Open code for the `OnClick` event handler for the Iterate button, and change it to that shown in Listing 5.1.

Listing 5.1   Code within the event handler `IterateClick`

```
1: var Count:Integer;
2: begin {this line was provided automatically!}
3:    for Count := 1 to 10 do
4:       ShowMessage('Here we are again');
5:    ShowMessage('Finished now!');
6: end;   {and so was this}
7:
```

---

7. Save the project, compile and run it.

The Iterate button will be initially focused, and so the user just needs to press the Enter key, to start the `OnClick` event for Iterate. If the other button marked Quit is selected, the messages in lines 4 and 5 will not be displayed at all.

The message box bearing the message

Here we are again

will be displayed, and the user must respond to the message box, 10 times. This is because line 4 has run 10 times.

In order to see how the variable `Count` changes, press the Quit button, to return to the Code window.

Change line 4 to

```
ShowMessage('Count is '+IntToStr(Count));
```

The whole unit is shown for completeness in Listing 5.2. Much of this is generated by Delphi. Beware that deleting the Delphi-generated code can lead to odd errors.

Listing 5.2   Complete unit to demonstrate **for** loops

```
1: unit U5_2;
2:
3: interface
4:
5: uses
```

```
 6:   Windows, Messages, SysUtils, Classes, Graphics,
 7:   Controls, Forms, Dialogs, StdCtrls;
 8:
 9: type
10:   TForm1 = class(TForm)
11:     Iterate: TButton;
12:     Quit: TButton;
13:     procedure QuitClick(Sender: TObject);
14:     procedure IterateClick(Sender: TObject);
15:   private
16:     { Private declarations }
17:   public
18:     { Public declarations }
19:   end;
20:
21: var
22:   Form1: TForm1;
23:
24: implementation
25:
26: {$R *.DFM}
27:
28: procedure TForm1.QuitClick(Sender: TObject);
29: begin
30:   Close;
31: end;
32:
33: procedure TForm1.IterateClick(Sender: TObject);
34: var Count: Integer;
35: begin {this line was provided automatically!}
36:   for Count:= 1 to 10 do
37:     ShowMessage('Here we are again');
38:   ShowMessage('Finished now!');
39: end;   {and so was this}
40:
41: end.
```

Compile and run the application with Listing 5.2, then experiment further by changing line 36 successively to

```
for Count:= 1 to 10 do;

for Count:= -10 to -1 do
```

then

```
for Count:= -1 to -10 do
```

In the last case, the message from line 38 of Listing 5.2 shows immediately, showing that if the initial value exceeds the final value, the action in line 37 is not executed at all.

Revert to the first version of line 36:

```
for Count:= 1 to 10 do
```

before finally saving the unit and project. It will be needed later.

(5.3)   Action of the **for** construct

The general form of the **for** construction that has been investigated in the previous section is

```
for control variable:= initial value to final value do action;
```

In Listing 5.2, Count was the control variable. The experiments in the previous section indicated that in that listing:

- On entry to the **for** construct the control variable, Count, is initialized to the initial value.
- At the start of the loop, line 36, this control variable is tested against the final value.
- If the control variable is less than or equal to the final value then control passes to the next statement, line 37: this is the action to be performed.
- Action takes place.
- The control variable is incremented.
- Control goes back to the code to test against the final value in line 36.
- If the control variable is now greater than the final value then control passes immediately to the statement following action (in Listing 5.2 this was line 38). Line 37 is not executed.
- A semicolon immediately following **do** causes a null statement to be done the relevant number of times; the subsequent statement (possibly intended to be a repeated action) is executed just once. This is a common error; sometimes extra semicolons do matter. The unit compiles and runs but produces the wrong results.

There is another variation where **to** is replaced by **downto** to give a backward running loop:

```
for control variable:= initial value downto final value do action;
```

To see how this works, replace line 36 in Listing 5.2 with

```
for Count:= -1 downto -10 do
```

and rerun the project. In this case each iteration changes the control variables by -1.

Note that the **for** construct in Pascal has no way of increasing or decreasing the control variable by a number greater than 1. Where the programmer wants this, a **while** loop or additional code within a **for** loop can be used. It is permissible to change the control variable within a **for** loop, but to do so is normally considered bad practice: the **for** construct increments or decrements the control variable automatically. The **for** construct is both easy for the programmer to use and efficient in execution.

After the **for** statement has finished normally, the value of the control variable is undefined, so do not assume that its value is the final value.

5.4 Non-integer control variables

Not surprisingly, control variables and initial and final values can be of type `Cardinal` (non-negative integer) rather than `Integer` as such. This is because `Cardinal` and `Integer` are both *ordinal* types. An ordinal type is one where each value, save the first and last, has a unique value preceding it and succeeding it. In fact control variables and initial and final values can be of any ordinal type, which includes characters. Assuming that

```
var Letter:Char;
```

the code fragment

```
for Letter := 'A' to 'J' do
  ShowMessage('Here we are again');
```

will again display 10 identical message boxes.

Floating-point types are not ordinal, so these cannot be used to control **for** loops.

The initial and final values employed so far are literals, such as `'A'` or `10`, but can be variables or expressions of the appropriate (assignment compatible) type.

5.5 Compound statements in **for** loops

The **for** constructs discussed so far have had only a single statement to be repeated. In the same manner as the **if** construct, a compound statement can replace a single statement as the action, and this is a more common option. The single statements that compose the compound statement are bracketed by a **begin end** pair.

We will now develop a project to total several numbers, and at the same time find the maximum and minimum of those numbers. The idea is that the user will first be asked how many values are to be summed, then an appropriate number of dialog boxes will ask for those individual values. A running total will be displayed in an edit box, as will current values of the maximum and minimum. A prototype form is shown in Figure 5.2.

1. Configure the form as shown in Figure 5.2 with five edit boxes, two buttons and labels.

2. Change the Name properties of the five edit boxes, starting from the top, to
   ```
   Count
   LastNo
   Max
   ```

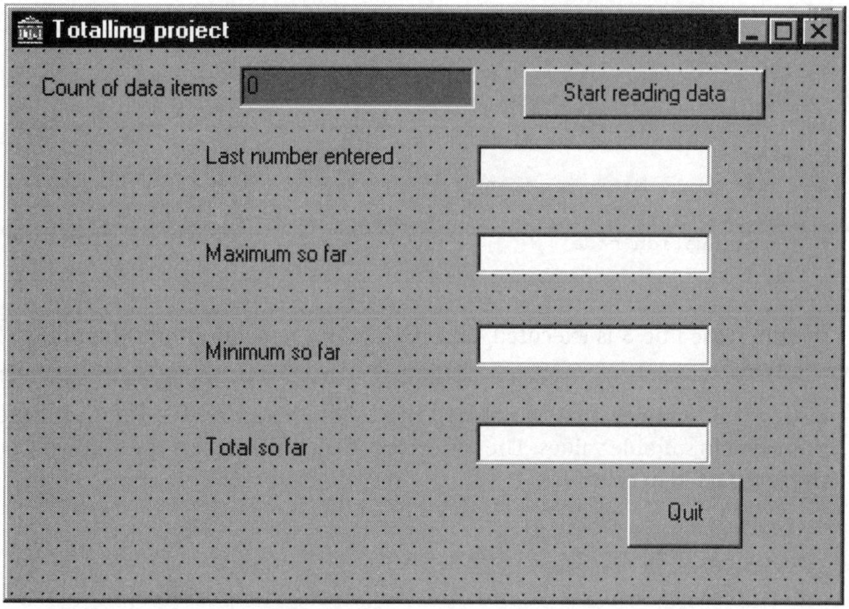

Figure 5.2 Prototype form for the totalling project.

```
Min
Tot
```

3. Change the `Color` property of the `Count` edit component as preferred, by selecting the Properties tab of the Object Inspector and choosing from the drop down menu to the right of `Color` (`clBlue` is one example), or double clicking there to show a palette from which to choose. This will highlight where the user is required to enter data directly into the form.

4. Change the `Text` property of `Count` to 0 (that is zero).

5. Change the `ReadOnly` property of the other edit boxes to `True`, so the user cannot alter those values directly, and change their `Text` properties to blank.

6. Change the `Caption` properties of the buttons and labels as shown in Figure 5.2.

7. Code the `OnClick` event of the Quit button as in earlier examples.

Now to design the underlying code to read and process the data. The basic process, after initialization, is to read another data item, then update the values of the maximum, minimum and total so far. The method will be described before explaining exactly where to type code into templates. Suitable code to find maximum, minimum and total might be as shown in Listing 5.3.
In Listing 5.3:

- Line 1 increments `Total` by `This`.
- Line 2 decides whether `This` is a new maximum, and if so line 3 is executed to update the maximum so far, and control passes to line 7.

Listing 5.3

```
1: Total:=Total + This;
2: if This > MaxSoFar then
3:    MaxSoFar:=This
4: else
5:    if This < MinSoFar then
6:        MinSoFar:=This;
7: {continuation code}
```

- Otherwise line 5 is executed, and if This is a new minimum then line 6 is executed.

Listing 5.3 assumes that variables Total, MaxSoFar and MinSoFar have been primed with suitable values. The easiest way to do this is to use the following code for the first data item only:

```
Total:=This;
MaxSoFar:=This;
MinSoFar:=This;
```

In addition, the values of variables MaxSoFar, MinSoFar, Total and This must be converted to string format and then used to update the appropriate edit boxes, by using code like the following:

```
Max.Text:=FloatToStrF(MaxSoFar,ffgeneral,5,2);
Min.Text:=FloatToStrF(MinSoFar,ffgeneral,5,2);
Tot.Text:=FloatToStrF(Total,ffgeneral,5,2);
LastNo.Text:=FloatToStrF(This,ffgeneral,5,2);
```

FloatToStrF was used in Chapter 3, to display currency. FloatToStr is easier to use than FloatToStrF, but the latter can produce superior looking output. The function heading is

```
function FloatToStrF(Value:Extended; Format:TFloatFormat;
    Precision,Digits:Integer): string;
```

- ffGeneral is a value of Format suitable for more general display of real numbers: the value is converted to an equivalent string using fixed or scientific format according to the value of Precision. Other alternatives to ffGeneral can be found in online help.
- Precision specifies the precision of the value displayed in decimal format, but if the value will not fit then scientific notation will be used instead.
- Digits specifies the minimum number of digits in the exponent, for scientific notation.

Enter this code for the OnClick event of the button which has the Caption

```
Start reading data
```

1. Between the procedure heading and **begin** insert:

    ```
    var
    This,MaxSoFar,MinSoFar,Total: Single;
    Index: Integer;
    ```

2. After the **begin** insert the code shown in Listing 5.4.
3. Compile it and run the code. Note that if you have not changed the names of the edit boxes as suggested, the code in Listing 5.4 will fail to compile. This version works satisfactorily in most cases, but if the count of data items entered is zero or negative, one item of data proper will be expected as line 2 causes an `InputBox` to be displayed. This could be avoided by inserting yet another **if** statement around lines 1 to 11. The other criticism of the code itself is that lines 8 to 11 are repeated in lines 25 to 28. One way of avoiding this is by use of procedures as explained in Chapter 9.

(**Listing 5.4**) Code to insert into event handler

```
 1: This:=
 2: StrToFloat(InputBox('Data Entry',
 3:   'Please enter next number','0'));
 4: Total:= This;
 5: MaxSoFar:= This;
 6: MinSoFar:= This;
 7: {update edit boxes}
 8: Max.Text:= FloatToStrF(MaxSoFar,ffgeneral,5,2);
 9: Min.Text:= FloatToStrF(MinSoFar,ffgeneral,5,2);
10: Tot.Text:= FloatToStrF(Total,ffgeneral,5,2);
11: LastNo.Text:= FloatToStrF(This,ffgeneral,5,2);
12: {deal with remaining data}
13: for Index:= 2 to StrToInt(Count.Text) do
14: begin
15:   This:=
16:   StrToFloat(InputBox('Data Entry',
17:     'Please enter next number','0'));
18:   Total:= Total + This;
19:   if This > MaxSoFar then
20:     MaxSoFar:= This
21:   else
22:     if This < MinSoFar then
23:       MinSoFar:= This;
24:   {update edit boxes}
25:   Max.Text:= FloatToStrF(MaxSoFar,ffgeneral,5,2);
26:   Min.Text:= FloatToStrF(MinSoFar,ffgeneral,5,2);
27:   Tot.Text:= FloatToStrF(Total,ffgeneral,5,2);
28:   LastNo.Text:= FloatToStrF(This,ffgeneral,5,2);
29: end;  {for}
```

Both these problems can be avoided in another way, by running the main loop from 1 to StrToInt(Count.Text) as shown in Listing 5.5 at line 12. Then if Count is zero or negative the main body of the loop starting on line 13 is never executed, thus avoiding the unwanted requests for data. Now an additional **if then else** is required, starting at line 17 and ending on line 31, to discriminate between the first data item and the rest, if any.

Listing 5.5 Improvements to the totalling project

```
 1: {-----------------------------------------------------------}
 2: {Improved version, avoids code repeats,                     }
 3: {also deals with negative input satisfactorily,             }
 4: {calculates maximum, minimum and total of a list of numbers}
 5: {by successively adding and comparing                       }
 6: {-----------------------------------------------------------}
 7:
 8: var
 9:    This,MaxSoFar,MinSoFar,Total: Single;
10:    Index: Integer;
11: begin
12:    for Index:= 1 to StrToInt(Count.Text) do
13:    begin
14:      This:=
15:      StrToFloat(InputBox('Data Entry',
16:        'Please enter next number','0'));
17:      if Index = 1 then
18:      begin
19:        Total:= This;
20:        MaxSoFar:= This;
21:        MinSoFar:= This;
22:      end
23:      else {index greater than 1}
24:      begin
25:        Total:= Total + This;
26:        if This > MaxSoFar then
27:          MaxSoFar:= This
28:        else
29:          if This < MinSoFar then
30:            MinSoFar:= This;
31:      end;{outer else}
32:      {update edit boxes}
33:      Max.Text:= FloatToStrF(MaxSoFar,ffgeneral,5,2);
34:      Min.Text:= FloatToStrF(MinSoFar,ffgeneral,5,2);
35:      Tot.Text:= FloatToStrF(Total,ffgeneral,5,2);
36:      LastNo.Text:= FloatToStrF(This,ffgeneral,5,2);
37:    end;  {for}
```

(5.6) Nested **for** loops

Much of the power of Pascal-like languages comes from nesting structures, as was shown with conditionals in Chapter 4. It is possible to nest one iterative structure, such as the **for** construct, within another iterative or conditional structure to any depth. The limitation is on the programmer's comprehension, and later in this book – in Chapter 9 – procedures will be introduced to simplify code.

To show how nested **for** loops work, open a new project which will show the running values of the control values of two loops, one inside the other. Set up a form like the prototype shown in Figure 5.3.

1. Place four edit boxes and six labels on it.

2. Change the Name properties of the edit boxes to StartOVal, StartIVal, StopOVal and StopIVal, and change the Caption property of the form as in Figure 5.3.

3. Place two buttons on the form.

4. Make one button a Quit button as in earlier projects, putting code to close in the OnClick event handler.

5. Change the Caption of the second button to

   ```
   Do nested loops
   ```

   which will use code in which one **for** loop is nested inside another **for** loop.

6. Insert lines 1 and 3 to 11 of Listing 5.6 into the OnClick event handler for this button. Lines 2 and 12 are generated automatically.

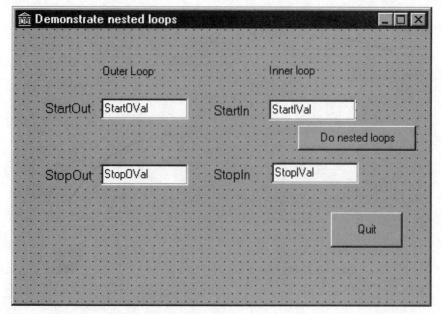

Figure 5.3 Prototype form to demonstrate nested loops.

Listing 5.6

```
 1: var Inner,Outer,StartIn,StopIn,StartOut,StopOut: Cardinal;
 2: begin
 3:    StartOut:= StrToInt(StartOVal.Text);
 4:    StopOut:= StrToInt(StopOVal.Text);
 5:    StartIn:= StrToInt(StartIVal.Text);
 6:    StopIn:= StrToInt(StopIVal.Text);
 7:    for Outer:= StartOut to StopOut do
 8:      for Inner:= StartIn to StopIn do
 9:        ShowMessage
10:          ('outer:'+IntToStr(Outer)+
11:              ' - inner:'+IntToStr(Inner));
12: end;
```

7. Compile and run the project. Choose limits for the outer loop of 5 and 7, and set limits of the inner loop as 9 and 12, then click the button whose Caption is Do nested loops and watch the way Outer and Inner change.

Figure 5.4 shows the screen with the second message box displayed. The value of Inner cycles completely through the values 9, 10, 11 and 12 before the value of

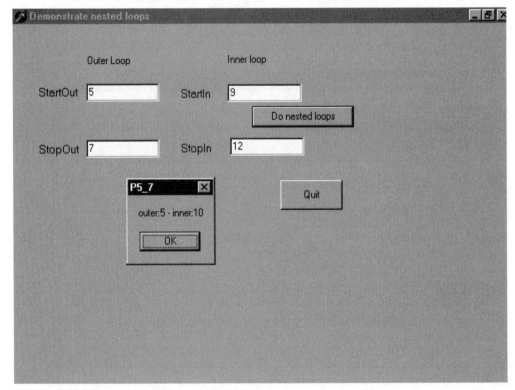

Figure 5.4   Running the nested loops demonstration.

`Outer` changes, showing 3 × 4 = 12 message boxes in total. In many applications a compound statement will replace the call to `ShowMessage`.

5.7 Summary of use of **for** loops

The control variable, the initial value and the final value must all be of the same ordinal type. In particular, the programmer cannot use floating-point types to control a **for** loop. The initial value and the final value can be literals, constants or variables.

The control variable changes automatically, so the programmer should not include code to change it. Some compilers do allow the programmer to change the value held in the control variable within the action statement, but it is most unwise to do so. Changing the control variable could be likened to altering the time on a clock whilst it is running.

The action statement can be single or compound. The programmer may always enter the **begin end** pair, even where only a single statement lies between them.

5.8 Graphics

In Chapter 2 a project pulled an image into a form using the Picture Editor, and the user could choose a particular bitmap image at run time. Many scientific and business projects require drawings, such as charts, to be done at run time rather than at design time. We can improve the triangle length calculation of Chapter 3 by redrawing the triangle once the angles and lengths have been calculated. Before looking at the triangle calculation, we will discuss a simple example of the graphics potential of the Delphi environment.

5.9 Using the shape component

The idea is to design a very simple game where every time the player clicks a circle, that circle jumps away. A prototype form is shown in Figure 5.5.

A circle is an example of a `TShape` component, the other possibilities being rectangles, squares and ellipses. `TShape` objects are easy for the programmer to handle, but are also efficient in terms of using computer resources at run time.

Open a new project and do as follows:

1. Place on the form a main menu component with caption `File`, with just one item with caption

   `Exit`

   For further details of how to do this see Chapter 2.

2. Place on the form a shape component. This is in the Additional page of the Component Palette, and the icon has an overlapping circle, square and triangle.

3. Change the `Name` property of `Shape1` to

   `Circle`

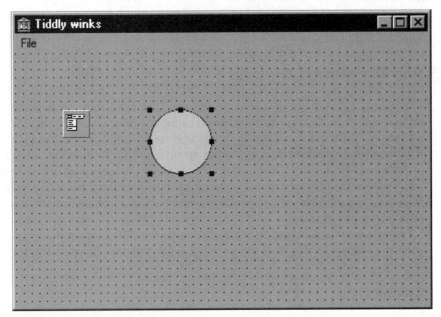

Figure 5.5   Form for the click the circle game.

4. Use the Object Inspector to change the shape property of `Circle` to `stCircle`, by choosing from the options available in the pull down list.

5. Use the Object Inspector again to change the `Brush` property of `Circle` to the colour you want, for example `clYellow`. This is done by selecting `Circle`, clicking on

   `+brush`

   to bring up a further menu, and then selecting the one wanted.

6. As in earlier projects, add

   `Close;`

   to the event handler for the Exit on the main menu File.

7. Change the form's caption as wanted.

8. Add the code that moves the circle to the `OnMouseDown` event handler for `Circle`. A shape component has no `OnClick` event associated with it, but the `OnMouseDown` event is rather similar. It occurs when the user presses the mouse button with its pointer over that component. Use the Events page of the Object Inspector to open the code template for the `OnMouseDown` event for the shape component and insert the code in Listing 5.7.

   In Listing 5.7:

   • Lines 16 and 17 are executed every time a mouse button is depressed within the circle; they cause the left and top properties of `Circle`, that is the x and y coordinates of the top left-hand corner of the circle relative to the form, to be increased or decreased.

Listing 5.7) Code to move a circle

```
 1:   if (Circle.Left > (Form1.ClientWidth - Circle.Width))
 2:      or (Circle.Left < 0)
 3:   then
 4:   begin
 5:      JumpHoriz:= -JumpHoriz;
 6:      Circle.Brush.Color:= clRed;
 7:   end;
 8:   if (Circle.Top > (Form1.ClientHeight - Circle.Height))
 9:      or (Circle.Top < 0)
10:   then
11:   begin
12:      JumpVert:= -JumpVert;
13:      Circle.Brush.Color:= clBlue;
14:   end;
15:
16:   Circle.Left:= Circle.Left+JumpHoriz;
17:   Circle.Top:= Circle.Top+JumpVert;
```

- The lines numbered 1 to 14 check how near that top left-hand corner is to the edge of the form. If it is near an edge, the sign of JumpVert or JumpHoriz is changed to send the circle moving back the other way, and the colour of the brush property of the circle is changed too. TShape objects have Height and Width properties with the obvious meanings, and these can be set at design time or run time.

- ClientHeight and ClientWidth properties of Form1 are used in preference to more obvious Form1.Height and Form1.Width to obtain the usable area of the form, excluding title bar and borders.

9. Insert

   var JumpVert,JumpHoriz: Integer;

   just below the line

   ```
   {$R *.DFM}
   ```

   but before any lines starting the procedure. This declares these two variables not merely within the procedure CircleMouseDown, but unit wide, that is, all event procedures can access them.

10. The variables JumpVert and JumpHoriz must be initialized. It is convenient to do this when the form is created, so insert

    ```
    JumpHoriz:= Circle.Width div 2;
    JumpVert:= Circle.Width div 2;
    ```

    into an event handler for OnCreate, accessed by using the Events page for Form1 of the Object Inspector.

11. Compile and run the whole project. The circle jumps each time the mouse is clicked on it, but changes direction (and colour) as it nears the edge of the form.

The magnitude of each jump is determined by the magnitude of `JumpHoriz` and `JumpVert`, and the programmer can adjust these, or change the size or shape of the `TShape` object to get different effects.

(5.10) Using the `Canvas` property

The previous example used the shape component, which gives a simple way of placing ellipses, circles, squares and rectangles on a form, and manipulating them at run time. Delphi also has versatile ways of drawing more general shapes, and lines and curves may be drawn on the form itself or on a component placed on a form. Forms and many components such as images have a `Canvas` property, and, by analogy with an artist, drawing is done on a specific canvas. Canvases themselves have properties such as a pen for drawing and a brush for colouring. The line drawing facilities can be used to draw graphs or other shapes, and they will be used in the next section to draw a general triangle to scale.

(5.11) The triangle problem revisited

In Chapter 3 we discussed a project to calculate an angle of a right-angled triangle. The triangle was illustrated by an imported image. We will now extend that project to draw a scaled triangle with the appropriate angles.

Figure 5.6 shows the prototype form. The triangle will not appear until run time, and will be drawn on the canvases of two images which are on the form itself.

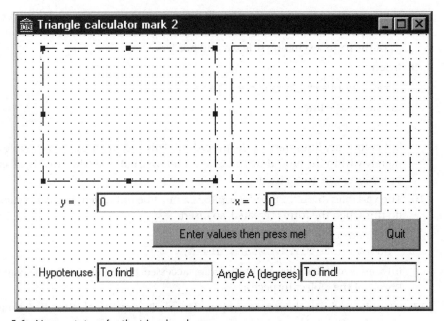

Figure 5.6   New prototype for the triangle solver.

1. Set up the prototype form as shown, changing the captions of the buttons to Quit and Enter values then press me! Initialize the Text properties of the edit boxes by use of the Object Inspector.

2. Place two image components side by side, changing their Name properties to LImage and RImage. Then change the initial value for the Visible property of LImage to False via the Object Inspector. This ensures that it will not show at run time until the code makes it visible, but RImage will show at the start of a run.

3. Change the Color property of the form to clWhite. This is to match the background of the image components.

4. In general, when Windows judges that a particular window needs redrawing, it calls an OnPaint event. FormPaint is the default name for the OnPaint event of a form, so in order to draw an initial triangle add the code shown in Listing 5.8 to the FormPaint event of the object Form1.

(**Listing 5.8**) Drawing a triangle on a canvas

```
 1:   Originx:= RImage.Width div 100;
 2:   Originy:= RImage.Height div 100;
 3:   Intx:= Form1.Width div 3;{makes triangle a reasonable size}
 4:   Inty:= Form1.Height div 3;
 5:   RImage.Canvas.MoveTo(Originx,Originy);
 6:   RImage.Canvas.LineTo(Originx,Originy+IntY);
 7:   RImage.Canvas.LineTo(Originx+Intx, Originy+Inty);
 8:   RImage.Canvas.LineTo(Originx,Originy);
 9:   RImage.Canvas.TextOut(Originx,Originy, 'A');
10:   RImage.Canvas.TextOut(Originx,Originy+Inty div 2,'y');
11:   RImage.Canvas.TextOut(Originx+Intx div 2,
12:      Originy+Inty,'x');
```

Drawing is done in terms of coordinates of pixels, starting at the top left of a component, and a typical form is a few hundred pixels high and wide. Coordinates are upside down compared with normal mathematical use.

Various components such as a form or an image have a TCanvas object; the properties and methods are the same. The basic methods for an object of type TCanvas used in the code above are shown in Table 5.1.

There are many more methods available for drawing and filling shapes at run time, and the online help gives details.

Table 5.1 Basic methods for object of type TCanvas.

MoveTo(x,y:Integer)	Moves the pen to the point (x,y)
LineTo(x,y:Integer)	Draws a line from the current position to the point (x,y), which then becomes the current position
TextOut(x,y:Integer; **const** s:**string**)	Outputs text at the point (x,y)

At run time lines 1 to 8 of Listing 5.8 will draw three lines to form the triangle, starting at a point (RImage.Width **div** 100, RImage.Height **div** 100), just inside the top left-hand corner, down the *y*-axis, along the *x*-axis and finally across the hypotenuse. The calls to TextOut in lines 9–12 provide the labelling.

5. The variables used must be declared, so insert

```
var Originx,Originy,Intx,Inty: Integer;
```

between the procedure heading of FormPaint and **begin**, to declare them locally.

6. Add

```
Close;
```

to the OnClick event of the Quit button.

7. Now insert the code in Listing 5.9 into the OnClick event handler for the Action button, which performs and displays the results of the calculation. If the project in Chapter 3 is available, the code can be copied from there, but otherwise type it in as shown in Listing 5.9.

(**Listing 5.9**) Calculation of side and angle
_____

```
y:= StrToFloat(Edit1.Text);
x:= StrToFloat(Edit2.Text);
z:= Sqrt(Sqr(x)+Sqr(y));
AngleA:= ArcTan(x/y)*180/Pi;
Edit3.Text:= FloatToStr(z);
Edit4.Text:= FloatToStr(AngleA);
```

_____

The variables introduced, x, y, z and AngleA, must be declared, as type Single, in the usual manner at the top of the procedural code immediately above the **begin**.

8. Compile and run the project.

Although it is apparently very similar to the version in Chapter 3, the drawing is now being accomplished at run time, in the manner that one could produce, for instance, a chart.

This project so far will not automatically redraw the triangle to scale.

(5.12) **Extending the triangle example***

This section demonstrates how an object can be made to move apparently, by drawing, erasing and then drawing again in a new position. To do this add Listing 5.10 underneath the final line of Listing 5.9.

In Listing 5.10:

● Line 1 just makes RImage invisible.

● Lines 4 to 13 scale the values of Intx and Inty so they will fit onto LImage.

● Line 14 then makes LImage visible.

Listing 5.10) Drawing triangle to scale

```
 1:   RImage.Visible:= False;
 2:   ShowMessagePos('Like to draw this triangle?',
 3:     Form1.Height div 2,0);
 4:   if x > y then
 5:   begin
 6:     Intx:= LImage.Width div 2;
 7:     Inty:= Trunc(y * Intx / x);
 8:   end
 9:   else
10:   begin
11:     Inty:= LImage.Height div 2;
12:     Intx:= Trunc(x * Inty / y);
13:   end;
14:   LImage.Visible:= True;
15:   LImage.Canvas.Pen.Color:= clRed;
16:   Originy:= 0;
17:   Originx:= 0;
18:   LImage.Canvas.MoveTo(Originx,Originy);
19:   LImage.Canvas.LineTo(Originx,Originy+IntY);
20:   LImage.Canvas.LineTo(Originx+Intx,Originy+Inty);
21:   LImage.Canvas.LineTo(Originx,Originy);
22:   LImage.Canvas.TextOut(Originx,Originy, 'A');
23:   LImage.Canvas.TextOut(Originx,Originy+ Inty div 2, 'y');
24:   LImage.Canvas.TextOut(Originx+Intx div 2,
25:     Originy+Inty,'x');
```

● Line 15 changes the colour of the Pen property for the canvas object of LImage.

● Lines 16 onwards draw the new, scaled triangle on LImage; they are equivalent to the code to draw the original triangle in Listing 5.8.

Compile and run this new version. An alternative approach is to erase the original triangle by using a special mode of the pen (pmNotXor), then the new scaled triangle could be drawn on RImage. In this project that is probably an unnecessary complication and it would double the drawing needed, but it can be a useful technique in other cases.

The last stage of the triangle project is to insert code to move it, first by using conventional methods, applicable in many languages, and finally by using a timer component available in Delphi.

1. Add the code in Listing 5.11 to the OnClick event handler for the action button, below line 25 of Listing 5.10.

   In Listing 5.11:

   ● Lines 2 to 6 of the code are repeated Count times.

   ● Line 3 increases the value of LImage.Left, that is it changes the x coordinate of the top left corner of LImage relative to the form.

Listing 5.11) Using a **for** loop to move the image

```
1:  for Move:= 1 to Count do
2:  begin
3:    LImage.Left:= LImage.Left + LImage.Width div Count;
4:    Refresh;
5:    for SlowIt:= 1 to TimeSlice do;
6:  end;
```

- Line 4 uses the `Refresh` method to erase and repaint the screen.

- Line 5 is a delay mechanism. It does nothing many times to delay the execution so that the user can actually see what is happening! The value to give best effect varies according to the speed of the PC. To start with, try setting `TimeSlice` to 100000 and `Count` to 30.

2. Add the declaration

    ```
    const TimeSlice=100000; Count=30;
    ```

   above the **var** declaration of this event handler, and add the new variables to the **var** declaration.

3. Compile and run this new version.

Finally, we use a more environment specific component to achieve a similar result.

4. Add a timer component from the Systems page of the Component Palette to the form. Whilst the form is in design mode the timer component will look like a clock, but it will be invisible at run time, so the position is immaterial.

5. Use the Object Inspector to change the `Enabled` property of `LImage` to `False`, so it is not active initially.

6. Add a further button, named Freeze. Your form should now look like Figure 5.7.

7. Add code to the `FreezeClick` event as follows:

    ```
    Timer1.Enabled:= False;
    ```

   Add this code to `Timer1Timer`, which will be called by the system at intervals determined by the interval property:

    ```
    LImage.Left:= LImage.Left + LImage.Width div 30;
    Refresh;
    ```

8. Replace lines 1 to 6 of Listing 5.11 with

    ```
    Timer1.Enabled:= True;
    Timer1.Interval:= 10;
    ```

   These turn on the timer and set the intervals between successive calls to `Timer1Timer`. An interval of 1 unit is approximately 0.001 seconds.

The final code is shown in Listing 5.12.

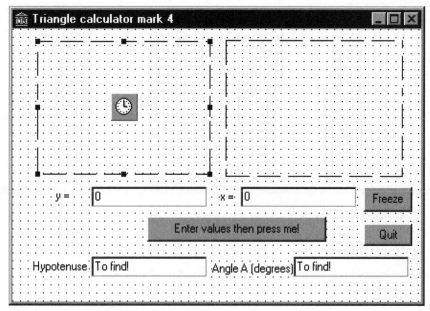

Figure 5.7 Triangle calculation with timer.

(Listing 5.12) Moving triangle program

```
 1: unit U5_12;
 2:
 3: interface
 4:
 5: uses
 6:    Windows, Messages, SysUtils, Classes, Graphics, Controls,
 7:    Forms, Dialogs, StdCtrls, ExtCtrls;
 8:
 9: type
10:    TForm1 = class(TForm)
11:       Edit1: TEdit;
12:       Edit2: TEdit;
13:       Edit3: TEdit;
14:       Edit4: TEdit;
15:       Button1: TButton;
16:       Button2: TButton;
17:       Label1: TLabel;
18:       Label2: TLabel;
19:       Label3: TLabel;
20:       Label4: TLabel;
21:       LImage: TImage;
22:       RImage: TImage;
23:       Timer1: TTimer;
24:       Freeze: TButton;
```

```
25:     procedure Button1Click(Sender: TObject);
26:     procedure Button2Click(Sender: TObject);
27:     procedure FormPaint(Sender: TObject);
28:     procedure FreezeClick(Sender: TObject);
29:     procedure Timer1Timer(Sender: TObject);
30:   private
31:     { Private declarations }
32:   public
33:     { Public declarations }
34:   end;
35:
36: var
37:   Form1: TForm1;
38:
39: implementation
40:
41: {$R *.DFM}
42:
43: procedure TForm1.Button1Click(Sender: TObject);
44: {----------------------------------------------------------}
45: {Given length of 2 adjacent sides of right-angled triangle }
46: {this procedure finds length of hypotenuse                 }
47: {plus angle opposite x in degrees                          }
48: {----------------------------------------------------------}
49: const TimeSlice=10000; Count=30;
50: var x,y,z,AngleA: Single;
51:     Originx,Originy,Intx,Inty,Move,SlowIt: Integer;
52: begin
53:   y:= StrToFloat(Edit1.Text);
54:   x:= StrToFloat(Edit2.Text);
55:   z:= Sqrt(Sqr(x)+Sqr(y));
56:   AngleA:= ArcTan(x/y)*180/Pi;
57:   Edit3.Text:= FloatToStr(z);
58:   Edit4.Text:= FloatToStr(AngleA);
59:   RImage.Visible:= False;
60:   ShowMessagePos('Like to draw this triangle?',
61:     Form1.Height div 2,0);
62:   if x > y then
63:   begin
64:     Intx:= LImage.Width div 2;
65:     Inty:= Trunc(y * Intx / x);
66:   end
67:   else
68:   begin
69:     Inty:= LImage.Height div 2;
70:     Intx:= Trunc(x * Inty / y);
71:   end;
72:   LImage.Visible:= True;
73:   LImage.Canvas.Pen.Color:= clRed;
74:   Originy:= 0;
75:   Originx:= 0;
```

```
76:    LImage.Canvas.MoveTo(Originx,Originy);
77:    LImage.Canvas.LineTo(Originx,Originy+IntY);
78:    LImage.Canvas.LineTo(Originx+Intx, Originy+Inty);
79:    LImage.Canvas.LineTo(Originx,Originy);
80:    LImage.Canvas.TextOut(Originx,Originy, 'A');
81:    LImage.Canvas.TextOut(Originx,Originy+Inty div 2, 'y');
82:    LImage.Canvas.TextOut(Originx+Intx div 2,
83:       Originy+Inty,'x');
84:    Timer1.Enabled:= True;
85:    Timer1.Interval:= 10;
86: end;
87:
88: procedure TForm1.Button2Click(Sender: TObject);
89: begin
90:    Close;
91: end;
92:
93: procedure TForm1.FormPaint(Sender: TObject);
94: {-----------------------------------------------------------}
95: {This event handler draws a triangle on the canvas of      }
96: {an image component, starting inside top left-hand corner   }
97: {-----------------------------------------------------------}
98: var Originx,Originy,Intx,Inty: Integer;
99: begin
100:    Originx:= RImage.Width div 100 ;
101:    Originy:= RImage.Height div 100;
102:    Intx:= Form1.Width div 3;
103:    Inty:= Form1.Height div 3;
104:    RImage.Canvas.MoveTo(Originx,Originy);
105:    RImage.Canvas.LineTo(Originx,Originy+IntY);
106:    RImage.Canvas.LineTo(Originx+Intx, Originy+Inty);
107:    RImage.Canvas.LineTo(Originx,Originy);
108:    RImage.Canvas.TextOut(Originx,Originy, 'A');
109:    RImage.Canvas.TextOut(Originx,Originy+Inty div 2,'y');
110:    RImage.Canvas.TextOut(Originx+Intx div 2,
111:       Originy+Inty,'x');
112: end;
113:
114: procedure TForm1.FreezeClick(Sender: TObject);
115: begin
116:    Timer1.Enabled:= False;
117: end;
118:
119: procedure TForm1.Timer1Timer(Sender: TObject);
120: begin
121:    LImage.Left:= LImage.Left + LImage.Width div 30;
122:    Refresh;
123: end;
124:
125: end.
```

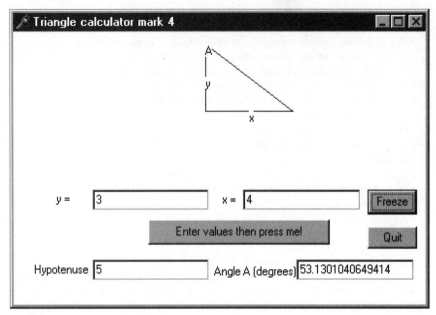

Figure 5.8   Triangle solver with timer running.

Compile and run this project. Unless variables Move and SlowIt have been removed, they will cause a warning message on compilation. The user must press a button in order to freeze the scaled triangle whilst it is in view, as in Figure 5.8.

5.13 Summary

In this chapter we discussed deterministic loops, and the properties of the **for** construct in Object Pascal. This included their use to simulate movement of graphics. In imperative languages such as Pascal, BASIC or ANSI C, the programmer must use a loop to simulate motion. A useful alternative in Delphi is the timer component. We introduced the powerful higher-level graphics capabilities of Delphi, including the use of the shape and image components. There are also facilities to manipulate individual pixels, which are beyond the scope of this chapter. The final version of the triangle program does not use a loop at all, because a timer component performs the iteration, which the user can halt by pressing a button. Thus in event-driven programming iteration does not occupy quite such a central position as it does in imperative programming.

Quiz

1. The control variable of a **for** loop should be
   (a) initialized before the action part
   (b) declared before the action part
   (c) referenced within the loop

2. The initial and final values of the control variable of a **for** loop should be
    (a) ordinal
    (b) constants
    (c) numeric

3. The control variable and the initial value should be
    (a) both variables
    (b) compatible
    (c) real

4. In order to find the maximum of several data items
    (a) an in-built function should be used
    (b) an **if** construction should be used
    (c) a **case** construct should be used

5. The action part of a **for** loop can be
    (a) only a simple statement
    (b) only a compound statement
    (c) either a simple or a compound statement

6. Changing the Name property of an edit box
    (a) always changes the Text property also
    (b) is not possible
    (c) is advisable only by using the Object Inspector

7. A shape (TShape) component has
    (a) a Shape property one of which is stCircle
    (b) an OnClick event
    (c) a Canvas property

8. The Canvas property of a component has
    (a) a Write method
    (b) a MoveTo method
    (c) a Brush.Color method

9. An image (TImage) component has
    (a) Bottom and Right properties
    (b) a Canvas property
    (c) a Canvas.Pen property

10. Timer (TTimer) components
    (a) can only be enabled one at a time
    (b) are useful for animation
    (c) have a Step property

Exercises

1. Use shape components to illustrate the sequence of colours of traffic lights. Colour should change when a button is clicked.

2.   Extend the above so the lights change automatically after a time interval.

3.   Write a program to test whether

$$1^4 + 2^4 + 3^4 + \ldots + n^4 = n(6n^4 + 15n^3 + 10n^2 - 1)/30$$

for the largest possible range of values of n available on your system (it is surprisingly small).

4.   Write an event handler to draw lines in random directions across the form, from top to bottom and from side to side, using a range of colours in turn.

Chapter 6

Non-deterministic loops and files

6.1 Introduction

Chapter 5 introduced loops in which the number of iterations was predefined, using the **for** construct in Delphi. Many real-world applications need a *non-deterministic loop* construct because until that cycling is under way the number of circuits is unknown. For instance, a programmer may want to add numbers to a series whilst the numbers are small, or to analyse a file and stop at the end of the file.

Windows users know the idea of a file: the left-hand item on almost all menu bars provides options on files such as saving and printing. Files provide a further means of input and output to programs, and files are better suited for transfer of large amounts of data than the input dialog boxes and edit boxes used in earlier chapters.

Pascal is an established programming language that was developed before Windows came into common use. Traditionally users entered data line by line at a console and viewed the results in the same manner.

6.2　Non-deterministic loops

There are two recognized ways of implementing non-deterministic iteration in Pascal:

- the **while** construct
- the **repeat** construct

In many cases, either construct could be used. The major difference between the two is that the **while** construct does a check before executing a statement whereas **repeat** executes a statement at least once, then checks. Hence the **while** is the more flexible of the two, and will be discussed first. The **repeat** construct was much used for display of menus in traditional Pascal, but in Delphi a GUI would normally be used to present a list of choices. A **repeat** construct can give more readable code in some algorithms.

6.3　Action of a simple **while** loop

The general form of the **while** construct is

　　while *something is true* **do** *action*;

For example, the following code will show an input box, and as long as the reply is anything except 'Y', it will go on to show a message to indicate that it is cycling round the loop. Once the user types 'Y', an appropriate message is shown and no more cycling occurs. If the response to the very first input box is 'Y', then execution passes to the second ShowMessage procedure, and 'Out of loop now' is displayed immediately.

```
while
   InputBox('Y stops this While loop ',
     'Stop ?, type Y or N','N') <> 'Y'
do
   ShowMessage('Round and round');
ShowMessage('Out of loop now');
```

As with the **if** construct discussed in Chapter 4, *something is true* is a Boolean expression. As an example of a more complex Boolean expression, it is frequently useful to cycle whilst two conditions both hold. The code shown in Listing 6.1 cycles until the user types a 'Y' or until Limit cycles have occurred.

Listing 6.1　Simple **while** loop with **if** construct following

```
1: Counter:= 1;
2: while
3:    (InputBox('type Y or N',
4:      'Stop ?, type Y or N','N') <> 'Y')
5:    and
```

```
 6:   (Counter < Limit)
 7: do
 8:    Inc(Counter);
 9: if Counter >= Limit then
10:    ShowMessage('out of loop : after' +
11:       IntToStr(Counter) + 'iterations')
12: else
13:    ShowMessage('out of loop : by request');
```

In Listing 6.1:

- Counter is a variable and as such must be declared in a **var** declaration.

- Limit may be declared as either a variable or a constant, but if its value is not changed within the unit it is preferable that it be a constant, as assumed in the code earlier. If it were a variable, it would need to be initialized.

- Counter is initialized in line 1. It is essential to arrange that the Boolean expression in lines 3 to 6 has an appropriate value for the first time it is checked.

- Inc was used in Chapter 4. It is an in-built procedure which adds 1 to Counter. Inc(Counter) can be replaced here by Counter:= Counter +1, but Inc generates more efficient code, which can be significant within nested loops. There is a matching procedure Dec which decrements a variable. (For upwards compatibility, the Pascal functions Pred and Succ are also available: see Section 9.8.)

- The **while** construct causes cycling, and in general the action in line 8 will be done several times. By contrast, the **if** construct starting in line 9 causes one or other action, starting in line 10 or line 13, to be executed just once.

- Removing lines 3 to 5 inclusive would reduce the **while** loop to one which just increments Counter and tests the value of Counter: this is better accomplished using a **for** loop. It is always possible to replace a **for** loop with an equivalent **while** loop, but it is not good programming practice to do so.

By its nature, it is quite possible for a **while** loop to execute indefinitely – or at least until the computer is rebooted. Obviously one aims to guard against this by careful design, and it is wise to save work before attempting to run a project. It may also be useful to add a counter to a **while** loop during development in the manner of line 6.

6.4 **while** loops with compound statements as action

The loops in the previous section had just one simple statement as an action. This is quite unusual. **while** constructs normally have a compound statement, that is a **begin** and **end** encompassing several statements, as an action. In part this is because the action of the loop must change the value of the Boolean to be tested. This is something that programmers should specifically check their code for, thus avoiding infinite loops.

Consider an example. A zoologist requires to know how much time will elapse before a colony of wild cats reaches a certain number. Observations indicate that, on average, kittens mature after 3 months, and mature cats produce double their number of kittens every 3 months, after 3 months' gestation. The basic algorithm, coded in Object Pascal, is shown in Listing 6.2.

(**Listing 6.2**) A basic model for an increasing population
_____

```
 1: while Cats+Kittens < MaxCat do
 2: begin
 3:   if (Months mod 3 = 0) and (Months > 0) then
 4:   begin
 5:     Cats := Cats+Kittens;
 6:     Kittens := 2*OldCats;
 7:     OldCats:= Cats;
 8:   end; {if}
 9:   Inc(Months);
10: end; {while}
```

Lines 2 to 10 inclusive are a compound statement, consisting of an **if** construct plus line 9, all encompassed by the outer **begin end** pair. All this code is executed repeatedly as long as the Boolean expression on line 1 is true.

A prototype form to demonstrate how the number of animals grows is shown in Figure 6.1. Edit boxes will show the input to, and the results from, the model. You

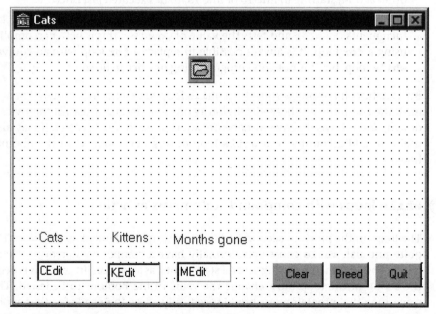

Figure 6.1   Prototype form for the cat population investigation.

will need a small bitmap image in order to complete this project. You could obtain a suitable image from a drawing or photograph using a scanner, or draw one using a paint package: many PCs have such software already installed. Alternatively clipart could be used.

1. Create a directory for this project.
2. Set up a prototype form as above.
3. Use the Object Inspector to change the `Color` property of the form to `clWhite`.
4. Use the Object Inspector to name the edit boxes `CEdit`, `KEdit` and `MEdit` respectively; they can be initialized using the Object Inspector or by code as we do in this example.
5. Use the Object Inspector to name the buttons Clear, Breed and Quit respectively.
6. Use the Object Inspector to change the colour assigned in the `Font` property of the labels to green. It is distinct from the `Color` property of the labels. To make the change, click on the `Font` property, then click on the ellipsis and fill in the dialog box. The method is similar to that used to load a picture in Chapter 2.
7. Add an OpenDialog component, from the Dialogs page of the Component Palette, to the form. Change the `Filter` property so the name is `Bitmaps` and the filter is `*.bmp`
8. Double click on the Quit button and type

   ```
   Close;
   ```

   into the `QuitClick` event handler.
9. Double click on the Clear button and type the code in Listing 6.3 into the `ClearClick` event handler.

(**Listing 6.3**) Code for clearing the form

```
1: Canvas.Brush.Color:= clWhite;
2: Canvas.FloodFill
3:   (Width div 2,Height div 2,clGreen,fsBorder);
4: KEdit.Text:= '0';
5: CEdit.Text:= '2';
6: MEdit.Text:= '0';
```

In Listing 6.3:

- Line 1 sets the `Color` property of the `Brush` for the `Canvas` to white, which will give a better appearance if the graphics to be added have a white background.
- Lines 2 and 3 start at the middle of the form and fill the form with the current brush colour (white) until the colour green is encountered. This is to avoid overwriting the captions on the labels. The last parameter is the fill option, and it has two alternatives. The one used here, `fsBorder`, fills until the colour specified is encountered.

● Lines 4 to 6 set initial values in the edit boxes. This has been done via the Object Inspector in previous examples, but initializing in code will enable the user to try several experiments without rerunning.

6.5 Adding graphics

The experiment can be demonstrated graphically by drawing the appropriate number of cat images at random points on the screen, but avoiding the edit boxes at the bottom of the window. The basic bitmap will be created, then loaded from a file. It can then be drawn at many positions in the window by using the draw method. The library function Random can be used to sprinkle the images round the window. The simplest way to do the drawing is:

```
for i:=1 to Cats do
  Form1.Canvas.Draw(Random(ClientWidth),
    Random(ClientHeight),BitMap);
```

● The **for** loop calls the Draw method a number of times, determined by the value in Cats.

● The first two parameters of Draw are the coordinates in pixels of the point where the top left corner of the image should be placed on the canvas of Form1.

● ClientHeight and ClientWidth are used in preference to the more obvious Form1.Height and Form1.Width to obtain the usable area of the form, excluding title bar and borders.

● The last parameter is the graphic to be drawn. In this case the identifier implies that it is a bitmap, but icons and metafiles could be used as alternatives.

● Random is a library function which generates a pseudo-random integer number in the range indicated by its actual parameter. If no parameter is given then the result is real and is in the range $0 \leq$ result < 1. In the new program the coordinates will be in the top part of the form, to avoid the buttons in the bottom third.

The problem with this simple approach is that the bitmap chosen may not be of a suitable size. Also the drawing may fall off the form. A more sophisticated approach, shown in Listing 6.4, is to use StretchDraw rather than Draw. This resizes a graphic, thus avoiding problems with large graphics.

Listing 6.4) Improving the graphics

```
1: for i:=1 to Cats do
2:   begin
3:     x:= Random(ClientWidth-ISize);
4:     y:= Random(ClientHeight-Bottom);
5:     Form1.Canvas.StretchDraw
6:       (Rect(x,y,x+ISize,y+ISize),BitMap);
7:   end;
```

In Listing 6.4:

- Lines 3 and 4 choose random coordinates for the top left corner of the drawing, whilst avoiding the right-hand side and bottom.
- Line 5 calls StretchDraw in place of Draw.
- In line 6, x, y, x+ISize, y+ISize are the four corners of the drawing wanted, thus specifying that the size be ISize by ISize.
- The in-built function Rect returns a specification of a rectangle as a single object of type TRect, as required by StretchDraw. The net result is to produce a drawing of size ISize square, whatever the original size.

1. Double click on the Breed button, then insert the constant and variable declarations at lines 7 to 9 of Listing 6.5 at the beginning of the event handler.

2. Now add lines 11 to 48 of Listing 6.5 between the existing **begin end** pair.

(**Listing 6.5**)   Main event handler for the population problem

```
 1: procedure TForm1.BreedClick(Sender: TObject);
 2: {-----------------------------------------------------------}
 3: {Requests input from user. Calculates time required, and  }
 4: {shows result in edit boxes.  Draws appropriate number of  }
 5: {scaled pictures.                                          }
 6: {-----------------------------------------------------------}
 7: const ISize=50; Bottom=150;
 8: var BitMap: TBitMap;
 9:     x,y,MaxCat,Cats,Kittens,OldCats,Months,i: Cardinal;
10: begin
11:   BitMap:= TBitMap.Create;
12:   OpenDialog1.Execute;
13:   BitMap.LoadFromFile(OpenDialog1.Filename);
14:   MaxCat:= StrToInt( InputBox('Data input required',
15:     'Number wanted?','20'));
16:   Kittens:= StrToInt(KEdit.Text);
17:   Cats:= StrToInt(CEdit.Text);
18:   Months :=0;
19:   OldCats:= Cats;
20:   Randomize;
21:   for i:= 1 to Cats do
22:   begin
23:     x:= Random(ClientWidth-ISize);
24:     y:= Random(ClientHeight-Bottom);
25:     Form1.Canvas.StretchDraw
26:       (Rect(x,y,x+ISize,y+ISize),BitMap);
27:   end;
28:   while Cats+Kittens < MaxCat do
29:   begin
30:     if (Months mod 3 = 0) and (Months > 0) then
31:     begin
```

```
32:        Cats:= Cats+Kittens;
33:        Kittens:= 2*OldCats;
34:        for i:=1 to Kittens do
35:        begin
36:          x:= Random(ClientWidth-ISize);
37:          y:= Random(ClientHeight-Bottom);
38:          Form1.Canvas.StretchDraw
39:             (Rect(x,y,x+ISize,y+ISize),BitMap);
40:        end;
41:        OldCats:= Cats;
42:        KEdit.Text:= IntToStr(Kittens);
43:        CEdit.Text:= IntToStr(Cats);
44:        MEdit.Text:= IntToStr(Months);
45:      end{if};
46:      Inc(Months);
47:    end; {while}
48:    Bitmap.Free;
49: end;
```

In Listing 6.5:

- Line 11 creates, or instantiates, `BitMap` at run time. The type of image is specified as `TBitMap`.

- Line 12 uses the `Execute` method to show a standard Windows dialog box, and the file chosen is loaded into `BitMap` in line 13.

- Alternatively, an image can be loaded from an icon (files with extension .ico) or a metafile (files ending .emf in Windows 95, but .wmf in Windows 3.1). Reference to bitmaps (including line 11) must be changed to reference the appropriate class.

- Lines 14 to 19 initialize variables.

- Line 20 calls `Randomize` to 'seed' the random procedure used for sprinkling bitmap images round the window.

Successive calls to `StretchDraw` add new images to the existing display, unless the user clicks the Clear button.

If the single line

```
ClearClick(Sender)
```

is added to the `OnCreate` event handler for the form, then the `ClearClick` event handler will be run automatically when the form is created. Alternatively the `ClearClick` event handler can be shared by the `OnCreate` event of `Form1`: select `Form1`, then the Events tab, and double click in the right-hand column opposite `OnCreate`. Choose `ClearClick` from the options.

The results of running the project, by clicking the Clear button and then the Breed button, are shown in Figure 6.2.

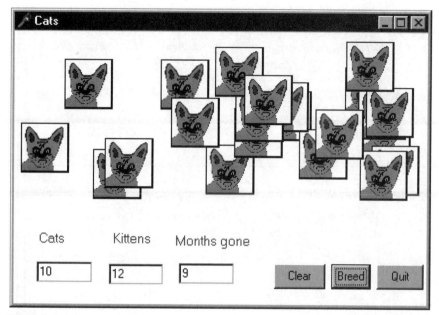

Figure 6.2 Running the cat population program.

6.6 Keeping results

The limitation of the methods of input and output used so far is their short life. In the previous project the answers are shown on the screen until the form window is closed, and the intermediate results – such as how many cats half-way through the experiment – are never shown at all. Traditional Pascal employed procedures such as read and write to write out constant strings, and the values of variables. These can be used in all versions of Delphi, but the ways of enabling them vary.

First we will show how to access the console from an event. Then we will develop applications which do not use event handlers. For this the programmer will put the Pascal code directly into the project file, rather than into the unit file. Techniques vary when using the older Delphi 1 and this will be explained.

6.6.1 Accessing a console from an event (not applicable to Delphi 1)

The programmer may wish to use the Delphi environment to run a complete Pascal program, possibly developed in Turbo Pascal. These are the steps to run old-style Pascal programs, using read and write:

1. Start a new project.
2. Choose Project|Options|Linker and check the Generate Console Application checkbox as shown in Figure 6.3.
3. Put a button with Caption 'Cat calculation' onto a form.

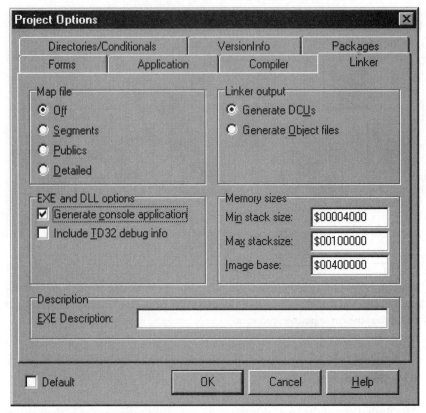

Figure 6.3 Choosing a console application.

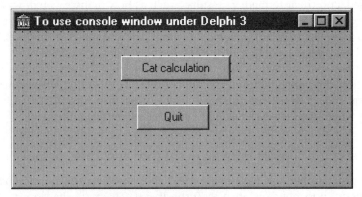

Figure 6.4 Form for running traditional Pascal code.

4. Put traditional Pascal code into the associated event handler `TForm1.Button1Click`: see Listing 6.6. This will usually include read and write procedures, which will be analysed later in this section.

5. Add a Quit button as in previous examples. The prototype form is shown in Figure 6.4.

Figure 6.5   Console window in Delphi 3.

6. Save all, and run in the normal way.

7. A black console window appears, as shown in Figure 6.5.

8. Press the Cat calculation button to run the main event handler.

9. Select the console window.

10. Data can be entered in the black console window and results output to it in the traditional manner.

An example of the finished unit appears in Listing 6.6.

Listing 6.6   Console application

```
 1: unit U6_6;
 2:
 3: interface
 4:
 5: uses
 6:    Windows, Messages, SysUtils, Classes, Graphics,
 7:    Controls, Forms, Dialogs, StdCtrls;
 8:
 9: type
10:    TForm1 = class(TForm)
11:       Button1: TButton;
12:       Button2: TButton;
13:       procedure Button1Click(Sender: TObject);
14:       procedure Button2Click(Sender: TObject);
15:    private
16:       { Private declarations }
17:    public
18:       { Public declarations }
19:    end;
20:
```

```
21: var
22:    Form1: TForm1;
23:
24: implementation
25:
26: {$R *.DFM}
27:
28: procedure TForm1.Button1Click(Sender: TObject);
29: {----------------------------------------------------------}
30: { Old-style Pascal code running under Delphi 2 or 3        }
31: { Console window opens when Button1 is clicked             }
32: {----------------------------------------------------------}
33: var Cats,Kittens,OldCats,MaxCat,Months: Integer;
34: begin
35:    Write('Enter initial number of cats: ');
36:    Read(Cats);
37:    if Cats < 0  then Cats:= 2;
38:    Write('Enter initial number of kittens: ');
39:    Read(Kittens);
40:    if Kittens < 0  then Kittens:= 0;
41:    Write('Number wanted: ');
42:    Read(MaxCat);
43:    Writeln('Months':10,'Cats':10,'Kittens':10);
44:    Months:= 0;
45:    OldCats:=Cats;
46:    while Cats+Kittens < MaxCat do
47:    begin
48:      if (Months mod 3 = 0) and (Months>0) then
49:      begin
50:        Cats:= Cats+Kittens;
51:        Kittens:= 2*OldCats;
52:        OldCats:= Cats;
53:        Writeln(Months:10,Cats:10,Kittens:10);
54:      end{if};
55:      Inc(Months);
56:    end; {while}
57: end;
58:
59: procedure TForm1.Button2Click(Sender: TObject);
60: begin
61:    Close;
62: end;
63:
64: end.
```

In Listing 6.6:

● Lines 35, 38 and 41 write strings to the console window.

● Lines 36, 39 and 42 read data values from the console window.

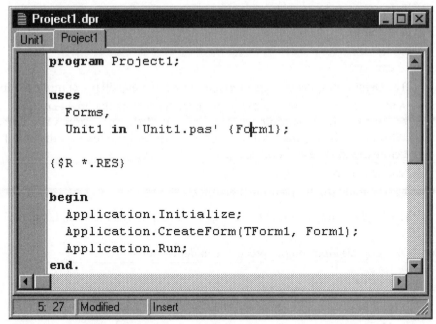

Figure 6.6 Project source in Delphi 3.

- Lines 37 and 40 perform data validation, and insert default values where necessary. This avoids the possibility of an infinite loop.

- In line 43 the `:10` indicates the width of the field available for a value. Essentially it enables the programmer to tabulate output in this example.

- In line 43 also, the use of `Writeln` as opposed to `Write` gives a new line on the output.

- Line 53 outputs values held in variables, rather than strings, to the console window.

6.6.2   Project source file (not applicable to Delphi 1)

An alternative approach is to place the Pascal program in the project source, which initially looks like Figure 6.6.

1. Delete the complete Unit1, either by selecting it and using menu on the right mouse button, or by choosing Project|Remove from Project|Unit.

2. Replace all the code after the first line with the code of the old-style Pascal Program, deleting `{$R *.RES}`.

3. Insert

```
{$Apptype Console}
uses Forms;
var Prop: Char;
```

between

program

and

var

The Delphi compiler expects a **uses** declaration, and will not compile without it.

4. Add a line such as `Readln(Prop)` immediately before the final **end**. This is necessary to keep the console window open until the user presses the Enter key. Without it, the program will run but the user sees the final results only briefly before the console window closes.

5. Save as a file of type `.dpr`.

6. Compile and run in the normal manner.

The finished program, in old-style Pascal, in Delphi 3, is shown in Listing 6.7.

Listing 6.7   Console input–output procedure under Delphi 3

```
 1: program P6_7;
 2: {$Apptype Console}
 3: uses Forms;
 4: var Prop: Char;
 5: {----------------------------------------------------------}
 6: { Old-style Pascal program running under Delphi 3          }
 7: { program code is in project window rather than unit window}
 8: {----------------------------------------------------------}
 9: var Cats,Kittens,OldCats,MaxCat,Months: Integer;
10: begin
11:   Write('Enter initial number of cats: ');
12:   Read(Cats);
13:   if Cats < 0  then Cats:= 2;
14:   Write('Enter initial number of kittens: ');
15:   Read(Kittens);
16:   if Kittens < 0  then Kittens:= 0;
17:   Write('Number wanted: ');
18:   Read(MaxCat);
19:   Writeln('Months':10,'Cats':10,'Kittens':10);
20:   Months:= 0;
21:   OldCats:= Cats;
22:   while Cats+Kittens < MaxCat do
23:   begin
24:     if (Months mod 3 = 0) and (Months>0) then
25:     begin
26:       Cats:= Cats+Kittens;
27:       Kittens:= 2*OldCats;
28:       OldCats:= Cats;
29:       Writeln(Months:10,Cats:10,Kittens:10);
30:     end{if};
31:     Inc(Months);
32:   end; {while}
```

```
33:    Write('Press enter to close console window');
34:    Readln(Prop);
35: end.
```

Listing 6.7 uses the same algorithm as discussed in Section 6.4.

The compiler directive in line 2 of Listing 6.7 is unnecessary if Project|Options| Linker is set as shown earlier in Figure 6.3. The other use for the read and write procedures is for debugging Delphi projects, but Delphi also has an excellent debugger which is described in Appendix A.

6.6.3 Using consoles in Delphi 1

In order to use the traditional Pascal write routines to interact with the console,

```
WinCrt
```

should be added to the **uses** clause near the top of the unit. Without this, although the unit may compile, it will give an input–output (IO) error at run time. The console window that appears may occlude the form that is running, but suitable positioning and sizing of windows will avoid this. To keep a record of the results, PrintScreen can be used, which copies the screen to the clipboard, and that clipboard can be pasted elsewhere, to a drawing package. Alt+PrintScreen copies the active window similarly.

These techniques could be of use for debugging code, but there are other alternatives such as use of the ShowMessage box, and a good integrated debugger (see Appendix A).

On the other hand the programmer may wish to use the Delphi environment to run a complete Pascal program, possibly developed in Turbo Pascal. These are the steps to run old-style Pascal programs, using Read and Write:

1. Start a new project.
2. Delete Unit1, which appears automatically, by selecting it, then clicking on the right-hand mouse button to show a menu. Then choose Delete Page. Alternatively use File|Delete to delete Unit1.
3. Save the project in a new file of type *program name*.dpr. Do not try to edit the program identifier, but let Delphi do the updating itself.
4. Use View|Project Source to show the underlying (default) project code.
5. Replace all the code after the first line with the code of the old-style Pascal program, deleting {$R *.RES}. Insert

   uses WinCrt;

   between

   program

   and

   var

   Listing 6.8 shows the code in the Project window.
6. Compile and run: see Figure 6.7.

Once the results have been studied, or copied to the clipboard, the console window in Figure 6.7 can be closed in the normal way. Leaving it open and minimizing will cause problems if the project is run again.

Under Delphi 1 the code should be as shown in Listing 6.8.

Listing 6.8   Console input–output procedures under Delphi 1

```
 1: program P6_8;
 2: {------------------------------------------------------------}
 3: {                                                            }
 4: {Old-style Pascal program, running under Delphi 1,           }
 5: {no read needed at the end to stop the form closing          }
 6: {                                                            }
 7: {------------------------------------------------------------}
 8: uses WinCrt;
 9: var Cats,Kittens,OldCats,MaxCat,Months: Integer;
10: begin
11:   Write('Enter initial number of cats: ');
12:   Read(Cats);
13:   if Cats < 0  then Cats:= 2;
14:   Write('Enter initial number of kittens: ');
15:   Read(Kittens);
16:   if Kittens < 0  then Kittens:= 0;
17:   Write('Number wanted: ');
18:   Read(MaxCat);
19:   Writeln('Months':10,'Cats':10,'Kittens':10);
20:   Months:= 0;
21:   OldCats:= Cats;
22:   while Cats+Kittens < MaxCat do
23:   begin
24:     if (Months mod 3 = 0) and (Months>0) then
25:     begin
26:       Cats:= Cats+Kittens;
27:       Kittens:=  2*OldCats;
28:       OldCats:= Cats;
29:       Writeln(Months:10,Cats:10,Kittens:10);
30:     end{if};
31:     Inc(Months);
32:   end; {while}
33: end.
```

We have seen that:

1. Write outputs a series of strings, or values of variables.

2. Writeln does the same as Write, but then adds a line feed marker, consisting of a carriage return and a line feed character.

3. The string or variable name in Write or Writeln can be followed by :*width*

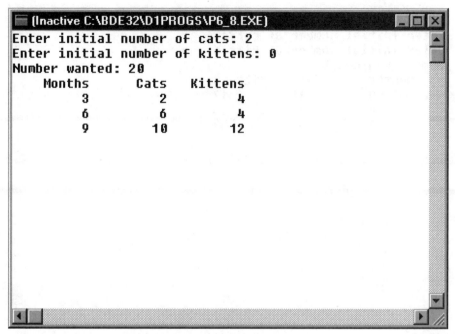

Figure 6.7   Running an old-style Pascal program under Delphi 1.

where *width* is the field width allowed for that item output, and the item is right adjusted within the field.

4. Read and Readln read values into variables. The action differs according to whether the variables are of numeric type or not:

- For numeric types of variable, white space (tabs and end-of-line markers as well as blanks) are skipped before reading the number. An error occurs if the numeric string does not match the variable type.

- For string type variables, all characters including white space are read. Readln skips to the next line after reading, but Read does not.

You should save, compile and run the program as for earlier Delphi projects. One such run is shown in Figure 6.8. Use the close box to close the execution window. In the execution window, first enter small positive values, then try a case when the number wanted is less than the initial number, and finally try a negative value for cats or kittens to start the program. This should indicate that an improved program should attempt to verify the user input before proceeding further.

6.7 The **repeat** loop

repeat loops are the second non-deterministic loop structure. The principal difference between the **repeat** and **while** is that the statement inside a **repeat** loop is always done at least once. This contrasts with the **while** loop, which was not

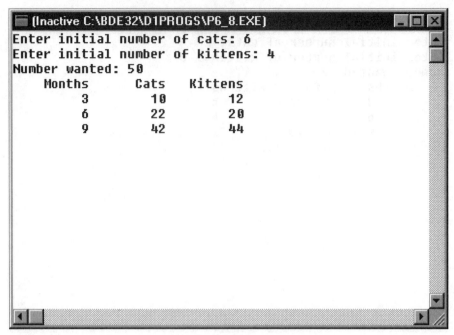

Figure 6.8 Further run of the cat program under Delphi 1.

executed above in the case where there were sufficient cats already! The **repeat** construct is thus well suited to checking data.

The general form of the **repeat** construct is

> **repeat** *action* **until** *something is true*

action can consist of several statements, and no **begin end** pair is required to bind them into a compound statement, unlike most Object Pascal constructs, because the **repeat** terminates at the **until**.

Copy the appropriate version of the old-style Pascal program into a new project file, then change it so that it reads as shown in Listing 6.9 for a Delphi 3 application. This new code will cycle until non-zero values are supplied by the user.

Compile and run the program for the same range of values that was used for the original program. The user is now asked for data repeatedly until positive numbers are entered. The program could be further improved by checking that the data values entered are not too large.

Listing 6.9 Using **repeat** to verify input

```
1: program P6_9;
2: {$Apptype Console}
3: uses Forms;
4: var Prop: Char;
5: {------------------------------------------------------------}
6: { Old-style Pascal program running under Delphi 3          }
```

```
 7: { checking of input added                                    }
 8: {-----------------------------------------------------------}
 9: var Cats,Kittens,OldCats,MaxCat,Months: Integer;
10: begin
11:   repeat {line added here}
12:     Write('Enter initial number of cats: ');
13:     Read(Cats);
14:     Write('Enter initial number of kittens: ');
15:     Read(Kittens);
16:   until (Cats >= 0) and (Kittens >= 0); {changed here}
17:   Write('Number wanted: ');
18:   Read(MaxCat);
19:   Writeln('Months':10,'Cats':10,'Kittens':10);
20:   Months:= 0;
21:   OldCats:= Cats;
22:   while Cats+Kittens < MaxCat do
23:   begin
24:     if (Months mod 3=0) and (Months>0) then
25:     begin
26:       Cats:= Cats+Kittens;
27:       Kittens:= 2*OldCats;
28:       OldCats:= Cats;
29:       Writeln(Months:10,Cats:10,Kittens:10);
30:     end{if};
31:     Inc(Months);
32:   end; {while}
33:   Readln(Prop);
34: end.
```

6.8 The memo component

We have already used edit boxes in several projects: they can be used both to input and output small amounts of data. Also we have seen how console-based programs, that is traditional Pascal, input and output larger amounts of data. Delphi has a memo component which is in some ways an extension of an edit box, in that it allows input and output of several lines of data.

Before using the memo component in a more ambitious project, let us use two memos in order to set up a rudimentary editing application.

1. Open a new project and set up a form like the prototype in Figure 6.9, with two memo components and one MainMenu. The main menu item File should have five options: Cut, Copy, Paste, Clear and Exit.

2. Put the initial contents of the memo boxes as shown in Figure 6.9 by using the Object Inspector and double clicking on the ellipsis following TStrings on the Lines property. The process is similar to that used to set filters on for the

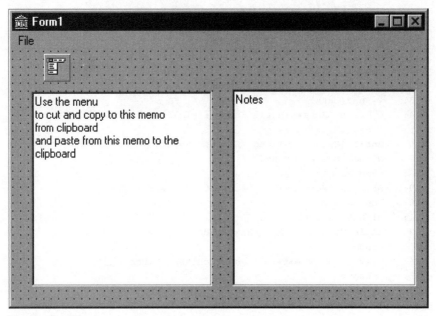

Figure 6.9   Simple editor.

OpenDialog box. An alternative is to add the text at run time, but it is sometimes useful to initialize in this manner.

3. Add code to the event handlers so the unit reads as shown in Listing 6.10.

Listing 6.10) Using editor commands in a memo component

```
 1: unit U6_10;
 2:
 3: interface
 4:
 5: uses
 6:    Windows, Messages, SysUtils, Classes, Graphics,
 7:    Controls, Forms, Dialogs, Menus, StdCtrls;
 8:
 9: type
10:    TForm1 = class(TForm)
11:      Memo1: TMemo;
12:      Memo2: TMemo;
13:      MainMenu1: TMainMenu;
14:      File1: TMenuItem;
15:      Cut1: TMenuItem;
16:      Copy1: TMenuItem;
17:      Paste1: TMenuItem;
18:      Clear1: TMenuItem;
19:      Exit1: TMenuItem;
20:      procedure Cut1Click(Sender: TObject);
```

```
21:      procedure Copy1Click(Sender: TObject);
22:      procedure Paste1Click(Sender: TObject);
23:      procedure Clear1Click(Sender: TObject);
24:      procedure Exit1Click(Sender: TObject);
25:    private
26:      { Private declarations }
27:    public
28:      { Public declarations }
29:    end;
30:
31: var
32:    Form1: TForm1;
33:
34: implementation
35:
36: {$R *.DFM}
37:
38: procedure TForm1.Cut1Click(Sender: TObject);
39: {Additions to Memo2 are just for information}
40: begin
41:    Memo1.CutToClipboard;
42:    Memo1.Lines.Add('');
43:    Memo2.Lines.Add('Selected items were');
44:    Memo2.Lines.Add('cut to clipboard');
45:    Memo2.Lines.Add('gone from memo');
46: end;
47:
48: procedure TForm1.Copy1Click(Sender: TObject);
49: {Additions to Memo2 are just for information}
50: begin
51:    Memo1.CopyToClipboard;
52:    Memo2.Lines.Add('');
53:    Memo2.Lines.Add('Selected items were');
54:    Memo2.Lines.Add('Copied to clipboard');
55:    Memo2.Lines.Add('but left on memo');
56: end;
57:
58: procedure TForm1.Paste1Click(Sender: TObject);
59: {Additions to Memo2 are just for information}
60: begin
61:    Memo1.PasteFromClipboard;
62:    Memo2.Lines.Add('');
63:    Memo2.Lines.Add('Pasted from clipboard');
64:    Memo2.Lines.Add('both here and there');
65: end;
66:
67: procedure TForm1.Clear1Click(Sender: TObject);
68: begin
69:    Memo1.Clear;
70: end;
```

```
71:
72: procedure TForm1.Exit1Click(Sender: TObject);
73: begin
74:   Close;
75: end;
76:
77: end.
```

The event handler `Paste1Click` (lines 58 to 65) pastes text from the standard window's clipboard into the left-hand memo box at the cursor, leaving the clipboard unchanged. The right-hand memo box merely receives comments on the action. `Copy1Click` and `Cut1Click` take whatever text is selected in the left-hand memo box and transfer it to the standard clipboard; the difference is whether or not that text remains in the memo box.

It is interesting to paste items that are already on the clipboard may be from another application.

Details of the many properties of the memo components can be found in the on-line help. Notice that the `Lines` property containing the actual text is an object of class `TStrings`. String objects are used by various other components as well as memos, and can be manipulated by the programmer.

6.9 Keeping results in a file*

Input and output from a series of model runs is more useful in electronic form, and as an example of text file handling within Object Pascal we will discuss a project to merge two previously ordered files, whilst maintaining the ordering. Text files can be written with an editor – such as that in the Delphi environment – or a word processor, and they are divided into separate lines. They should always be saved as type `.txt`. Object Pascal can also use binary files and typed files. Binary files are quick to process, but they can be tricky to program. Typed files are useful in conjunction with records.

The basic algorithm is much as one might merge two piles of papers manually:

1. Take the first item from each file. These are 'in hand'. The files are assumed to be non-empty.

2. Compare the two items 'in hand', decide which should be first, and put it into the output. Read a replacement from the same file. As long as neither of the files is empty, go on comparing items 'in hand'.

3. When end-of-file is encountered, put a sentinel 'in hand'. This is a string further through the alphabet than any string obtained from either file; in this case 'zzzzzz' is a reasonable choice. This is one of many occasions where the addition of a dummy value or sentinel simplifies the overall algorithm. Without the sentinel, the main loop will have to stop when the first file is exhausted, and **while** or **repeat** loops would be required to deal with the tail left in the second file, which could be of any length.

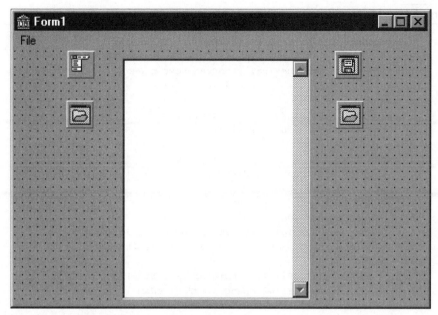

Figure 6.10   Prototype form for the file merging project.

4. Finally, put the final item on the output file, and copy the contents of the output file into the memo, so the user can see a copy of the text file produced.

As with piles of paper, merging is not to be done lightly, because vital information may be lost. In our example the input files must be sorted alphabetically and the output file must be brand new, or unwanted.

Filters will be set so that .txt files are targeted – merging other types of files is inadvisable.

A simple prototype form for the file merging project is shown in Figure 6.10.

1. Open a new Delphi project.

2. Add a main menu component, a memo component, two OpenDialog components and a SaveDialog component to the form.

3. Change the first main menu caption to &File and add two items to that drop down menu, &Merge and E&xit.

4. Use the Properties tab of the Object Inspector to change the default filters on the three dialog boxes to *.txt to ensure only text files are offered.

5. Add

```
Close;
```

to the Exit1Click event handler.

6. Add lines 10 to 52 of the Listing 6.11 code to the OnClick event handler for Merge1.

Listing 6.11 Merging sorted text files

```
 1: procedure TForm1.Merge1Click(Sender: TObject);
 2: {----------------------------------------------------------}
 3: {To merge 2 alphabetically sorted text files              }
 4: {----------------------------------------------------------}
 5: var
 6:    InFile1,InFile2,OutFile: TextFile;
 7:    InString1,InString2: string;
 8:
 9: begin
10:    ShowMessage('Choose 2 distinct i/p files, 1 o/p file');
11:    if OpenDialog1.Execute
12:      and OpenDialog2.Execute
13:      and SaveDialog1.Execute
14:      and (MessageDlg('Write to'+SaveDialog1.FileName
15:        ,mtwarning, [mbYes,mbNo],0 ) =mrYes) then
16:    begin
17:      AssignFile(InFile1,OpenDialog1.FileName);
18:      AssignFile(InFile2,OpenDialog2.FileName);
19:      AssignFile(Outfile,SaveDialog1.FileName);
20:      Reset(InFile1);
21:      Reset(InFile2);
22:      Rewrite(OutFile);
23:      Readln(InFile1,InString1);
24:      Readln(InFile2,InString2);
25:      while
26:        not Eof(InFile1) or not Eof(InFile2) do
27:      begin
28:        if (InString1 < InString2) then
29:        begin
30:          Writeln(OutFile,InString1);
31:          if not eof(InFile1) then
32:            Readln(InFile1,InString1)
33:          else InString1:='zzzzzz';
34:        end
35:        else
36:        begin
37:          Writeln(OutFile,InString2);
38:          if not Eof(Infile2) then
39:            Readln(InFile2,InString2)
40:          else InString2:='zzzzzz';
41:        end; {else}
42:      end {while};
43:      if Eof(InFile1) then
44:        Writeln(OutFile,InString2);
45:      if Eof(InFile2) then
46:        Writeln(OutFile,InString1);
47:      CloseFile(InFile1);
48:      CloseFile(InFile2);
```

```
49:      CloseFile(OutFile);
50:      Memo1.Lines.LoadFromFile(SaveDialog1.FileName);
51:    end {then}
52:    else ShowMessage('File Problem');
53: end;
```

7. Add the variable declarations of lines 5 to 7.

   As the name implies, `TextFile` is the type which should be used for text files, replacing the type `Text` used in earlier versions of Pascal. `Text` may be used, but it is used for other purposes in Delphi.

8. Save both project and file. Use a word processor or editor to set up two files, each containing an alphabetic list. The project will detect end-of-file, so it is unnecessary to insert the 'zzzzzz' in the files.

9. Compile and run the project.

In Listing 6.11:

● Lines 11 to 15 evaluate the Boolean expression:

```
OpenDialog1.Execute
and OpenDialog2.Execute
and SaveDialog1.Execute
and (MessageDlg('Write to'+SaveDialog1.FileName
   ,mtwarning, [mbYes,mbNo],0 ) =mrYes)
```

The expression will only be true if all three calls to the `Execute` method return true (the user having pressed the OK button every time) and the user replies Yes to the message dialog box that appears. If that expression is true, lines 16 to 51 will then be executed, otherwise an error message will be shown by line 52.

● Lines 11 to 13 also obtain the value `FileName` property for each file; they are of type **string**.

● Lines 17 to 19 connect these three actual external files with the three variables of type `TextFile`: `InFile1`, `InFile2`, `OutFile`.

● Lines 20 and 21 open two files for reading only, and line 22 opens the final file for writing only. In each case the file pointer is set at the start of the file. `Rewrite` will overwrite an existing file of the same name. The in-built `Reset` and `Rewrite` procedures are slightly different in the case of binary files.

● Lines 23 and 24 obtain the first two items from each input file.

● Lines 25 to 42 are the main loop, which cycles as long as one of the files is not at the end. `Eof` is an in-built function which returns true if the current position of the file pointer is beyond the data, and otherwise false.

● Within a single iteration of the loop either lines 29 to 34 or 36 to 41 are executed, according to the alphabetical ordering of `InString1` and `InString2`. In ASCII ordering, lower case letters appear after the upper case ones, hence 'zzzzzz' is a reasonable choice for a sentinel. It could be replaced by a constant.

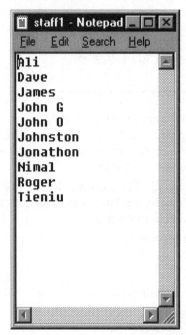

Figure 6.11 First input to file merge.

- Lines 30 to 32 write one line to the output file, and then input another from InFile1, placing it in InString1. If Eof is true, then the sentinel value is placed in InString1 in line 33.
- Once InString1 contains the sentinel value, it will always be greater than values InString2, unless end-of-file has been reached there too. Hence the **else** branch of the **if** statement in line 28 will be executed, that is lines 36 to 39.
- InString2 is treated similarly to InString1.
- Lines 43 to 46 write to file the one item that remains 'in hand'.
- Line 49 closes OutFile.
- Line 50 uses the LoadFromFile method to copy the entire file into Memo1.

The inputs and outputs from a typical run are illustrated in Figures 6.11 to 6.13.

(6.10) Summary

This chapter extended the concept of iteration to the important idea of non-deterministic loops, in which the number of iterations is not preset. We have demonstrated techniques for running old-style Pascal programs in the Delphi environment. File handling of text files was introduced; this is essential for many projects.

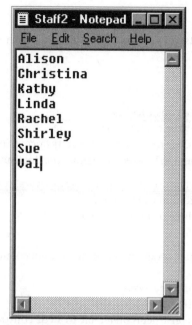

Figure 6.12   Second input to file merge.

Figure 6.13   Text file output from the file merging project.

Quiz

1. What Pascal constructs can a programmer use to implement non-deterministic loops?
    (a) `for`
    (b) `while`
    (c) `repeat`

2. What is true of a `while` construct in Pascal?
    (a) It can cause code to be executed several times.
    (b) It can only cause code to be executed exactly once, or not at all.
    (c) It causes a statement to be executed before the Boolean condition is evaluated.

3. Can a `while` construct be used to cycle as long as several conditions hold?
    (a) No, only one condition can be used.
    (b) Yes, but at most three conditions can be tested.
    (c) Yes.

4. For what reasons might a programmer test the number of iterations in a `while` or `repeat` construct?
    (a) To guard against infinite loops.
    (b) Because the step size is not 1.
    (c) Because a `while` construct is preferable to a `for` construct.

5. Why might a programmer prefer a `repeat` construct over a `while` construct?
    (a) The action statement of a `while` construct is always executed at least once.
    (b) The action statement of a `repeat` construct is always executed at least once.
    (c) The action statement of a `while` construct can only be a simple statement.

6. Which features does an `InputBox` have?
    (a) It can be positioned appropriately on the screen.
    (b) It provides a user-friendly way to both input and output data.
    (c) It provides a user-friendly way to input data.

7. The `Draw` method of a `Canvas` can be used:
    (a) to draw bitmaps, metafiles or icons on any `Canvas`
    (b) to draw items of type `TShape` on a `Canvas`
    (c) only to draw bitmaps, metafiles or icons on the `Canvas` of a form

8. A memo component:
    (a) can include several lines
    (b) can be used for output from a project, but not for input
    (c) can contain only one line of text

9. To run a standard Pascal program under Delphi:
    (a) Write code in the unit file, adding **uses** `WinCrt`.
    (b) Write code in the project file, adding **uses** `WinCrt`.
    (c) Write code in the project file, adding `{$Apptype Console}` and a **uses** clause.

10. Files are useful:
    (a) to store data from run to run

(b) for debugging purposes

(c) for displaying data

Exercises

1. Write a program that finds the greatest power of 2 that is less than a number entered by the user via an `InputBox`.

2. Write a program that counts down from 100 to 1, then shows a message box with the message 'Blast off'.

3. Extend the previous exercise so that after 'Blast off' a rocket shape moves up the screen.

4. Write an application to read an unknown number of real numbers from a text file and average them.

5. Write a program to count the words in a line of text in an edit box by counting spaces until a full stop or period is entered.

Chapter 7

Arrays, subranges and strings

7.1 Introduction

In this chapter we introduce the array data structure. An array is a bounded collection of elements of the same type. The bounds are represented as subranges. Each element of an array is accessed via an index. The array is an example of a Pascal structured data type, that is a type constructed from other types. Arrays may be one, two, three or more dimensional, but in all cases elements are arranged sequentially and stored contiguously in memory.

Arrays are found in almost all programming languages, as they provide a convenient way of associating a group of data values with a single name, while providing an indexing mechanism for accessing individual elements.

Subrange types are derived from existing ordinal types and are used to restrict the range of the *base* type. We use subranges to represent the bounds of arrays and as a type in their own right.

A number of Delphi's components echo the array concept. List boxes (on the Standard page of the Component Palette) can be used to represent one-dimensional arrays, whereas string grids (on the Additional page) can represent two-dimensional arrays.

Delphi strings are essentially arrays of characters. There are inherently two different string types: static, with a fixed maximum size, and dynamic, which expand and contract as necessary. In earlier chapters strings were used but their underlying anatomy was not explained. In this chapter we will explain the inner workings of strings, the explanation of which will require an understanding of arrays.

7.2 One-dimensional arrays

A one-dimensional array can be visualized as a row of elements, each of identical type. Figure 7.1 illustrates a one-dimensional array with 10 floating-point elements. Such one-dimensional arrays are also called vectors.

6.2	4.2	3.1	−1.2	−7.1	−1.2	6.2	21.2	21.0	9.2

Figure 7.1   A one-dimensional array.

The general form of a one-dimensional array **type** declaration is

type *array type name* = **array** [*subrange*] **of** *a type* ;

An array of 10 real `Single` numbers can be defined by

type TTenSingles = **array** [1..10] **of** Single;

Note that square brackets must be used around the range of arrays, but round brackets are used in expressions and procedures. A **type** definition describes how data is stored and accessed, while a variable definition reserves memory for storing data. The name of a type can be any legitimate identifier. It is good practice to choose meaningful names for identifiers; however, sometimes this leads to confusion in the programmer's mind between what is a type and what is a variable of that type. This confusion can be avoided by putting a 'T' at the start of the name of each user-defined type.

Pascal array bounds do not have to start at 1. They do not even have to be numbers; the lower value of the subrange can be any value of the base type. So the following are valid array types:

type TLetterCount= **array** ['A'..'Z'] **of** Integer;
type TNegativeTen= **array** [-10..-1] **of** Boolean;

The first declares a type of array with 26 elements labelled 'A' to 'Z', and the second an array of Boolean elements labelled −10 to −1, each of which can hold the value True or False.

Type declarations, such as those above, do not create any space in memory to store arrays. In order to create space for arrays, variable declarations must be made, for example as follows:

```
var TopTen: TTenSingles;
var LetterArray: TLetterCount; NegativeArray: TNegativeTen;
```

Individual elements of an array can be accessed using subscripts in square brackets. For instance to put the number 6.2 in the first element of TopTen:

```
TopTen[1]:= 6.2;
```

To assign half the value of the first element of TopTen to the third:

```
TopTen[3]:= TopTen[1] / 2;
```

To put the number 82 into the second element of LetterArray:

```
LetterArray['B']:= 82;
```

To set the first element of NegativeArray to False:

```
NegativeArray[-10]:= False;
```

It is often useful to use a counted loop to initialize or reset all values of an array:

```
for Count:= 1 to 10 do
  TopTen[Count]:= 0.0;
```

will initialize all elements of TopTen to zero. Count is a previously declared integer variable.

Setting all elements of LetterArray to 1 would need a previously declared character variable, such as AChar below:

```
for AChar:= 'A' to 'Z' do
  LetterArray[AChar]:= 1;
```

7.3 Subrange types

The programmer can define a subrange type and use it to narrow the choices available from a *base* type. They are particularly useful for declaring the bounds of an array.

A subrange type is derived from an existing ordinal type, by restricting the range of this base type. A subrange of all integers between −10 and 10 can be declared as

```
type TTens= -10..10;
```

The elements of the subrange type must be consecutive values of the base type. For example, it is not possible to create a subrange of all integers between −10 and 10 except 0.

The subrange type TTens can be used in an array type declaration:

```
type TTenSingles1= array [TTens] of Single;
```

A subrange of the lower case letters of the alphabet could be

```
type TLowerCase= 'a'..'z';
```

This could be used in the following **array** declaration:

```
type TLowerLetterArray= array [TLowerCase] of Boolean;
```

The general form of a subrange **type** declaration is

```
type type name = constant1 .. constant2;
```

Both *constant1* and *constant2* must be of the same ordinal type.

(7.4) Variables of subrange types

Variables of a predefined subrange type can be declared by using a variable declaration:

```
var SmallNumber: TTens; SmallLetter: TLowerCase;
```

It is also possible to define variables, without a separate type definition, using an anonymous user-defined type; for example:

```
var BigLetter: 'A'..'Z';
```

declares that the variable BigLetter is a character value between 'A' and 'Z'. However, if the same type is used more than once, it is good practice to use a named type. In the above example it would be possible in one definition to inadvertently type a lower case 'z'; this would not lead to a compile time error but might lead to a very puzzling run time error.

Variables of a subrange type have all the properties of the base type, but their run time values must be within the specified range. By default Delphi does not generate checks to ensure that variables are within the allowed range. The programmer can force such *run time* checks to be included by the use of range-checking directives. Within a unit this is achieved by adding a {$R+} to the unit code; if no longer required this range-checking can be turned off later in the unit by a {$R-}. Compiler directives are enclosed in comment braces (curly brackets) and can be placed anywhere that a comment can appear, but the first character of a compiler directive is always a $ symbol. Unlike ordinary comments, compiler directives carry important information for the compiler. Ordinary comments are discarded by the compiler.

The fragment of code in Listing 7.1 illustrates the use of a subrange type.

(Listing 7.1)   The use of a subrange type

```
1: {$R+}
2:
3: type TTens= -10..10;
```

```
 4:
 5: procedure TForm1.Button1Click(Sender: TObject);
 6: var SmallNumber: TTens;
 7: begin
 8:   SmallNumber:= StrToInt(Edit1.Text);
 9:   Button1.Caption:= IntToStr(SmallNumber);
10: end;
```

What happens when the user clicks the button will depend on the contents of the string in the edit box, accessed by line 8 of Listing 7.1.

- If the string in Edit1.Text represents an integer number between −10 and 10 then the subsequent statement will be executed and the button's caption will be set to the appropriate number.

- If the value in Edit1.Text is not an integer an exception is raised and an error message is displayed. This will be of the general form: 'this is not an integer'. Once the user accepts this message the program will continue, but without attempting to set the button's caption or execute any other statements in this event handler. Chapter 11 explains more about the role of exceptions.

- If Edit1.Text contains any integer value outside the range −10 to 10 then an error message will be displayed, because the range checking has been turned on by the compiler directive {$R+}. The message will tell the user that the value is out of range. The user can accept this and allow the program to continue, but it will not attempt to set the button's caption or execute any other statements in this event handler. The application will continue to execute and respond to new events.

- If the range-checking directive is turned off by {$R-} or never turned on (the default) and Edit1.Text contains any integer value outside the range −10 to 10, the subsequent statements will be directly executed and the button's caption set. There will be no error message.

Range checking does not correct the out-of-range fault; it merely points it out. It is the programmer's responsibility to ensure that there is code in place to take appropriate action if the values are erroneous. In Chapter 4 an event handler was developed that attempted to ensure input was valid. This event handler is shown in Listing 7.2.

Listing 7.2) Verification of input

```
1: procedure TForm1.Edit1KeyPress
2:              (Sender: TObject; var Key: Char);
3: {-----------------------------------------------------------}
4: { Accept inputs of digits and backspace                     }
5: { Do comparison when enter pressed                          }
6: { Ignore all other key presses                              }
7: {-----------------------------------------------------------}
8: const BackSpace= #8; Null= #0; Enter= #13;
9: begin
```

```
10:    case Key of
11:    '0'..'9',BackSpace:
12:       ;{Key is a digit or backspace so no action necessary}
13:    Enter:
14:    begin
15:       Key:= Null; {don't include the enter key with the number}
16:       CompareButtonClick(Sender);
17:       Edit1.SelectAll;
18:    end
19:    else
20:       Key:= Null;   {all other key presses replaced by null}
21:    end;
22: end;
```

- This procedure transmits only on certain key presses, whereas others are set to null.

- At line 11 the range of Key is set as '0' to '9' and backspace to allow the user to correct a mistyped value. Realizing that the user may wish to correct a mistyped character is a result of consideration of the user's requirements. Range checking is an aid, not a substitute for careful design.

Range checking can be set for a whole project using the Compilers Option page. This is accessed via Project|Options from the main menu bar (Options|Project in Delphi 1).

By enabling range checking the programmer forces the compiler to generate checks that all uses of subranges are within bounds, including scrutiny of all subscripts of arrays. The by-product is that the program is larger and runs slower. It is usual practice only to use range checking where it is needed during development and debugging, then to incorporate suitable checks before using the program in earnest.

At points where a variable may go out of range the programmer should develop checks and add code that takes remedial actions. The programmer may choose to modify the example given in Listing 7.1 to the version shown in Listing 7.3 so that when the number entered is outside the range −10 to 10, it is reset to 0 and no further action takes place until another event occurs.

Listing 7.3 Programmer-developed checking

```
1: Temp:= StrToInt(Edit1.Text);
2: if Abs(Temp)>10 then
3:    Edit1.Text:= '0'
4: else
5: begin
6:    SmallNumber:= Temp;
7:    Button1.Caption:= IntToStr(SmallNumber);
8: end;
```

The in-built functions `Low` and `High` can be used to determine the lowest and highest values in a range respectively. This is particularly useful in the case of passing open arrays to procedures: see Chapter 9.

If the programmer added the statement

```
ANumber:= Low(SmallNumber);
```

to the code in Listing 7.1 it would set `ANumber` to −10, likewise:

```
High(SmallNumber)
```

will return 10.

The range of an array cannot be changed at run time, but the programmer may change the range as a program develops, using a small array in early versions and later changing to larger arrays. To cope with such change the `Low` and `High` functions can be used to ensure the whole array is always accessed. They are also used when an open array is passed as a parameter to a procedure (see Chapter 9). The following code illustrates these functions:

```
for Count:= Low(TopTen) to High(TopTen) do
   TopTen[Count]:= 0.0;
```

7.5 Strings

Every version of Delphi provides an in-built type **string** that can be visualized as an array of characters. With Delphi 1 the longest string size available was 255 characters. After Delphi 1 the implementation of the default **string** type was enhanced to allow for much longer strings. The improvement to the implementation means that for subsequent releases of Delphi there is no predefined maximum length of a string: the Delphi Help pages give a theoretical limit of 2 GB (gigabytes) of memory.

With later releases of Delphi (from Delphi 2) the default string is dynamic. This means that memory is allocated for the string at run time and is taken only as needed. These strings are known as long strings.

The Delphi 1 string is static, as in most versions of the Pascal language. Memory is reserved for the string at compile time and as such is unavailable for other use. The programmer can fix the size of the string or accept the default size of 255 characters. Either is perfectly acceptable for a small number of strings each with only a few characters, but can be problematic when a program has potentially a large number of strings of which only a few are used in any particular run. Later releases of Delphi allow the use of these static strings for compatibility, calling them short strings, but the use of long strings is usually superior.

All versions of Delphi support another category of strings known as *null terminated* strings. Null terminated strings have their roots in the C programming language, so here we call them *C strings*. They are widely used by C and C++ programmers and they also play a significant role in Windows programming. Delphi provides C strings to allow for easy interface to other programming languages and to the Windows API (Application Programming Interface). C strings also allow Delphi 1 programmers to create strings longer than 255 characters.

Table 7.1 Summary of string types.

Type of string	Name in Delphi 1	Name in later versions	Usage
Long strings	not available	**string** or AnsiString	in later versions `var LStr:`**`string`**`;`
Fixed-length short strings	**string**	**string**	in all versions `var SStr:`**`string`**`[12];`
Default-length short strings	**string**	*use not recommended*	in Delphi 1 `var DStr:`**`string`**`;`
C strings (null terminated)	**array of** Char	**array of** Char	in all versions `var CStr:`**`array`** `[0..11]` **`of`** `Char;`

Note: boundaries where given can vary; 12 elements are used in the table as an example

---

The plethora of string types is confusing. Table 7.1 summarizes the names of strings and their usage. A programmer using later versions of Delphi (from 2 onwards) should concentrate on long strings. On the other hand a Delphi 1 programmer will find it easier to start with fixed-length short strings. Advanced programmers will need to master C strings, but the beginner can postpone study of that material.

7.5.1 Long strings (not available in Delphi 1)

A long string does not have a fixed predefined maximum length. It will dynamically expand and contract as the contents of the string alter. Delphi automatically allocates memory when a string changes and *garbage collects* memory released. The actual implementation of long strings is based on pointers (see Chapter 14). However, the programmer can access strings as though they were arrays of characters. The predefined identifier AnsiString can be used as an alternative to the reserved word **string**, which is useful if a programmer cannot avoid using both short and long strings.

The general format of a definition for a long string variable is

```
var string variable: string;
```

For example:

```
var Salutation: string;
```

Values can be assigned to strings by assignment, such as:

```
Salutation:= 'Hello World!';
```

Salutation can be displayed using an edit box:

```
Edit1.Text:= Salutation;
```

which displays the text

```
Hello World!
```

Individual characters within a string can be accessed using the same index mechanism as arrays. For example, the two statements

```
Salutation[10]:= 'd';
Salutation[11]:= 's';
```

would change the contents of Salutation to

```
Hello Words!
```

Long strings start at element 1. The in-built function Length can be used to return the length of the current string. The current value of Length(Salutation) will be 12, that is the number of characters in the message (including the space and the exclamation mark).

The functions High and Low, introduced in Section 7.3, are not applicable to long strings.

The character immediately after the end of a long string is a null character. The null character is not part of the string, and long strings should not be confused with C strings (null terminated strings).

7.5.2   Fixed-length short strings (all versions of Delphi)

In a fixed-length short string an array is used to store the characters of the string. The first element of the array (the 'zeroth' element) is used to represent the current length of the string and the remaining elements contain the characters of the string. The number of elements in the array is fixed by the **type** statement and cannot be more than 255.

The general format of a definition for a fixed-length short string type is

```
type string type name = string [ length ];
```

So a string type to hold 12 characters could be defined as

```
type TGreeting= string[12];
```

A variable of this type can be declared as

```
var Salutation: TGreeting;
```

Unlike the long string equivalent this will actually have 13 elements, the zeroth element being used to store the current size of the string. Within a unit's code:

```
Salutation:= 'Hello World!';
```

assigns text to Salutation. This text will be stored in an array of characters as shown in Figure 7.2.

#12	H	e	l	l	o		W	o	r	l	d	!

Figure 7.2   The array of characters representing the string Salutation.

As earlier, `Salutation` can be displayed using an edit box:

```
Hello World!
```

would appear in the box. Again, if these assignments are performed:

```
Salutation[10]:= 'd';
Salutation[11]:= 's';
```

then Salutation redisplayed in the edit box would show the text

```
Hello Words!
```

If the value of the zeroth character is changed the string length will alter, although the elements not used remain available:

```
Salutation[0]:=#5;
```

#5 is used because the right-hand side of this assignment statement must be a character, not an integer. This would result in displaying only the first five characters of the fixed-length short string:

```
Hello
```

The other characters are still there, just not accessible.

The programmer should use this facility sparingly as it does not work with long strings, which are the default in later versions of Delphi.

The value of `Length(Salutation)` would currently be 5, corresponding to the result that would be obtained from the equivalent long string.

The functions `Low` and `High` can be used with short strings. The `Low` function will return 0 for any string, while `High` gives the maximum number of elements. As these functions do not work with long strings it is advisable to avoid them.

Mixtures of short strings and long strings can be used in assignments and expressions. The compiler will ensure the necessary string type conversions take place. However, the programmer should consider carefully if it is essential to mix these two types before doing so.

7.5.3   Default-length short strings (only recommended for use with Delphi 1)

Short strings do not need to be given a length and will automatically be given a default length of 255. However, because of the enhancements available in later versions of Delphi such strings should be used with care.

The type of a default-length short string could be declared by the use of a **type** statement in Delphi 1 of the general form

```
type string type name = string;
```

The Delphi 1 type **string** is usually used directly in a variable declaration, of the general form:

```
var string variable name : string;
```

A Delphi 1 string declared in this manner will have a length of 255, but by assignment or setting the zeroth element a shorter string can be manipulated, as with a string with a length fixed by the programmer.

In Delphi 1 a variable of this type can be declared as

```
var D1Salutation: string;
```

and assigned by

```
D1Salutation:= 'Hello World!';
```

This can be visualized as the array of characters in Figure 7.2 with another 243 elements containing no useful information. Where a program uses only a small number of strings this wasted space is insignificant, but when large numbers of strings are needed this squandered resource can be detrimental to the program's performance.

For compatibility, programmers using later versions of Delphi can have access to this sort of string, by either using the type ShortString or setting compiler options. However, long strings are more efficient and should be used where possible.

7.5.4   C strings (all versions of Delphi)*

A C string consists of a series of non-null characters followed by the null character (#0). Delphi provides C strings to allow for easy interface with other programming languages (including C and C++) and to the Windows API. A number of procedures are available for converting between C strings and long and short strings. In the online help C strings are referred to as null terminated strings; we find that term confusing and so prefer to use the term C strings.

With later versions of Delphi there is no limit on the number of characters in a C string (like long strings there will be a physical limit based on the underlying hardware). With Delphi 1 there is a maximum of 65,535 characters in a C string. Delphi 1 programmers use C strings to hold larger amounts of characters than are permitted in short strings.

A C string is stored in an array of characters. For example:

```
var ArrayOfChar: array [0..14] of Char;
```

declares an array capable of holding up to 14 characters. The procedure StrPCopy can be used to place a string into the array, creating a C string:

```
StrPCopy(ArrayOfChar,'Hello World!');
```

The array can be visualized as shown in Figure 7.3.

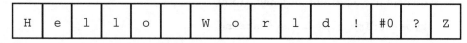

| H | e | l | l | o | | W | o | r | l | d | ! | #0 | ? | Z |

Figure 7.3   A C string.

The first character of the string ('H') is in element 0 of the array, unlike short strings where this contains the length of the string. The character after the '!' is a null character (#0); this is stored as part of the string, unlike long strings where the null is not part of the string. The characters after the null are not part of the current string, but can be anything, usually what were left in that part of memory. They are there because the assignment statements assigned only characters 0 to 11 of an array with range 0 to 14.

Individual characters can be accessed using the array's index. Because C strings are zero index based, the access index will always be one less than for the corresponding short or long string. ArrayOfChar[0] contains the letter 'H'.

In Chapter 4 we introduced message boxes. By using C strings it is possible to make wider use of the facilities provided by Windows. More details of message boxes and related functions can be found on the Help pages. Text messages to this function must be in the form of C strings. Listing 7.4 illustrates the use of MessageBox.

Listing 7.4) Using MessageBox

```
1: var
2:    ArrayOfChar:array [0..14] of Char;
3:    Title:array [0..14] of Char;
4: begin
5:    StrPCopy(ArrayOfChar,'Hello World!');
6:    StrPCopy(Title,'Example');
7:    MessageBox(0,ArrayOfChar,Title,MB_OK);
8: end;
```

When this is executed a box like the one in Figure 7.4 will be displayed.

- Lines 5 and 6 use StrPCopy to put literal strings into C strings.
- Line 7 activates the message box passing the C string for display.

Figure 7.4 Message box.

The programmer must be aware that such arrays of characters cannot be replaced by either long or short strings. Such code will not compile.

Long strings can be directly assigned to C strings, of a sufficient length. They can also be typecast to be treated as though they were C strings. So:

```
PChar(long string)
```

can be used in the place of a C string. This casting does not work with short strings.

7.6 Two-dimensional arrays

Arrays can have any number of dimensions. One-dimensional arrays, as seen in Section 7.2, have many applications. Two-dimensional arrays are frequently used to represent tables of information.

Multidimensional arrays are stored as a vector in memory, the indices being used to pick out elements in each dimension.

The programmer is free to choose what an index represents. Commonly a two-dimensional array will be envisaged to have rows and columns. Whether the first index is chosen to represent the rows or columns of the table is up to the programmer and as long as the programmer is consistent in the use of indices the program will work correctly. The normal mathematical convention is *row major*, that is the first index represents the rows and the second the columns. The Delphi components for visualizing two-dimensional objects are *column major*, that is the first index represents the column and the second the row. Here we follow the Delphi approach.

A two-dimensional array for holding integers can be declared as follows:

```
const NoCols= 10; NoRows= 12;
type
  TATable= array[1..NoCols,1..NoRows] of Integer;
```

The type can be used to declare variables that can hold a 10 by 12 table of integers, for example by declaring:

```
var TimesTable: TATable;
```

This variable array could be used to hold the results of calculating the *times table*. The following code performs the necessary calculations:

```
for i:= 1 to NoCols do
  for j:= 1 to NoRows do
    TimesTable[i,j]:= i*j;
```

where i and j are integers.

7.7 DrawGrid

The component DrawGrid allows the user to display two-dimensional arrays of both text and graphics. The power of a DrawGrid is that its cells can contain almost anything. The cost of this is that the onus is on the programmer to ensure the data is manipulated in a legitimate manner. If a grid is to be used only to display text it is much better to use a StringGrid (see Section 7.8). However, if graphics are to be incorporated a DrawGrid is appropriate.

Here we develop a project that illustrates the use of a DrawGrid. The project allows the user to choose a bitmap file; the contents of the bitmap will be revealed by clicking on squares of the DrawGrid. A display on the right will indicate the row and column of the element within the grid that were selected.

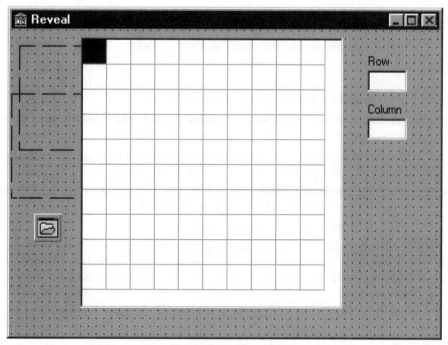

Figure 7.5 Prototype form illustrating the use of DrawGrid.

The prototype form will look like Figure 7.5.

1. Create a new directory for this, open Delphi and store the project and unit in the directory.

2. Place the following components on the form:

   - Two images (Image1 and Image2); their positions are not important as they will not be visible at run time.

   - An OpenDialog component. Set the Filter property so that bitmaps will be read (as in Section 2.6 and as illustrated in Figure 2.12).

   - Two edit boxes (Edit1 and Edit2) with their texts set blank.

   - Two labels named Row and Column above Edit1 and Edit2 respectively.

   - A DrawGrid (DrawGrid1), from the Additional page of the Component Palette. A number of properties need to be set so that DrawGrid1 represents the grid on the prototype form. Those changed from their default values are:

     ```
     ColCount          10
     Color             clWhite
     DefaultColWidth   24
     DefaultDrawing    False
     FixedCols         0
     FixedRows         0
     Height            270
     ```

```
RowCount          10
Width             270
```

The final precision of the `Width` and `Height` will be set in the code, to ensure there is no need for scroll bars.

3. Double click on the `OnMouseDown` event of `DrawGrid1`. This will produce an event handler template with the following header:

```
procedure TForm1.DrawGrid1MouseDown(Sender: TObject;
     Button: TMouseButton; Shift: TShiftState; X, Y: Integer);
```

The `X` and `Y` parameters represent the pixel position of the point where the mouse was clicked. The parameters `Button` and `Shift`, which indicate what state the mouse was in when clicked, will not be used in this example. Add these local declarations, after the header and before the **begin**:

```
var CurrentRow,CurrentCol: Integer;
```

If a Delphi 1 or 2 version of the program is being developed, `CurrentRow` and `CurrentCol` will need to be declared as `LongInt`, to be compatible with `RowCount` and `ColCount` which are `LongInt` in Delphi 1 and 2 but `Integer` in later versions.

Add this code to the body of the event handler (between **begin** and **end**):

```
DrawGrid1.MouseToCell(X,Y,CurrentRow,CurrentCol);
Edit1.Text:= IntToStr(CurrentRow);
Edit2.Text:= IntToStr(CurrentCol);
```

When the program is run and the user clicks the mouse on a cell of the DrawGrid the edit boxes will show the row and column pointed to. Note that the top row is row 0 and the leftmost column is also 0.

4. The program can now be developed to get the correct sizing of the DrawGrid and to set the graphic. Two images are used, one to hold the picture and one to hold a copy stretched to be the size of the DrawGrid. This will all be done at the time the form is activated, by adding code to the `OnActivate` event of the form. The `OnActivate` event handler is in lines 51 to 78 of the full unit in Listing 7.5. The programmer adds:

- the comments and declaration at lines 52 to 56

- the code from lines 58 to 77.

Lines 51, 57 and 78 are generated automatically when the programmer double clicks on the form's `OnActivate` event in the Object Inspector.

(**Listing 7.5**) Revealing an image

```
1: unit U7_5;
2:
3: interface
4:
5: uses
6:   Windows, Messages, SysUtils, Classes, Graphics, Controls,
```

```
 7:    Forms, Dialogs, Grids, StdCtrls, ExtCtrls;
 8:
 9: type
10:    TForm1 = class(TForm)
11:       Image1: TImage;
12:       Image2: TImage;
13:       OpenDialog1: TOpenDialog;
14:       Edit1: TEdit;
15:       Edit2: TEdit;
16:       Label1: TLabel;
17:       Label2: TLabel;
18:       DrawGrid1: TDrawGrid;
19:       procedure DrawGrid1MouseDown(Sender: TObject;
20:         Button: TMouseButton; Shift: TShiftState;
21:         X, Y: Integer);
22:       procedure FormActivate(Sender: TObject);
23:    private
24:       { Private declarations }
25:    public
26:       { Public declarations }
27:    end;
28:
29: var
30:    Form1: TForm1;
31:
32: implementation
33:
34: {$R *.DFM}
35:
36: procedure TForm1.DrawGrid1MouseDown(Sender: TObject;
37:    Button: TMouseButton; Shift: TShiftState; X, Y: Integer);
38: {------------------------------------------------------------}
39: { Indicate which cell selected and reveal the contents     }
40: {------------------------------------------------------------}
41: var CurrentRow,CurrentCol: Integer;{use LongInt not Integer}
42:      MyRect: TRect;                  {with Delphi 1 and 2   }
43: begin
44:    DrawGrid1.MouseToCell(X,Y,CurrentRow,CurrentCol);
45:    Edit1.Text:= IntToStr(CurrentRow);
46:    Edit2.Text:= IntToStr(CurrentCol);
47:    MyRect:= DrawGrid1.CellRect(CurrentRow,CurrentCol);
48:    DrawGrid1.Canvas.CopyRect(MyRect,Image2.Canvas,MyRect);
49: end;
50:
51: procedure TForm1.FormActivate(Sender: TObject);
52: {------------------------------------------------------------}
53: { Initialization routine: makes all cells visible,         }
54: { selects an image, scales to fit and makes invisible      }
55: {------------------------------------------------------------}
56: var MyRect: TRect;
```

```
57: begin
58:    {Make all the cells visible within the space available
59:       this could be done at design time}
60:    DrawGrid1.BorderStyle:= bsNone;
61:    DrawGrid1.Width:= DrawGrid1.ColCount*
62:       (DrawGrid1.DefaultColWidth+DrawGrid1.GridLineWidth);
63:    DrawGrid1.Height:= DrawGrid1.RowCount*
64:       (DrawGrid1.DefaultRowHeight+DrawGrid1.GridLineWidth);
65:    {Choose an image}
66:    OpenDialog1.Execute;
67:    Image1.Picture.LoadFromFile(OpenDialog1.FileName);
68:    {Scale Image1 into Image2 to fit the size of the grid }
69:    Image2.Height:= DrawGrid1.Height;
70:    Image2.Width:= DrawGrid1.Width;
71:    Image2.Top:= DrawGrid1.Top;
72:    Image2.Left:= DrawGrid1.Left;
73:    MyRect:= Rect(0,0,Image2.Width,Image2.Height);
74:    Image2.Canvas.StretchDraw(MyRect,Image1.Picture.Graphic);
75:    {hide both images}
76:    Image1.Visible:= False;
77:    Image2.Visible:= False;
78: end;
79:
80: end.
```

In the event handler:

- Lines 60 to 64 change the grid size to allow for the number of elements.
- Lines 66 and 67 load an image selected by the user from the file store.
- Lines 69 to 72 make Image2 the same size as DrawGrid1.
- The function Rect (at line 73) returns a variable of type TRect, which is required by StretchDraw (at line 74) to stretch the graphic from Image1 into Image2.
- Lines 76 and 77 hide the images, so they are invisible at run time.

5. Extend the DrawGrid1MouseDown event handler to copy the graphic to the appropriate cell of the DrawGrid, by adding the local declaration of MyRect at line 42 of Listing 7.5 and the statements at lines 47 and 48.

  - The function CellRect (line 47) returns a variable of type TRect matching the size of the current cell.
  - The procedure CopyRect (line 48) takes a rectangle of Image2 and puts it on the current cell of the DrawGrid. If Image2 was not aligned with the DrawGrid, it would be necessary to add an offset based on the differences between the tops and lefts.

7.8 StringGrid

The Delphi type `TStringGrid` is a descendant of `TDrawGrid` and is a refinement to handle text strings easily using the `Cells` property. As with a DrawGrid the number of rows and columns composing a StringGrid can be set at design time using the Object Inspector. They can also be changed by the code at run time using statements such as

```
StringGrid1.ColCount:= 11;
```

This is different from standard arrays which cannot have their size changed at run time.

The intersection of a row and a column is called a *cell*, and this can contain a string. Access to the contents of `Cells` is in a similar manner to arrays, so element [1,1] is assigned like this:

```
StringGrid1.Cells[1,1]:= '10';
```

which would assign the string 10. StringGrids are numbered from zero, so the top left element is [0,0]. The column index is the first item in the square brackets; the row index is the second. A number of rows and columns can be fixed, that is these rows and columns remain visible when the remainder are scrolled. Fixed rows and columns can be used for any reason but are particularly useful for showing the index of a row or column, using the top row to show the indices of the columns and the leftmost column to show the indices of the rows. Spreadsheet users will be familiar with the idea of fixed rows and columns.

The following code displays the column indices along the top row and the row indices along the leftmost column:

```
for i:= 1 to NoCols do
   {set the top row to the column numbers}
   StringGrid1.Cells[i,0]:= IntToStr(i);
for j:= 1 to NoRows do
   {set the leftmost column to the row numbers}
   StringGrid1.Cells[0,j]:= IntToStr(j);
```

The elements of `TimesTable` set in Section 7.6 can be copied one by one to `StringGrid1` as follows:

```
for i:=1 to NoCols do
   for j:= 1 to NoRows do
      StringGrid1.Cells[i,j]:=IntToStr(TimesTable[i,j]);
```

All of this code can be associated with a Calculate button's `OnClick` event as shown in Listing 7.6.

Listing 7.6 `OnClick` for Calculate button

```
1: procedure TForm1.CalculateClick(Sender: TObject);
2: var i,j: Integer;
```

```
3: var TimesTable: TATable;
4: begin
5:    for i:= 1 to NoCols do
6:       for j:= 1 to NoRows do
7:          {Calculate multiplication table}
8:          TimesTable[i,j]:= i*j;
9:
10:   for i:= 1 to NoCols do
11:      {set the top row to the column numbers}
12:      StringGrid1.Cells[i,0]:= IntToStr(i);
13:   for j:= 1 to NoRows do
14:      {set the leftmost column to the row numbers}
15:      StringGrid1.Cells[0,j]:= IntToStr(j);
16:
17:   for i:= 1 to NoCols do
18:      for j:= 1 to NoRows do
19:         {copy TimesTable elements to StringGrid1 cells}
20:         StringGrid1.Cells[i,j]:= IntToStr(TimesTable[i,j]);
21: end;
```

The properties of StringGrid1 can be altered to give the correct numbers of columns and rows. This will be one more than the dimension of TimesTable to allow for the fixed row and column indicating the position in the table. To avoid a scroll bar appearing, the grid size and column width should be altered. Properties changed from the defaults are summarized below:

ColCount	11
DefaultColWidth	32
Height	350
RowCount	13
Width	400

When executed this will produce an output as shown in Figure 7.6.

7.9 Multidimensional arrays

Arrays with many dimensions are used less frequently than one- and two-dimensional arrays, though they are a convenience in some situations allowing groupings of related tables of information. Multidimensional arrays can be found in financial modelling, scientific calculations and games.

The general format of an **array** type declaration is:

array [list of index types] **of** type

where list of index types is a list of one or more ordinal types, separated by commas. For example a subrange type TWeek could be declared as:

type TWeek= 1..7;

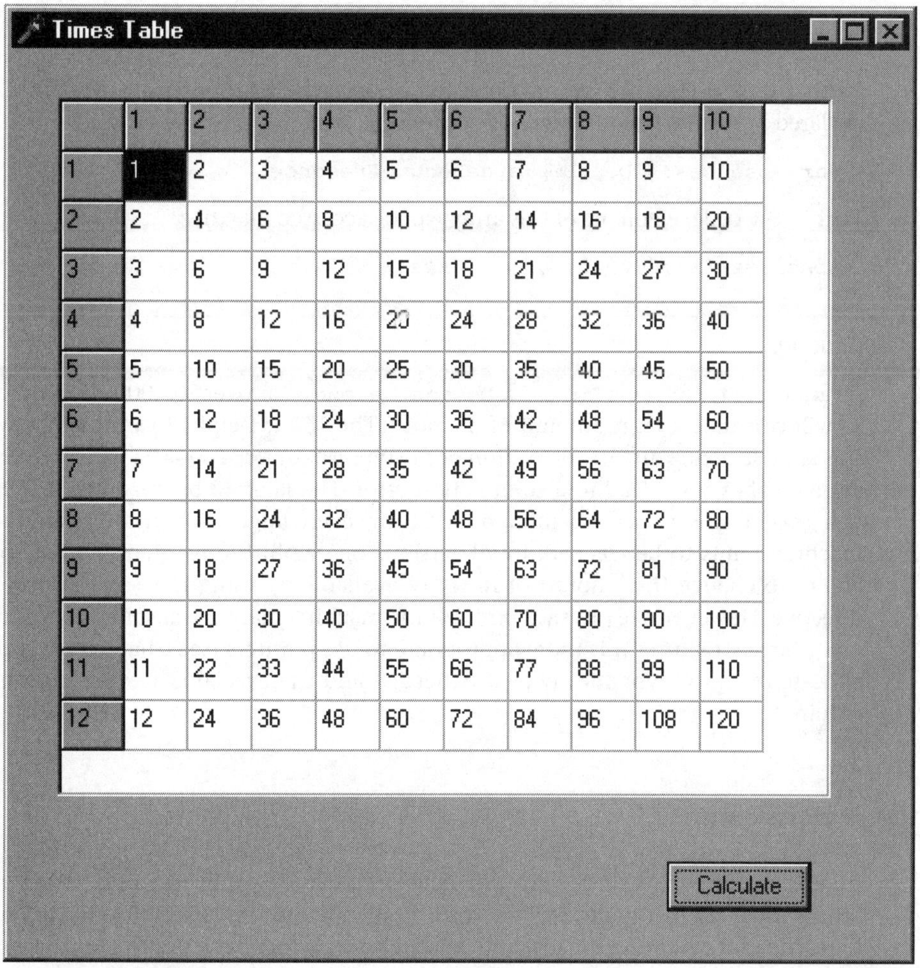

Figure 7.6 A StringGrid.

In Chapter 12 we will show how this can be made more meaningful by creating an enumerated type for representing days of the week. The existing subrange type can be used as the index of a one-dimensional array type TWeeklyPresence of Booleans.

```
type TWeeklyPresence= array[TWeek]of Boolean;
```

It can also be used as an index of a two-dimensional array:

```
type TYearlyPresence= array[1..52,TWeek]of Boolean;
```

or in a three-dimensional array:

```
type TDecadePresence= array[TDecade,1..52,TWeek] of Boolean;
```

where TDecade has been previously defined as a subrange, 2000 to 2009. This could be extended to a five-dimensional array for each of 10 employees (numbered 0 to 9), in each of six departments (numbered 112 to 117):

```
type TDeptEmployeeDecadePresence=
  array[112..117,0..9,TDecade,1..52, TWeek] of Boolean;
```

Further dimensions can be incorporated in an array as appropriate. Variables are declared in the normal manner, for example:

```
var Absences: TDeptEmployeeDecadePresence;
```

Within the code, elements of this array will be accessed like this:

```
Absences[112,0,2000,1,3]:= False;
```

Caution!

A variable of type TDeptEmployeeDecadePresence has over 200,000 elements and so will consume a large amount of memory. The 16-bit Delphi 1 cannot cope with this large structure and the definition of the type TDeptEmployeeDecadePresence as given above will lead to a compilation error. The later 32-bit versions of Delphi will accept this structure, though declaring even larger dimensions can cause machine limits to be reached. In all versions of Delphi the programmer has some ability to change the amount of memory available by using the {$M } compiler directive. However, the physical limits of the machine mark the absolute maximum.

For large structures it is more appropriate to use pointers (see Chapter 14) and to allocate memory dynamically as it is needed and then reclaim it when no longer required.

7.10 A word game

In this section we will design and develop a word game that uses arrays and StringGrids. The computer will generate a table of random letters. By clicking on a letter the user will make the row and column containing that letter rotate. The aim is for the user to find a real word. As there is no intelligence behind the generation of random letters it is possible that there will be times when no words can be found; a New option on the main menu will allow the user to request a different set of letters.

1. Create a prototype form as shown in Figure 7.7. The components on the form are a StringGrid and a MainMenu. The Caption of the form is changed to:

   ```
   Word Game
   ```

   The MainMenu is given the menu item Caption:

   ```
   &File
   ```

   with two options &New and E&xit separated by a bar, as in earlier examples.

   A number of properties are changed for the StringGrid so it will be of an appropriate size, as shown below:

   ```
   ColCount          5
   DefaultColWidth   42
   DefaultRowHeight  64
   ```

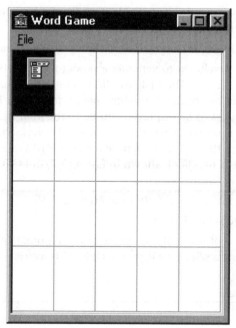

Figure 7.7 Prototype form.

FixedCols	0
FixedRows	0
Font	Courier new|Bold|36 point
Height	265
Name	WordGrid
RowCount	4
Width	220

The programmer can choose a different font.

The programmer should alter the design time size of the form so that the grid will be fully visible at run time. Alternatively the advanced programmer may prefer to set the size of the form at run time.

2. Declare a number of unit-wide constants and an array in the implementation section as shown in lines 37 to 41 of the full program: see Listing 7.7.

  - NoRows and NoCols have the same values as the RowCount and ColCount property of StringGrid. These constants are used to set the count properties at run time, but if they differ from the design time values the form will need resizing to show all the letters, which would require additional code.

  - NoChoices is the number of different values each element can take.

  - The type TLetters is set to the capital letters subrange of characters, but it could be changed to lower case letters or even a different alphabet, if one was available.

  - The type TLetterArray declares a three-dimensional array type. The subscripts start at 0 to match the StringGrid; the order of subscripts (column then row) also matches StringGrid.

- The variable `LetterArray` is an instance of type `TLetterArray`.

3. Code will be developed to generate a random set of letters in the three-dimensional `LetterArray`. The first two dimensions are columns and rows; the third dimension can be imagined moving *from the front to the back*, in the manner of a z-axis. The letters to be displayed will be in the *front* of the array (that is all the columns and rows associated with the zeroth choice). The code developed will be associated with the `OnEnter` event of the StringGrid called `WordGrid`.

The full event handler is shown in Listing 7.7, lines 43 to 68. The programmer should enter:

- the comments and declarations at lines 44 to 48
- the code from line 50 to 67.

The remainder of the `OnEnter` procedure is automatically generated, when the `OnEnter` event is selected within the Object Inspector.

Listing 7.7   Word game
_____

```
 1: unit U7_7;
 2:
 3: interface
 4:
 5: uses
 6:   Windows, Messages, SysUtils, Classes, Graphics, Controls,
 7:   Forms, Dialogs, Menus, Grids;
 8:
 9: type
10:   TForm1 = class(TForm)
11:     WordGrid: TStringGrid;
12:     MainMenu1: TMainMenu;
13:     File1: TMenuItem;
14:     New1: TMenuItem;
15:     N1: TMenuItem;
16:     Exit1: TMenuItem;
17:     procedure WordGridEnter(Sender: TObject);
18:     procedure Exit1Click(Sender: TObject);
19:     procedure WordGridMouseDown(Sender: TObject;
20:       Button: TMouseButton; Shift: TShiftState;
21:       X, Y: Integer);
22:   private
23:     { Private declarations }
24:   public
25:     { Public declarations }
26:   end;
27:
28: var
29:   Form1: TForm1;
```

```
30:
31: implementation
32:
33: {$R *.DFM}
34: {----------------------------------------------------------}
35: { Unit-wide constants, types and array                     }
36: {----------------------------------------------------------}
37: const NoCols= 5; NoRows= 4; NoChoices= 4;
38: type TLetters= 'A'..'Z';
39: type TLetterArray= array [0..NoCols-1,0..NoRows-1,
40:   0..NoChoices-1] of TLetters;
41: var LetterArray: TLetterArray;
42:
43: procedure TForm1.WordGridEnter(Sender: TObject);
44: {----------------------------------------------------------}
45: { Set each element of LetterArray to a random letter       }
46: { Display the first two dimensions in WordGrid             }
47: {----------------------------------------------------------}
48: var i,j,k,a: Integer;
49: begin
50:   WordGrid.ColCount:= NoCols;
51:   WordGrid.RowCount:= NoRows;
52:   Randomize; {seed random number generator }
53:   for i:= 0 to NoCols-1 do
54:     for j:= 0 to NoRows-1 do
55:     begin
56:       for k:= 0 to NoChoices-1 do
57:       begin
58:         {force a random letter between 'A' and 'Z'
59:           using High and Low means it is easy to change the
60:           alphabet or subrange }
61:         a:= Random(Ord(High(TLetters))-Ord(Low(TLetters))+1);
62:         {must add 1 or the range will never include last
63:           element in subrange}
64:         LetterArray[i,j,k]:= Chr(Ord(Low(TLetters))+a);
65:       end;
66:       WordGrid.Cells[i,j]:= LetterArray[i,j,0];
67:     end;
68: end;
69:
70: procedure TForm1.Exit1Click(Sender: TObject);
71: begin
72:   Close;
73: end;
74:
75: procedure TForm1.WordGridMouseDown(Sender: TObject;
76:   Button: TMouseButton; Shift: TShiftState; X, Y: Integer);
77: {----------------------------------------------------------}
78: { When the mouse is pressed rotate characters in the       }
79: { current row and column                                   }
```

```
80: {------------------------------------------------------------}
81: var i,j,k: Integer;
82:     temp: TLetters;
83: begin
84:   {rotate current row}
85:   for i:= 0 to NoCols-1 do
86:   begin
87:     temp:= LetterArray[i,WordGrid.Row,0];
88:     for k:= 0 to NoChoices-2 do
89:       LetterArray[i,WordGrid.Row,k]:=
90:         LetterArray[i,WordGrid.Row,k+1];
91:     LetterArray[i,WordGrid.Row,NoChoices-1]:= temp;
92:     WordGrid.Cells[i,WordGrid.Row]:=
93:       LetterArray[i,WordGrid.Row,0];
94:   end;
95:   {rotate current column, but not the current element
96:     as that was rotated with the row}
97:   for j:= 0 to NoRows -1 do
98:     if j<>WordGrid.Row then
99:     begin
100:       temp:= LetterArray[WordGrid.Col,j,0];
101:       for k:= 0 to NoChoices-2 do
102:         LetterArray[WordGrid.Col,j,k]:=
103:           LetterArray[WordGrid.Col,j,k+1];
104:         LetterArray[WordGrid.Col,j,NoChoices-1]:= temp;
105:         WordGrid.cells[WordGrid.Col,j]:=
106:           LetterArray[WordGrid.Col,j,0];
107:     end;
108:
109: end;
110:
111: end.
```

In Listing 7.7:

- Line 48 declares local variables used as the control variable of the loops and to hold a random number for accessing the letters. The control variables could be cardinals as they never hold negative values.

- Lines 50 and 51 set the WordGrid to have the same number of columns and rows as LetterArray.

- Line 52 seeds the random number generator, that ensures a different set of values is generated each time the game is played.

- Lines 58 to 64 generate a random character in the range dictated by the subrange TLetters. This code could be simplified if we only require the letters to be between 'A' and 'Z'.

- The loop from lines 56 to 65 generates all the choices for a given row and column of the WordGrid.

- Line 66 puts the front choice from the array into the `WordGrid`.

- The loops starting at lines 53 and 54 to line 67 cycle through all rows and columns to set all the elements of the array.

4. The functionality is now added to the main menu. Double click on the Exit option of the main menu and put the `Close` instruction between the **begin** and **end**, as in earlier examples. For the New option, associate the `OnClick` event with the `WordGridEnter` event as shown in Figure 7.8. By reusing the code that initially sets all the letters, this generates a new set of letters each time New is chosen.

Figure 7.8 `WordGridEnter`.

5. Save the unit and project and then run. The programmer can check that letters are generated and the New and Exit options work, before adding the code to rotate letters.

6. The functionality for rotating letters is now added to the `MouseDown` event of `WordGrid`, as shown in Listing 7.7, lines 75 to 107. The programmer adds lines 77 to 82 and lines 84 to 107; the remainder are generated automatically when the `MouseDown` event is selected via the Object Inspector.

- Local variables are declared in lines 81 and 82; the variables in line 81 are control variables for the loops, and `temp` is used for temporarily holding a letter as the rotation takes place.

- Lines 85 to 94 rotate the entire row containing the element on which the mouse was pushed down. The property `WordGrid.Row` indicates which row the mouse was in when the mouse's button was pushed. The front element is copied to `temp`, and each of the other cells is moved forward. The letter in `temp` is then copied to the back.

- Lines 97 to 107 rotate the column in a similar fashion.

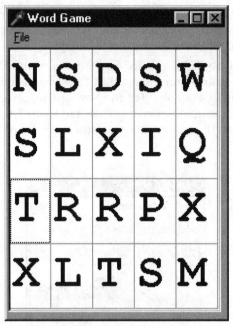

Figure 7.9 The running letters game.

● The conditional at line 98 ensures the element on which the mouse rests is not rotated twice.

7. The program is now complete, it can be run and the letters manipulated: see Figure 7.9.

7.11 Summary

In this chapter we introduced the concept of arrays. First, one-dimensional arrays were introduced and the related topic of strings. The variants of strings available to Delphi programmers were described, along with techniques for handling them. The subrange type was introduced both as a type in its own right and for use in indexing arrays. Two-dimensional arrays were presented along with the Delphi components DrawGrid and StringGrid which allow the display of two-dimensional arrays on a form. The concept of two-dimensional arrays was then extended to multidimensional arrays.

The chapter concluded with an example, based around a three-dimensional array of characters that can be viewed and manipulated by a StringGrid.

Quiz

1. What is the type **array** an example of?
   (a) a Pascal structured data type

(b) an enumerated type

(c) an integer

2. A subrange type must be derived from:
(a) an ordinal type
(b) a real type
(c) a string

3. When does range checking occur?
(a) at compile time
(b) every time the program is run
(c) when range checking is turned on and the program run

4. What is the in-built function `High` used for?
(a) finding how much memory is free
(b) finding the highest value in a range
(c) setting a constant

5. What sort of brackets indicates the range of an array?
(a) round brackets
(b) curly brackets
(c) square brackets

6. What value must array bounds start at?
(a) 0
(b) 1
(c) any ordinal value

7. Which of the following string types are allocated dynamically?
(a) `ShortString`
(b) `LongString`
(c) `AnsiString`

8. What does the first index of a DrawGrid's cell position refer to?
(a) the row
(b) the column
(c) the front

9. The number of columns for a StringGrid:
(a) can be altered at run time
(b) must be fixed via the Object Inspector
(c) must match an array declared within the program

10. Which of these is the general format for an **array** type declaration?
(a) **array** [*list of index types*] **of** *type*;
(b) **array** [*subrange*] **of** *type*;
(c) **string** [*length*];

Exercises

1. Write a program that will ask the user for a word. Then display this word in all capitals as the caption of the form.

2. Write a program to count the occurrences of each of the letters of the alphabet in a line of text.

3. Adapt the word game in Section 7.10 so that only the letters 'D', 'E', 'L', 'P', 'H' and 'I' are displayed. Expand the grid so that it contains six columns and ten rows. Add a Check option to the menu. When Check is clicked the program will look for any rows that say DELPHI and an appropriate message will be displayed via a message box.

4. A square of numbers is said to be *magic* if the sum of every row, column and diagonal is the same. Write a program to check if a given user-supplied square is magic.

5. Write a program to generate magic squares.

   Hint: An odd-order magic square can be generated by writing 1 at the top of the middle column. Then follow a diagonal up from this position (wrapping round the top–bottom and sides of the square) placing successive numbers in each space. When a space is already filled the next number ($n+1$) is written directly beneath the previous number (n). Table 7.2 shows a magic square generated by this algorithm.

Table 7.2 A five-order magic square.

17	24	1	8	15
23	5	7	14	16
4	6	13	20	22
10	12	19	21	3
11	18	25	2	9

Chapter 8

Scope, records and multiple forms

8.1 Introduction

The term 'scope' is used to indicate the parts of a program in which a variable or other item is available. In some programming languages all variables are available to all parts of the program. This does not create many problems with small programs, but can cause chaos in larger programs, with two variables with the same name contaminating each other. In this chapter we introduce the concept of *scope*. We then discuss the effects on larger programs including records and their data structure, objects created at run time, and multiple forms.

8.2 Scope

Within Delphi, visual components have a number of properties that affect their appearance. These properties have meaningful names like `Top`, `Left` and `Height`, the same named property existing for many components. For example, all visual components have a property `Top`, which can be altered to move the component up and down on the screen. To move a component `Button1` down by one pixel the following statement would be executed:

```
Button1.Top:= Button1.Top+1;
```

If a programmer uses the statement:

```
Top:= Top+1;
```

then the `Top` that is currently in scope will be the one that moves. Normally this will be the first component created, that is the form. The result will be that the form itself moves down the screen.

8.3 Declaring variables

In earlier chapters the programmer predominantly declared variables in two places:

● just below the **implementation** statement of the unit code
● between the procedure header of an event handler and the associated **begin**.

Variables declared in the implementation section of a unit are in scope to all the code in that section and can be accessed and altered; these are sometimes called *unit-wide variables*. It is usual to leave the compiler directive `{$R *.DFM}` immediately after the word **implementation**; it must not be deleted. See Section 13.2 for further details.

Variables declared below the procedure header are only in scope for that procedure. They cannot be accessed or altered outside the procedure and are referred to as *local variables*, to indicate that they are local to that event handler. Within an event handler local variables can be either dynamic or static:

● Dynamic variables are usually just referred to as variables. Once the procedure is completed the dynamic variables go out of scope and their values are lost. If the procedure is called again a dynamic variable will once again be created but it will not hold any values previously assigned. Delphi does not normally initialize variables, so it is the programmer's responsibility to assign values to variables.
● Static variables are called *typed constants* in Delphi and declared by statements such as

```
const NumberOfTimes: Integer = 0;
```

This is in fact not a constant, rather it is a *persistent* variable, which will keep its value from one call of the event handler containing it to the next. In our example the value of `NumberOfTimes` is kept from one call of the event handler to the next. The event handler can change `NumberOfTimes` and it is the most recent value that is available to the next invocation. NumberOfTimes is not accessible outside the event handler where it is declared.

Constants and types can be declared in the same sections of a unit as variables. A constant declaration of

```
const NumberOfMonths = 12;
```

creates a proper constant and the programmer cannot alter the value of NumberOfMonths in the code.

8.4 Declarations local to a form

At design time Delphi automatically generates code both declaring the type of a form and creating a variable of this type, as shown in Listing 8.1. Lines 1 to 7 declare the type TForm1, while lines 9 and 10 create an instance, called Form1, of a variable of type TForm1.

Listing 8.1 TForm1

```
1: type
2:    TForm1 = class(TForm)
3:    private
4:       { Private declarations }
5:    public
6:       { Public declarations }
7:    end;
8:
9: var
10:    Form1: TForm1;
```

As components and events are added to the form the **type** definition will expand to include details of the components and their events. For example, consider the **type** definition shown in Listing 8.2.

Listing 8.2 TForm1 with added components and events

```
1: type
2:    TForm1 = class(TForm)
3:       Edit1: TEdit;
4:       Label1: TLabel;
5:       Label2: TLabel;
6:       CompareButton: TButton;
7:       QuitButton: TButton;
8:       procedure QuitButtonClick(Sender: TObject);
9:       procedure FormCreate(Sender: TObject);
10:      procedure CompareButtonClick(Sender: TObject);
```

```
11:    private
12:       { Private declarations }
13:    public
14:       { Public declarations }
15:    end;
```

This shows that the form has the following components:

- an edit box called Edit1, defined at line 3
- two labels, called Label1 and Label2, defined on lines 4 and 5
- two buttons, called CompareButton and QuitButton, defined on lines 6 and 7.

There are also three events that have been coded: QuitButtonClick, FormCreate and CompareButtonClick as defined by lines 8 to 10. The role of the private and public parts (lines 11 to 14) will be discussed in Chapter 10.

When the programmer added the components and then opened the code for the event handler, Delphi automatically added these definitions to the initial type statement for the form shown in Listing 8.1.

Each event for a unit will be defined in two places:

1. Within the **type** declaration of the form, Delphi will automatically add a definition for each event handler the programmer adds, for example:

   ```
   procedure CompareButtonClick(Sender: TObject);
   ```

2. Within the implementation part of the unit the programmer provides the implementation of the procedure within the skeleton template provided, for example:

   ```
   procedure TForm1.CompareButtonClick(Sender: TObject);
   begin

   end;
   ```

If any of the definitions within the form's **type** statement are removed or renamed by the programmer, the program may fail to compile or raise an execution error at run time. If a component is no longer needed, the safest way to remove it is to delete it on the design time form. If an event is no longer required the body of the procedure declaration (the code added by the programmer) should be removed plus any variable declarations. In both cases the Delphi environment will then safely remove the definition parts it earlier added automatically. Occasionally the programmer may inadvertently delete the whole of an event handler's procedure declaration (in the implementation section), in which case the next step is to delete the corresponding definition in the **type** statement (in the interface section).

8.5 Records

In Chapter 7 we used the **array** type to declare variables that could store several items of data of the same type. The **array** type is sometimes referred to as a homogeneous structured data type. A record, like an array, can be used to store several items of data, but with a record the items do not have to be of the same type. The **record** type is a heterogeneous structured data type: it is made up of fields of any type. Whole records can be manipulated, as can individual fields. Whereas we access items of arrays via subscripts, in square brackets, fields of records are accessed via their names. A **record** type for storing dates may be declared as

```
type
  TDate = record
    DayNo: 1..31;
    MonthNo: 1..12;
    Year: 1900..2100;
  end;
```

A variable of this type can then be declared as

```
var StartDate: TDate;
```

The fields of this record can be assigned as follows:

```
StartDate.DayNo:= 1;
StartDate.MonthNo:= 10;
StartDate.Year:= 1990;
```

Whole records can be assigned: for example, given a second record DateJoinedLibrary of type TDate, this can be set to the same value as StartDate by the following assignment:

```
DateJoinedLibrary:= StartDate;
```

The fields of a record can be of any type; for example a Boolean could be a field in a record type:

```
type
  TAnimalRec = record
    Name, Species: string;
    DoB: TDate;
    Male: Boolean;
  end;
```

which also includes fields of the type **string** and TDate. This assumes that TDate was in scope.

The statement:

```
type
  TAnimalRegister= array [1..20] of TAnimalRec;
```

declares a type that is an array of records, which is a very useful structure used in many programs.

The statement:

```
var
  PetRegister: TAnimalRegister;
```

declares a variable of this type.

The name field of the first animal in the register can be achieved by

```
PetRegister[1].Name:= 'Jennie';
```

Setting her year of birth:

```
PetRegister[1].DoB.Year:= 1998;
```

8.6 The `with` statement

When records are used the programmer often needs to assign values to several fields. Hence Pascal provides a **with** statement that acts as shorthand to save the programmer having repeatedly to enter the full record name in front of the field identifier. For example, the assignments to the fields of StartDate could be rewritten as

```
with StartDate do
begin
  DayNo:= 1;
  MonthNo:= 10;
  Year:= 1990;
end { with StartDate };
```

The comment after the **end** is useful for matching the end of a **with** with the **begin**. The comment is not essential but is useful for keeping track of nested **with** statements such as those shown in Listing 8.3.

We can set a complete record entry in PetRegister using the code shown in Listing 8.3.

Listing 8.3   Nested **with** statements

```
 1: with PetRegister[2] do
 2:   begin
 3:     Name:= 'Fluffy';
 4:     Species:= 'Hamster';
 5:     with DoB do
 6:     begin
 7:       DayNo:= 5;
 8:       MonthNo:= 3;
 9:       Year:= 1996;
10:     end { with DoB };
11:     Male:= False; { she's female }
12:   end { with PetRegister[2] };
```

The statement at line 7 is equivalent to:

```
PetRegister[2].DoB.DayNo:= 5;
```

Records are part of standard Pascal and the **with** statement will be familiar to Pascal programmers. Delphi offers the programmer the ability to use other structures called *objects*. Components are objects with a number of properties and in many ways these are similar to records with a number of fields. Procedures for operating on objects are called methods and are discussed in more detail in Chapter 10.

The programmer can use the **with** statement to access the fields and *methods* of any object. The edit component has a number of properties which the code can set at run time. For example:

```
Edit1.Top:= 10;
Edit1.Left:= 10;
```

repositions the box. Alternatively using the **with** statement:

```
with Edit1 do
begin
  Top:= 10;
  Left:= 10;
end { with Edit1 };
```

does the same.

The Text field of this edit box can be set to the hamster's name by

```
with Edit1 do
  Text:= PetRegister[2].Name;
```

Alternatively nested **with** statements could be used:

```
with Edit1 do
  with PetRegister[2] do
    Text:= Name;
```

In both of the above examples **begin end** pairs are unnecessary as there is only a single statement (not a compound statement).

Care must be taken when using nested **with** statements. Both the components Edit1 and PetRegister[2] have a field called Name. The statements above give the results shown in Figure 8.1.

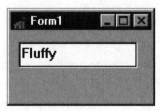

Figure 8.1 PetRegister[2].Name in scope.

However, if we exchange the two **with** statements to give:

```
with PetRegister[2] do
  with Edit1 do
    Text:= Name;
```

then the Name that is in scope belongs to the nearest **with** statement which is now Edit1 and the result will be as shown in Figure 8.2.

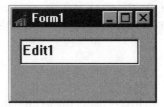

Figure 8.2   Edit1.Name in scope.

Inside a **with** statement, each variable referred to is first checked to see if it can be interpreted as a field of the record or object. If so, it is always interpreted as belonging to the closest, even if a variable or other field with the same name is also accessible.

8.7 Possible errors due to multiple declarations

Pascal allows multiple declarations of a single identifier. A programmer can declare a variable MyNumber in the implementation section of a unit and then use the same variable name as a local variable. As we showed earlier, all visible components have a property Top and the **with** statements or the dot notation can be used to ensure the correct one is accessed. However, this feature sometimes leads to unexpected errors.

For example, if the programmer changes the name of a button to Close, this Close is now in scope and occludes (hides) the Close method of the form that normally closes the form. Likewise a programmer may define an enumerated type for the months of the year using the common three-letter abbreviations. The value Dec (short for December) will occlude the in-built procedure Dec that is used for decrementing.

Experienced programmers do reuse identifiers, especially identifiers such as *i* for an index. Beginners frequently get confused with such reuse, so it may be wiser to use unique identifiers.

8.8 Sender **and** Self

Every event procedure has a Sender parameter of type TObject. When creating an OnClick event for a component Button1 the following template is produced:

```
procedure TForm1.Button1Click(Sender: TObject);
begin

end;
```

Sender is a reference back to the object that initiated the event, for example the specific button that was clicked. Self is an implicit parameter within every method, referencing the object that contains the method. In the above example that is Form1. The use of Sender and Self is illustrated in Listing 8.4.

Listing 8.4) Using `Sender` and `Self`

```
1: procedure TForm1.Button1Click(Sender: TObject);
2: begin
3:   if Sender=Button1 then
4:     Button1.Caption:= 'that''s me';
5:   if Self=Form1 then
6:     Form1.Caption:= 'myself';
7: end;
```

In Listing 8.4:

◉ The automatically generated line 1 specifies `Sender` as a parameter.

◉ `Self` is not specified but is implicitly available and within this procedure will be `Form1`.

◉ Line 3 compares `Sender` with the object `Button1`, and if they are the same the button's `Caption` changes.

◉ Line 5 compares `Self` with `Form1`, and if they are the same changes the form's `Caption`.

◉ Normally this event, belonging to `Form1`, will occur as a result of clicking `Button1` and so we would expect that both `Caption` properties will change.

`Self` is used as a shorthand to the containing object, which is particularly useful when there may be multiple instances of an object. We will refer to `Self` in Chapter 10 when discussing the use of objects.

Verifying the `Sender` is useful when the event `Button1Click` has been associated with an additional component. For example if a second button (`Button2`) is placed on the form, the event `Button1Click` can be associated with it via the Object Inspector – see Figure 8.3.

By selecting the `Button1Click` from the pull down list the `OnClick` event for `Button2` is linked to the same event handler (`Button1Click`) as the `OnClick` event for `Button1`, as we did in Section 7.10.

However, the original code for `Button1Click` takes effect only if the button pressed is `Button1`. The code can be made more general by replacing the body of the procedure as shown in Listing 8.5.

Listing 8.5) Use of **is** and **as**

```
1: procedure TForm1.Button1Click(Sender: TObject);
2: begin
3:   if Sender is TButton then
4:     (Sender as TButton).Caption:= 'that''s me';
5: end;
```

Figure 8.3   Linking an existing event to a new component.

In this code two new operators (**is** and **as**) are used. Their use is explained below:

- At line 3 the operator **is** is used to verify that the Sender object is of type TButton: this is called *type checking*. This will return true only if the Sender was a button component. The event Button1Click can be linked to any component, though an error would arise at line 4 if an attempt was made to cast a non-button object as a TButton. The precedence of the **is** operator is the same as relational operators (for example = and <).

- At line 4 the operator **as** is used to cast the type of Sender to a TButton. The brackets are essential, as the precedence of the **as** operator is the same as multiplication; without the brackets the compiler would try to cast Sender as the button's Caption.

- The **as** operator forces the compatibility of Sender and TButton to be established at run time. If Sender could not be treated as though it were of type TButton there would be a run time error; the conditional at line 3 prevents this from occurring.

When this code runs, whichever button is clicked will display the message – see Figure 8.4.

Use a conditional statement to protect the casting of Sender. When the same event is linked to a number of components a conditional can ensure the castings are always applied to the correct types. Consider the example in Listing 8.6.

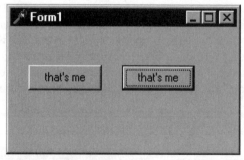

Figure 8.4   Buttons linked to the same event.

(Listing 8.6)   Casting objects

```
 1: procedure TForm1.Button1Click(Sender: TObject);
 2: begin
 3:   if Sender is TButton then
 4:     (Sender as TButton).Caption:= 'I''m a button'
 5:   else if Sender is TPanel then
 6:     (Sender as TPanel).Caption:= 'I''m a panel'
 7:   else if Sender is TEdit then
 8:     (Sender as TEdit).Text:= 'I''m an edit box'
 9:   {else take no specific action for that click};
10:   Label2.Caption:= IntToStr(StrToInt(Label2.Caption)+1);
11: end;
```

Suppose this event is linked to all components on the prototype form shown in Figure 8.5, including the form itself.

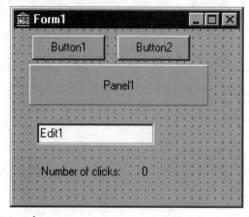

Figure 8.5   Prototype form.

Then, each time the project is run, wherever the form is clicked the number in the Caption property of Label2 will be incremented. If either of the buttons or the panel is clicked, their Caption property changes to indicate what they are, and if the edit box is clicked, its Text property changes to *I'm an edit box*.

It is neater to use a **with** statement to cast Sender as several different objects. Listing 8.7 contains the code for an OnDblClick event written for a Label1.

Listing 8.7 Casting using a **with** statement

```
 1: procedure TForm1.Label1DblClick(Sender: TObject);
 2: begin
 3:   if Sender is TLabel then
 4:     with (Sender as TLabel) do
 5:     begin
 6:       Color:= clWhite;
 7:       with Font do
 8:       begin
 9:         Style:= [fsBold,fsItalic];
10:         Size:= 24;
11:       end;
12:     end;
13: end;
```

All the code between lines 5 and 12 operates with the Sender cast as TLabel. The inner **with** statement on line 7 refers to the Font property of the label. The Style property is assigned values in square brackets because it is a **set** (sets are discussed in Chapter 12). When the user runs the project containing this event handler, double clicking on Label1 produces output like that shown in Figure 8.6.

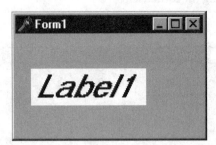

Figure 8.6 Double click on label.

This event can be linked to any component's click events, either single or double click in the case of a label. However, the event will produce a changed output only for an object of type TLabel, because the condition at line 3 of Listing 8.7 ensures the remainder of the code is executed only for labels.

8.9 Creating instances of components at run time

Most of the visual objects used so far have been created at design time. In Chapter 5 when a number of cats were displayed at run time, their bitmap was created at run time. In this section we will demonstrate the run time creation of other visual components. The association of events with the new creations will also be presented.

Listing 8.8 shows how to create a shape component within the form's `OnCreate` event. The object `NewShape` must be declared previously, and if it is to be used unit wide then this should be within the **implementation** section:

```
var NewShape: TShape;
```

The form must explicitly include the name of the Delphi unit which contains `TShape`. This is done by adding the name `ExtCtrls` to the end of the **uses** list at the start of the current unit, for example:

```
uses
   Windows, Messages, SysUtils, Classes, Graphics, Controls,
   Forms, Dialogs, ExtCtrls;
```

The simple alternative is to put the required component on the form at design time and run the program once; Delphi will add the required unit name. Then remove the temporary component; Delphi will not remove `ExtCtrls` from the **uses** list. The role of **uses** lists will be discussed in more detail in Chapter 13.

Listing 8.8   Creating `NewShape`

```
 1: procedure TForm1.FormCreate(Sender: TObject);
 2: begin
 3:   NewShape:= TShape.Create(Self);
 4:   with NewShape do
 5:   begin
 6:     Top:= 25;
 7:     Left:= 25;
 8:     Parent:= Self;
 9:   end;
10: end;
```

In Listing 8.8:

- Line 3 brings the object `NewShape` into existence, passing `Self` to `Create` to make the form the `Owner` of the shape.
- Lines 4 to 9 set properties of the new object.

More details of the role of `Owner` and `Parent` will be presented in Chapter 10.

Events can also be assigned to an object. In Chapter 5 we presented an example where a ball bounced across the screen. In the following project the program creates an array of balls. The programmer will assign events to each ball from those belonging to an initial object. When the program runs, the user will be able to bounce many balls across the screen.

1. Assume a unit-wide declaration such as:

   ```
   const ShapeSize= 20;
   ```

   in the implementation part of the code.

2. Adapt the OnMouseDown event for the shape Circle, given in Listing 5.7, so that it will work for any Sender that is a TShape, as shown in Listing 8.9.

Listing 8.9   Generalized shape mover

```
 1: procedure TForm1.CircleMouseDown(Sender: TObject; Button:
 2:   TMouseButton; Shift: TShiftState; X, Y: Integer);
 3: const JumpHoriz: Integer= ShapeSize;
 4:    JumpVert: Integer= ShapeSize;
 5: begin
 6:   if Sender is TShape then
 7:     with Sender as TShape do
 8:     begin
 9:       if (Left > (Form1.ClientWidth - Width))
10:       or (Left < 0)
11:       then
12:       begin
13:         JumpHoriz:= -JumpHoriz;
14:         Brush.Color:= clRed
15:       end;
16:       if (Top > (Form1.ClientHeight - Height))
17:       or (Top < 0)
18:       then
19:       begin
20:         JumpVert:= -JumpVert;
21:         Brush.Color:= clBlue;
22:       end;
23:       Left:= Left+JumpHoriz;
24:       Top:= Top+JumpVert;
25:     end;
26: end;
```

3. This will still work for the existing shape Circle, where Sender will be Circle. The programmer can verify this by compiling and running the project.

4. Declare a constant for the number of shapes and an array type that will be available to the form, by putting the following:

   ```
   const NumShapes= 10;
   type TArrayOfCircles= array[1..Numshapes] of TShape;
   ```

   before the type declaration for the form.

5. Declare an array of `TShape` objects, that will be unit wide, by adding the declaration to the **implementation** section:

```
var Circles: TArrayOfCircles;
```

6. Each of the array of circles needs to be created at run time. An appropriate place will be in the `OnCreate` event for the form: see Listing 8.10.

Listing 8.10 Creating an array of shapes

```
 1: procedure TForm1.FormCreate(Sender: TObject);
 2: var i: Integer;
 3: begin
 4:   for i:= 1 to NumShapes do
 5:   begin
 6:     Circles[i]:= TShape.Create(Self);
 7:     with Circles[i] do
 8:     begin
 9:       Parent:= Self; { Self is Form1 in this event handler }
10:       Shape:= stCircle;
11:       Brush.Color:= clYellow;
12:       Width:= ShapeSize;
13:       Height:= ShapeSize;
14:       Top:=((Form1.ClientHeight-Height)*i) div (NumShapes+1);
15:       Left:= ShapeSize;
16:       OnMouseDown:= CircleMouseDown;
17:     end {with};
18:   end{for};
19: end;
```

The code performs the following actions:

- Lines 4 to 18 ensure that all the array of circles are properly created and initialized.

- Lines 14 and 15 place the newly created circles evenly down the form; the random function could be used to create an alternative set of starting positions.

7. The original `TShape Circle`, from Chapter 5, is no longer needed and can be deleted from the prototype form.

8. The project can now be run and each of the created circles can be made to move around the form.

This project illustrates the use of `Sender` and the creation of objects. It is noticeable that the original `TShape Circle` was used to develop the `OnMouseDown` event, but finally the shape `Circle` was removed. In many instances the use of a temporary object will help rapid development of a program. The programmer can test all the actions on a single object and then, when that object works as required, link the events into all relevant objects. Further work may still be needed. For example, in the above the user may find that it is possible to force the circles off the top of the form. The `OnMouseDown` event would need to be refined to prevent this.

8.10 Adding an About box

In earlier chapters we used the standard Window dialog boxes to exchange information with users. Delphi allows the programmer to design and use multiple forms in a variety of formats. The later releases and more expensive versions of Delphi offer a wider range of forms for the programmer and there are some minor differences in how these choices are accessed. We will illustrate the addition of a secondary form by creating an About box for an existing project.

1. Choose a project that already has a main menu and add a menu item called `&About`.

2. Add an Additional form. With Delphi 3 choose the option File|New... If the Professional Edition of Delphi 3 is in use, this will display a set of options as shown in Figure 8.7. Select the tab marked Forms, see Figure 8.8. Highlight the About box and press OK.

   Most versions of Delphi work in a similar way to Delphi 3 Professional, although there are varying tab options and different choices offered under Forms. With Delphi 1, choose the option File|New Form. This will display the options shown in Figure 8.9, from which the programmer can select the About box.

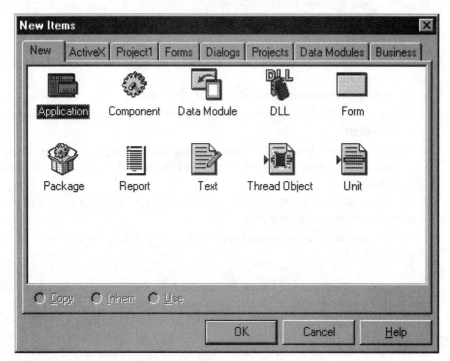

Figure 8.7   The new option for Delphi 3 Professional Edition.

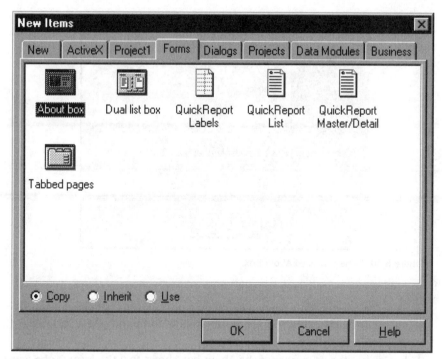

Figure 8.8   The Forms tab.

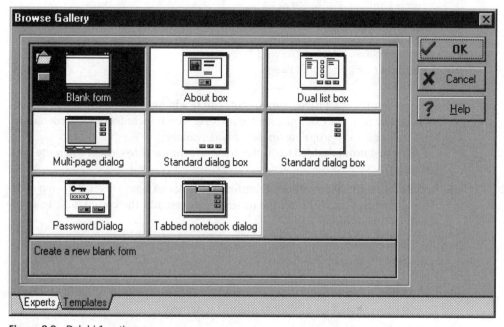

Figure 8.9   Delphi 1 options.

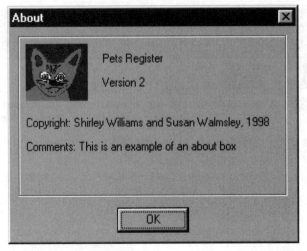

Figure 8.10   A personalized About box.

3. Save the project. Note there are now two unit files (by default called Unit1 and Unit2), one that corresponds to the original form and one associated with the new form (the About box).

4. Looking at the properties of the About box shows that the form is of a new type, TAboutBox, and that this contains seven components:

   ```
   Comments        TLabel
   Copyright       TLabel
   OKButton        TButton   (TBitBtn in Delphi 1)
   Panel1          TPanel
   ProductName     TLabel
   ProgramIcon     TImage
   Version         TLabel
   ```

   The appearance of all these components can be changed in the usual way to personalize the box. For example, see Figure 8.10, which includes our own details in the labels and an appropriate image we had available.

   Code must now be added to display the About box and to close it when the user has read it.

5. Add an OnClick event to the OK button in the About box. This will open a code template within Unit2, then the programmer can add the command Close as shown at line 3 below.

   ```
   1: procedure TAboutBox.OKButtonClick(Sender: TObject);
   2: begin
   3:    Close;
   4: end;
   ```

6. To make the About box accessible add this statement:

   ```
   uses Unit2;
   ```

after the implementation line of Unit1. The role of the **uses** statement is explained in Chapter 13.

7. To make the About box appear, add an OnClick event to the About option of the main menu; this will be in the code of Unit1:

```
1: procedure TForm1.About1Click(Sender: TObject);
2: begin
3:   AboutBox.Show;
4: end;
```

By adding line 3 above, the programmer has instructed the About box to be displayed.

8. Save and run the project. Clicking the About option on the main menu will cause the Pets Register About box to be displayed.

(8.11) Second forms*

As well as adding previously designed forms the programmer can add blank forms and customize them as required. A new form can be added via the same tabbed options as used for adding the About box. With newer versions of Delphi it is also possible to choose File|New Form, or use the New Form speed button. On creation of a new form an associated new unit is also created.

This new form can be designed in exactly the same way as a single form: components placed, properties set and events programmed. To change the form that is currently being edited use the View menu to select another form, or the Select Form From List speed button.

Some event associated with the first form must call the second form before it can appear. The second form's unit must be listed amongst the **uses** of the unit associated with the first form (in this discussion called Form1). Displaying a second form, called Form2, can be achieved by executing any of the following statements in Form1:

```
{a}         Form2.Show;
{ or b}     Form2.ShowModal;
{ or c}     Form2.Visible:= True;
```

Statement {a} will cause Form2 to be displayed and become the active form (the bar at the top will be highlighted). The original form (Form1) will continue with its processing and by selecting any part of Form1 it will become the active form, even though the supplementary form (Form2) is still open. A second execution of the Show method will cause Form2 to again become the active form.

Statement {b} also displays Form2 and makes it the active form. However, the original form (Form1) is disabled and its unit does not process until the modal form (Form2) is closed. Statement {c} also causes Form2 to be displayed. It will not necessarily become the active form: if the form is not visible it will become visible and the active form. However, if the form (Form2) is already visible it will not become the active form.

The following example will be used to illustrate how a date can be obtained for an original form via a second form.

1. Open Delphi and create the prototype form shown in Figure 8.11 containing a label, an edit box and a button.

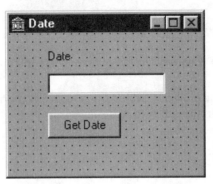

Figure 8.11 Prototype main form.

2. Use the Delphi File menu to add a second form and create a prototype consisting of three labels, three edit boxes and two bit buttons, as shown in Figure 8.12.

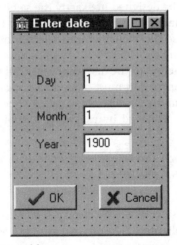

Figure 8.12 Prototype second form.

3. On the second form change the names of the labels to DayLabel, MonthLabel and YearLabel respectively, and the names of the edit boxes to DayBox, MonthBox and YearBox. This will avoid clashes of names between the two forms. Alter the initial values of components to match the prototype form.

4. Save the unit code for the new form (here saved as U8_11.pas to match the

listing number). Save the unit code for the original form (here saved as U8_12.pas to match the listing) and save the project.

5. The user will click OK if the date entered in the second form is correct and Cancel if it is not. A variable OK will pass this information back to the main form. To make this variable OK readily accessible it will be placed in the public part of the declaration of Form2 – see line 28 of the full unit listing in Listing 8.11. Note the word **var** is not used in the public part of the type. Chapter 10 discusses the role of the public and private parts of objects.

Listing 8.11 Unit code for the second form

```
 1: unit U8_11;
 2: {---------------------------------------------------------}
 3: { Displays a box for entering a date, variable OK        }
 4: { indicates success                                      }
 5: {---------------------------------------------------------}
 6: interface
 7:
 8: uses
 9:    Windows, Messages, SysUtils, Classes, Graphics, Controls,
10:    Forms, Dialogs, StdCtrls, Buttons;
11:
12: type
13:    TForm2 = class(TForm)
14:       DayLabel: TLabel;
15:       MonthLabel: TLabel;
16:       YearLabel: TLabel;
17:       DayBox: TEdit;
18:       MonthBox: TEdit;
19:       YearBox: TEdit;
20:       BitBtn1: TBitBtn;
21:       BitBtn2: TBitBtn;
22:       procedure BitBtn1Click(Sender: TObject);
23:       procedure BitBtn2Click(Sender: TObject);
24:       procedure FormCreate(Sender: TObject);
25:    private
26:       { Private declarations }
27:    public
28:       OK: Boolean;
29:    end;
30:
31: var
32:    Form2: TForm2;
33:
34: implementation
35:
36: {$R *.DFM}
37:
```

```
38: procedure TForm2.BitBtn1Click(Sender: TObject);
39: begin
40:    OK:= True;
41:    Close;
42: end;
43:
44: procedure TForm2.BitBtn2Click(Sender: TObject);
45: begin
46:    OK:= False;
47:    Close;
48: end;
49:
50: procedure TForm2.FormCreate(Sender: TObject);
51: begin
52:    OK:= False;
53: end;
54:
55: end.
```

6. The bit buttons' events for OnClick are added as shown in lines 38 to 48 of Listing 8.11, the programmer adding lines 40, 41, 46 and 47, and the remainder being automatically generated.

- Lines 40 and 41 are executed if BitBtn1 is clicked by the user, setting OK to True and closing the current form (Form2).

- Lines 46 and 47 are executed if BitBtn2 is clicked, setting OK to False and closing the current form (Form2).

7. The value of OK can be initialized by adding an OnCreate event for Form2 (see lines 50 to 53 of Listing 8.11), the programmer adding the assignment to set OK initially to False in line 52.

(Listing 8.12) Unit code for the main form

```
1: unit U8_12;
2:
3: interface
4:
5: uses
6:    Windows, Messages, SysUtils, Classes, Graphics, Controls,
7:    Forms, Dialogs, StdCtrls;
8:
9: type
10:    TForm1 = class(TForm)
11:       Edit1: TEdit;
12:       Label1: TLabel;
13:       Button1: TButton;
14:       procedure Button1Click(Sender: TObject);
15:    private
```

```
16:       { Private declarations }
17:    public
18:       { Public declarations }
19:    end;
20:
21: var
22:    Form1: TForm1;
23:
24: implementation
25:
26: {$R *.DFM}
27: uses U8_11;
28:
29: procedure TForm1.Button1Click(Sender: TObject);
30: {----------------------------------------------------------}
31: { Show the second form, wait for the user to complete it   }
32: { display the date in European format or an error message  }
33: {----------------------------------------------------------}
34: begin
35:    Form2.ShowModal;
36:    with Form2 do
37:      if OK then
38:        Edit1.Text:= (DayBox.Text + '/' +
39:                      MonthBox.Text + '/' +
40:                      YearBox.Text)
41:      else
42:        Edit1.Text:= 'date not entered';
43: end;
44:
45: end.
```

8. Add line 27 of Listing 8.12 to the unit code of the main (first) form to allow it to use the second form.

9. An OnClick event needs to be added to the button with the caption 'Get Date', as shown in lines 29 to 43 of Listing 8.12. In this event:

   ● ShowModal is used at line 35 to ensure processing is suspended until the user has entered a date.

   ● The **with** statement from line 36 to line 42 saves writing Form2 in front of all the variables and objects from Form2.

   ● The condition at line 37 will test the value of OK from Form2. If OK is True then the date will be displayed, otherwise an error message will be displayed.

When this program is run and the Get Date button pressed the two screens in Figure 8.13 will be displayed.

When OK is pressed the date will be displayed in the required format, as shown in Figure 8.14.

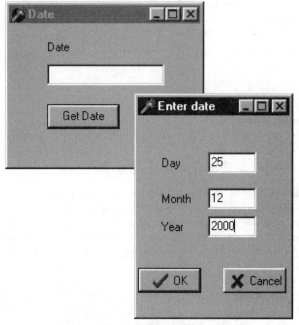

Figure 8.13   Get Date pressed.

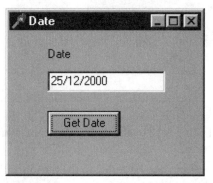

Figure 8.14   Date displayed.

(8.12) Multiple forms*

The Delphi programmer is not limited to two forms but can add many forms to a project. The accessing of variables, events, etc., belonging to another form is limited only by the following two factors:

- A **uses** statement in the calling unit must include any units to which it refers.
- The object referred to in another unit must be publicly declared in its own unit.

Two forms can refer to each other's objects, for instance a secondary form may consult an entry on the main form and the main form may fetch information from the secondary form. In doing this it is especially important to ensure the relevant **uses** are in the implementation section. If they are just added to the system-generated **uses** list in the interface section (near the top of the unit) an error will be generated owing to unresolved circular references. The roles of the interface and implementation parts of a unit are discussed in more detail in Chapter 13.

8.13 Summary

In this chapter we introduced a number of concepts related to the issue of scope. Issues of scope can be simply summarized as *what is accessible from where.*

We described the structured data type record and illustrated the accessing of individual fields. Objects were created at run time and we used techniques for assigning properties and methods, along with the Sender parameter to determine which component had initiated an event.

The chapter finished with an illustration of the use of multiple forms.

Quiz

1. What does the statement:

    ```
    Left:= Left+1;
    ```

    do?
    (a) Moves all visual components left one pixel.
    (b) Moves all visual components right one pixel.
    (c) Moves the visual component that is in scope.

2. A record is best used for storing:
    (a) several items of data of the same type
    (b) several items of data of different types
    (c) strings

3. What purpose does a **with** statement serve?
    (a) It saves the programmer having to enter the full record name repeatedly.
    (b) It allows several statements to be executed simultaneously.
    (c) It allows several fields to be assigned the same values.

4. To what does the parameter Self refer?
    (a) the object that contains the method
    (b) the object that initiated the event
    (c) the programmer

5. To what does the parameter Sender refer?
    (a) the mouse
    (b) the form
    (c) the object that initiated the event

6. Which of the following statements is true?
    (a) For every form there must be an associated unit.

(b) For every project there must be a form.

(c) The second form in a project must always be an About box.

7. What does this expression:

```
Sender as TButton
```

do?

(a) Evaluates to true if Sender is a button.

(b) Casts Sender as a button.

(c) Creates a new button object.

8. Which of the following describes a modal form?

(a) While it is open other forms in the project cannot be accessed.

(b) While it is open other forms in the project can be accessed.

(c) While it is open no other window can be accessed.

9. What does the expression:

```
TPanel.Create(Self)
```

do?

(a) It creates a Panel object at run time; this object should be assigned to a previously declared variable of type TPanel.

(b) It creates a Panel object at that design time that will appear on the prototype form.

(c) It recursively creates panels, one inside the other.

10. What is the maximum number of forms in a project?

(a) 2

(b) 10

(c) A large number, limited only by the total resource required by the project and available on the computer.

Exercises

1. Adapt the program developed in Section 8.9 so that the balls all remain within the form.

2. Adapt the date project so that the data containing the date is stored in a record in the unit associated with the main form. Add an About box.

3. Write a program that will allow the user the option of presenting dates in a variety of international formats.

4. Design a record structure to store rainfall, wind speed and dominant wind direction for one day. Use it in an array type to store the daily weather information for a week. Use a secondary form to enter data and a grid component on the main form to display it.

5. Define an array of record types, each value of which denotes a point on a second form. Write a program that asks the user for four pairs of values, representing the vertices of a quadrilateral, in cyclic order. The program should validate the input. Then draw the shape on the second form and display a label indicating whether the shape is a square, a rectangle or some other shape.

Chapter 9

Procedures and list boxes

9.1 Introduction

By the nature of Delphi's event-driven programming, an event such as clicking on a component of a form calls a procedure, known as an event handler. Object Pascal also has in-built functions for common operations such as type conversions. This chapter extends these ideas to programmer-coded functions and procedures, which are essential in projects of any size. They make for more readable code, and facilitate its reuse.

We will introduce a new visual component, the list box. As the name implies, a list box displays a list of items which the programmer can manipulate in various ways. It gives yet another way for the user to interact with the program.

9.2 Event-handling procedures

The Delphi environment is event driven by design, which means that events such as mouse clicks or key presses determine the code to be executed. It is also possible to run old-style Pascal programs, as was shown in Chapter 6. In these programs, code execution starts at the beginning, and progresses through the code with selection and iteration as programmed. Common programming languages in use before 1990, including BASIC, FORTRAN and C, all worked in that manner. Event-driven programming was restricted to expert programmers using specialized tools such as Guide under UNIX™ until visual languages became available.

As early as the first chapter, when the project illustrated in Figure 1.11 was run, clicking Button1 on Form1 caused a procedure named TForm1.Button1Click to execute. In that case the finished procedure was:

```
procedure TForm1.Button1Click(Sender: TObject);
begin
  Label1.Visible:= True;
end;
```

The programmer had only typed the one line

```
Label1.Visible:= True;
```

because the Delphi environment provided the skeleton of the event handler. The **begin end** pair are compulsory; they enclose the statements which constitute the procedure. In this example, unusually, there is precisely one statement. The code within parentheses,

```
Sender: TObject
```

is a *formal parameter*. The purpose of parameters generally is to transmit information into and out of that procedure, but this particular parameter is capable only of receiving information into the event handler, not of transmitting information out again. The information received via Sender is which component (for example Button1 or Button2) triggered this event.

Many of the event handlers used so far have a similar parameter list to that of the OnClick event of Button1, but some have more parameters. For example, an event handler for the OnMouseDown event used in Listing 7.5 had five parameters:

```
procedure TForm1.DrawGrid1MouseDown(Sender: TObject;
  Button: TMouseButton; Shift: TShiftState; X, Y: Integer);
```

In the above

- Button communicates which of the mouse buttons is pressed.
- Shift communicates whether other keys such as Shift or Alt are down.
- X and Y are the horizontal and vertical coordinates in pixels of the point where the mouse was clicked, relative to the top left-hand corner of the DrawGrid.

To see such parameters in use in a StringGrid (a descendant of DrawGrid), try this short example:

1. Start a new project.
2. Add two edit boxes, two labels X and Y and a StringGrid.
3. Alter the RowCount and ColCount properties of the StringGrid to 12 each.
4. Open the TForm1.StringGrid1MouseDown event handler via the Object Inspector.
5. Zero the FixedRows and FixedCols properties using the Object Inspector.
6. Change the code as in Listing 9.1.

(**Listing 9.1**) Using parameters

```
 1: procedure TForm1.StringGrid1MouseDown(Sender: TObject;
 2:   Button: TMouseButton; Shift: TShiftState; X, Y: Integer);
 3: {-----------------------------------------------------------}
 4: {This event handler copies the values of coordinates,      }
 5: {in pixels, into the appropriate edit box                  }
 6: {-----------------------------------------------------------}
 7: begin
 8:   Edit1.Text:= IntToStr(X);
 9:   Edit2.Text:= IntToStr(Y);
10: end;
```

7. Compile and run the project, then watch the changes that happen in the edit boxes as the mouse is clicked in different regions of the form and of the StringGrid. Figure 9.1 shows the result of clicking somewhere within the cell in column 0 and row 3.

These parameters can be examined within the event handler, but they cannot communicate information out again. We call them *value parameters*. Note that in this formal parameter list semicolons separate several parameter declarations, whereas commas separate lists of identifiers of the same type, such as X and Y. See the syntax diagram in the help files.

A few events, such as the OnMeasureItem event for list and combo boxes, have a parameter declaration which starts with the reserved word **var**. This indicates that the parameter can transmit information outwards from the event handler, rather than merely receiving. We call these *variable parameters*. Variable parameters use a

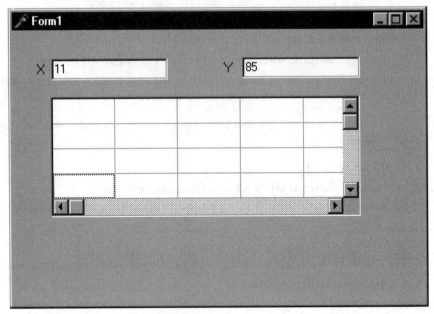

Figure 9.1 Using parameters in an event handler.

different mechanism from value parameters: the computer stores the address of the value rather than the value itself, and thus makes two-way communication possible.

9.3 A simple programmer-defined procedure

It is all too easy for an event handler to grow and grow. What seems a simple algorithm requires special code to deal with unusual cases, and the additional code required lengthens the procedure. This was the case in the file merging project discussed in Chapter 6. Soon it expands beyond one screen of code and then beyond one printed sheet. This is seldom good news. It is hard to persuade long procedures to compile, let alone execute appropriately. Ideally, procedures should normally be less than 30 lines of code. This leads on to creating procedures which are not themselves event handlers. The programmer should put some of the detailed code in a procedure, and test it by itself, then use it in an event handler procedure. In some languages procedures are known as subroutines, while in others, C for example, they are known as functions.

First we give an illustration of the manner of implementing and using procedures.

1. Open a new project.
2. Add a main menu component to give the choice of Demo or Exit.
3. Add `Close` to the `Exit1Click` event handler.
4. Add code to the `Demo1Click` event handler so it reads as shown in Listing 9.2.

Listing 9.2) Simple procedures

```
 1: procedure TForm1.Demo1Click(Sender: TObject);
 2: const A: Integer= 98;    {Starting value for whole project}
 3:   procedure OwnPFirst;
 4:   begin
 5:     ShowMessage('In procedure OwnPFirst, and A is '
 6:        + IntToStr(A));
 7:     Inc(A);
 8:   end {procedure OwnPFirst};
 9:
10: begin   { Demo1Click }
11:   ShowMessage('In procedure Demo1Click, and A is '
12:      + IntToStr(A));
13:   OwnPFirst;
14:   ShowMessage('In procedure Demo1Click, and A is '
15:      + IntToStr(A));
16: end;
```

5. Save the unit and project in appropriate locations.

6. Compile and run.

When the user chooses the Demo option the message boxes shown in Figures 9.2 to 9.4 appear.

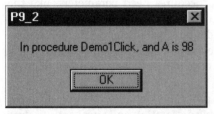

Figure 9.2 First message box.

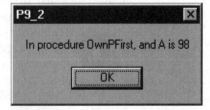

Figure 9.3 Second message box.

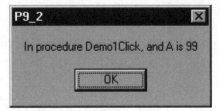

Figure 9.4 Third message box.

Notice that

● We declare **procedure** OwnPFirst inside the event handler, after any variable declarations. OwnPFirst is a procedure which is local to the event handler Demo1Click.

- Its basic structure is the same as that of the event-handling procedures.

- The declaration commences with the reserved word **procedure**, followed by an identifier OwnPFirst, which the programmer chooses.

- A **begin end** pair bracket the executable statements; this pair is needed even if there is only one executable statement.

- Procedure OwnPFirst is not executed immediately after File|Demo is pressed: the code at line 11 is executed making the message box of Figure 9.2 show (and the user must respond) before OwnPFirst is called.

- Procedure OwnPFirst is executed when *called* in line 13 of Listing 9.2. The call simply involves using the identifier OwnPFirst.

- A is a *typed constant*, as discussed in Chapter 8. It is a variable which is initialized just once, rather than each time the procedure is executed. To see this, try choosing the Demo option from the menu more than once.

- A is within scope in procedure OwnPFirst; OwnPFirst increments the value of A, and Figure 9.4 shows the new value.

9.4 Programmer-defined procedures with value and variable parameters

The procedure OwnPFirst as defined and used above had no parameters. To be precise, it was defined without parameters and it was called without parameters. This is a relatively unusual situation: normally procedures need parameters, like the event-handling parameters used throughout this text, to drive them appropriately. In standard Pascal procedures, the number and type of parameters in the declaration and the calling sequence must match. Some relaxation is allowed in Delphi's Object Pascal, but the programmer should weigh up the particular situation before abandoning strong typing.

In order to see how standard Pascal handles procedures, change the project started above by adding new lines – including a variable declaration and another procedure – and extend the Demo1Click event handler so that the main unit reads as shown in Listing 9.3. The lines added are 31, 40–47 and 55–57.

Listing 9.3   An illustration of procedure implementation and calls

```
 1: unit U9_3;
 2:
 3: interface
 4:
 5: uses
 6:    Windows, Messages, SysUtils, Classes, Graphics,
 7:    Controls, Forms, Dialogs, Menus;
 8:
 9: type
10:    TForm1 = class(TForm)
```

```
11:      MainMenu1: TMainMenu;
12:      file1: TMenuItem;
13:      Demo1: TMenuItem;
14:      Exit1: TMenuItem;
15:      procedure Demo1Click(Sender: TObject);
16:      procedure Exit1Click(Sender: TObject);
17:    private
18:      { Private declarations }
19:    public
20:      { Public declarations }
21:    end;
22:
23: var
24:    Form1: TForm1;
25:
26: implementation
27:
28: {$R *.DFM}
29:
30: procedure TForm1.Demo1Click(Sender: TObject);
31: var Param: string;
32: const A: Integer= 98;    {Starting value for whole project}
33:    procedure OwnPFirst;
34:    begin
35:      ShowMessage('In procedure OwnPFirst, and A is '
36:         + IntToStr(A));
37:      Inc(A);
38:    end {procedure OwnPFirst};
39:
40:    procedure Second(B: Char;var C: string);
41:    begin
42:      ShowMessage('In procedure Second,B is '
43:         + B + ': C is '+ C );
44:      C:= 'now defined';
45:      ShowMessage('In procedure Second,B is '
46:         + B + ': C is '+ C );
47:    end{ procedure Second};
48:
49: begin   { Demo1Click }
50:    ShowMessage('In procedure Demo1Click, and A is '
51:       + IntToStr(A));
52:    OwnPFirst;
53:    ShowMessage('In procedure Demo1Click, and A is '
54:       + IntToStr(A));
55:    Second('X', Param);
56:    ShowMessage('In procedure Demo1Click, and Param is '
57:       + Param);
58: end;
59:
60: procedure TForm1.Exit1Click(Sender: TObject);
```

```
61: begin
62:   Close;
63: end;
64:
65: end.
```

Save the project and unit, then compile and run the new project.

The general form of a procedure header is

procedure *procedure_identifier(formal parameter list);*

where *procedure_identifier* obeys the usual rules for identifiers.

- The first three message boxes from OwnPFirst are as shown in Figures 9.2 to 9.4.

- The fourth one comes from the new procedure, Second. Its exact contents will vary but should indicate that C contains rubbish when referenced in line 43, as shown in Figure 9.5.

- The next message box shown in Figure 9.6 shows that C has been initialized (in line 44).

- The final message box in Figure 9.7 indicates that the same value is available in Param.

- Param is a formal variable parameter, as indicated by the reserved word **var**. This means that on entering the procedure the pointer or address of the actual parameter is passed. Then changes in the formal parameter made within the procedure change the same part of memory as that used by the actual parameter. The effect is as if the formal and actual parameters were two names for the same memory location.

- The identifier B, used in line 40, is a formal value parameter. There is no preceding **var**.

- In line 55, 'X' is a corresponding actual value parameter. In this case the actual parameter is a literal, but it could be a variable.

- In cases where the actual value parameter is a variable, as is commonly the case, even if the corresponding formal parameter is changed within the procedure, those changes will not be reflected in the actual variable. This is because a copy is made of the actual parameter into the formal parameter on entry to the procedure, and it is that copy rather than the original which is changed. There are two separate memory locations.

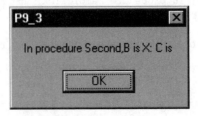

Figure 9.5 Fourth message box of application P9_3.

Figure 9.6 Fifth message box of application P9_3.

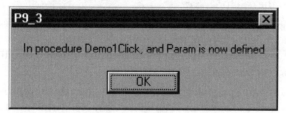

Figure 9.7 Sixth and final message box of application P9_3.

9.5 Positioning procedures

In the previous section we placed the procedures OwnPFirst and Second appropriately, within the event handler which used them. It is good practice to declare procedures, like variables, locally if possible. In fact, if we need a procedure Third, which
will be needed only by procedure Second, then we can declare it and call it inside
Second:

Listing 9.4

```
 1:   procedure Second(B: Char;var C: string);
 2:   var MyD,MyE: Char;
 3:     procedure Third(var D: Char;E: Char);
 4:     begin
 5:       D:= 'D';
 6:       E:= 'E';
 7:     end {procedure Third};
 8:
 9:   begin
10:     ShowMessage('In procedure Second,B is '
11:       + B + ': C is '+ C );
12:     C:= 'now defined';
13:     ShowMessage('In procedure Second,B is '
14:       + B + ': C is '+ C );
15:     MyD:= '?';
16:     MyE:= '?';
17:     Third(MyD,MyE);
18:     ShowMessage(' MyD is '+ MyD + ': MyE is '+ MyE );
19:   end {Second};
```

Save the unit and project in new files, then extend procedure Second as shown in Listing 9.4.

1. Add the local variable declarations in line 2.

2. Add the declaration of Third in lines 3 to 7.

3. Add code to initialize the new variables and call the new procedure Third in lines 15 to 17.

4. Add a call to ShowMessage in line 18 to examine the values of the new local variables after the call to Third.

5. If wished, the original message boxes could be edited out, or merely surrounded with { } to hide them from the compiler. Note that successive commenting out of code can also be an excellent way of locating elusive compiler errors. However, comment brackets cannot be nested.

6. Save the unit and project, then compile and run the new project. A new message box should be as shown in Figure 9.8. Only MyD, which is a variable parameter, has been changed.

Figure 9.8 Nesting procedures.

Just like variables and types, procedure declarations can be visible or not from other procedures.

● The procedure Third is within the scope of Second, as are the variables MyD and MyE.

● In the declaration of Third at line 3 of Listing 9.4, D is a formal variable parameter but E is a value parameter.

● It is not possible to call Third from either Demo1Click or OwnPFirst. Third is local to Second, and only in scope there.

● Procedures may be nested to any depth.

● If OwnPFirst and Second are both declared at the same level, it is possible to call OwnPFirst from within Second; but attempting to call Second from within OwnPFirst gives an error message, as Figure 9.9 shows.

OwnPFirst and Second are within the scope of the event handler Demo1Click, but the compiler has no knowledge of the identifier Second when it processes OwnPFirst. Pascal provides a way of allowing OwnPFirst to call Second also. A *forward directive* to the compiler placed before either procedure definition is the solution, as shown in line 33 of Listing 9.5.

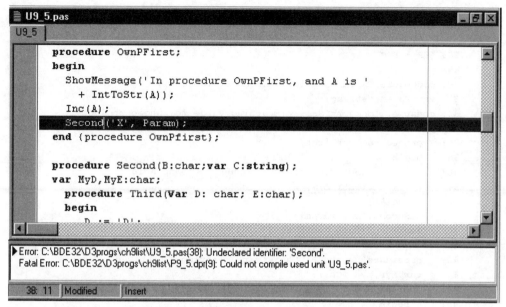

Figure 9.9   Error in scope of procedure declarations.

(Listing 9.5)   Ordering of procedures

```
 1: unit U9_5;
 2:
 3: interface
 4:
 5: uses
 6:    Windows, Messages, SysUtils, Classes, Graphics,
 7:    Controls, Forms, Dialogs, Menus;
 8:
 9: type
10:    TForm1 = class(TForm)
11:      MainMenu1: TMainMenu;
12:      file1: TMenuItem;
13:      Demo1: TMenuItem;
14:      Exit1: TMenuItem;
15:      procedure Demo1Click(Sender: TObject);
16:      procedure Exit1Click(Sender: TObject);
17:    private
18:      { Private declarations }
19:    public
20:      { Public declarations }
21:    end;
22:
23: var
24:    Form1: TForm1;
```

```
25:
26: implementation
27:
28: {$R *.DFM}
29:
30: procedure TForm1.Demo1Click(Sender: TObject);
31: var Param: string;
32: const A: Integer= 98;    {Starting value for whole project}
33: procedure Second(B: Char;var C: string);forward;
34:    procedure OwnPFirst;
35:    begin
36:      ShowMessage('In procedure OwnPFirst, and A is '
37:         + IntToStr(A));
38:      Inc(A);
39:      Second('X', Param);
40:    end {procedure OwnPfirst};
41:
42:    procedure Second(B: Char; var C: string);
43:    var MyD,MyE: Char;
44:      procedure Third(var D: Char; E: Char);
45:      begin
46:        D:= 'D';
47:        E:= 'E';
48:      end {procedure Third};
49:
50:    begin {Second}
51:      ShowMessage('In procedure Second,B is '
52:         + B + ': C is '+ C );
53:      C:= 'now defined';
54:      ShowMessage('In procedure Second,B is '
55:         + B + ': C is '+ C );
56:      MyD:= '?';
57:      MyE:= '?';
58:      Third(MyD,MyE);
59:      ShowMessage(' MyD is '+ MyD + ': MyE is '+ MyE );
60:    end {Second};
61:
62:
63: begin   { Demo1Click }
64:    ShowMessage('In procedure Demo1Click, and A is '
65:       + IntToStr(A));
66:    OwnPFirst;
67:    ShowMessage('In procedure Demo1Click, and A is '
68:       + IntToStr(A));
69:    Second('X', Param);
70:    ShowMessage('In procedure Demo1Click, and Param is '
71:       + Param);
72: end { Demo1Click };
73:
74: procedure TForm1.Exit1Click(Sender: TObject);
75: begin
```

```
76:    Close;
77: end;
78:
79: end.
```

The reader may like to experiment further by moving the declaration of both A and OwnPFirst from the position inside the event handler to immediately after the compiler directive on line 28 of Listing 9.5.

OwnPFirst would then be a unit-wide procedure, and the project will compile and run just the same. Further, OwnPFirst is within scope of other event handlers or procedures added to this unit. If it is required to access OwnPFirst from other units, it must be added to the interface part too.

9.6 Procedures with open array parameters

So far we have used formal parameters of simple types but Pascal parameters can be of any previously defined type such as array types, strings and records. Consider the procedure to find the sum of the values of the elements of an array in Listing 9.6.

Listing 9.6

```
 1: type TTen= 1..10;
 2:      TTenSingles= array[TTen] of Single;
 3:
 4: procedure SumArray(MyTen: TTenSingles;var Sum: Single);
 5: { These parameters will be improved! }
 6: var Index: Cardinal;
 7: begin
 8:   for Index:= Low(MyTen) to High(MyTen) do
 9:     Sum:= Sum + MyTen[Index];
10: end; { procedure SumArray }
```

The functions Low and High used in Listing 9.6 locate the bounds of arrays (see Section 7.4). Although it is useful to be able to pass the array as a parameter to a procedure, that procedure can only be used for arrays of type TTenSingles. A much better method is to use an open array. The procedure header changes to

```
procedure SumArray(MyTen: array of Single; var Sum: Single);
```

but the calling sequence could remain the same, for example it could be

```
SumArray(TopTen, TopSum);
```

or

```
SumArray(TopTwenty, TopSum);
```

Open arrays are only applicable to one-dimensional arrays.

9.7 Procedures with `const` parameters

Object Pascal in the Delphi environment has an additional parameter type which overcomes a weakness in the earlier versions of Pascal. It has a **const** parameter type which guarantees no change within its procedure. In many cases, programmers should use it where they would have used a value parameter in earlier versions of Pascal. Technically the method of passing **const** parameters is like that used for variable parameters, in that pointers are used. This is more efficient than the method used for value parameters, and this is particularly important where those parameters are arrays, in terms of not only execution time but also memory use. In earlier languages it was often recommended that array parameters be variable, or that global arrays be used instead. These workarounds should no longer be necessary in Delphi.

Thus the header for `SumArray` should be

```
procedure SumArray(const MyTen: array of Single; var Sum: Single);
```

9.8 In-built functions

The concept of a function existed in the early versions of Pascal; in fact there were two types of function, in-built functions and programmer-defined functions. Some languages such as C++ and Java only have functions; they do not have procedures.

Earlier in this text there have been many uses of in-built functions. Simple examples are

```
SmallNumber:= StrToInt(Edit1.Text);
```

and

```
z:= Sqrt(Sqr(x)+Sqr(y));
```

`Sqrt` and `Sqr` are examples of mathematical functions, similar to those available in many computing languages, but `StrToInt` converts from **string** to `Integer` type: useful where a number is entered in an edit box and then used in a calculation. To display these lists in later versions of Delphi, go to Help contents, then choose Object Language Reference, and Language Reference. To see a list of such predefined functions, look under *functions and procedures* if you are using Delphi 1. The functions are part of the Delphi Run Time Library (RTL), and are in units such as `System` and `SysUtils`. They may vary slightly from version to version.

Functions are like procedures in their use of parameters, the difference to the programmer being that a function *returns* one and only one result. In Pascal and similar languages that result can be imagined as replacing the function call within an expression. By contrast a procedure call like

```
Third(MyD,MyE);
```

or

```
ShowMessage('In procedure Demo1Click, and Param is '+ Param);
```

stands as a statement by itself. Unlike some similar languages, the result type can be nearly any user-defined type (file types are not allowed).

Delphi's Object Pascal has some pairs of procedures and functions which perform much the same processes, such as Inc and Succ: Inc is a procedure whereas Succ is a function. Use of the online help shows this, and it also shows that Inc takes a variable parameter but Succ takes a constant parameter. The other interesting feature of Inc is that it can take a second optional parameter, of type LongInt, which determines the size of the increment.

So

```
Inc(Number,1);
```

or

```
Number:= Succ(Number);
```

can be used, but one or other might read better in a particular context.

9.9 Programmer-defined functions

The programmer can define functions much as procedures. To illustrate such a simple procedure, a growth function will be defined and used, as in Gleick (1993). The idea is to model population changes by using an equation

$$x_n = \Lambda\, x_{n-1}(1-x_{n-1})$$

where Λ is a constant parameter, x_n is the population after n years, and $0 \leqslant x_n \leqslant 1$. This represents a population whose size is a constant multiple of that population from the year before, but with a $(1-x_{n-1})$ term to allow for the fact that a population declines after a certain point due to lack of shared resources. Thus Listing 9.7 shows a function to represent growth in Object Pascal.

Listing 9.7

```
1: function Growth(const x,Lambda: Double): Double;
2: {------------------------------------------------------------}
3: {Double gives more accuracy than Single                     }
4: {------------------------------------------------------------}
5: begin
6:   Growth:= Lambda * x *(1-x);
7: end;
```

An Object Pascal function may be declared within an event handler, within a programmer-defined procedure, or unit wide. The **forward** directive may be used as for procedures.

The header of the function must have the form

function *function identifier(formal parameter list): result type;*

Precise syntax diagrams are available in the online help.

The function returns one result of the type stated in the header. As for in-built functions, most types of return value are permitted. In Delphi, it is possible for the programmer to define functions which can be used in a standalone way like procedures, in the manner of C++, by using the compiler directive {$X+}. The result is discarded. The facility is best used sparingly.

In standard Pascal, the result is assigned to the identifier *function identifier* within the function, such as Growth in line 1 of Listing 9.7. The function cannot be used on the right-hand side of a statement in the manner of an ordinary variable.

In addition in Delphi, there is a predefined variable Result within a procedure, and assigning to it has the same effect. So the growth function could be coded as

```
function Growth(const x,Lambda: Double): Double;
begin
  Result:= Lambda * x *(1-x);
end;
```

Technically, functions are allowed to have variable parameters, but again these should be used sparingly. It is normally preferable to use a procedure in such cases.

In many cases, it is a question of taste whether to code a subprogram as a function or a procedure, but a function is normally preferred where there is just one value to be transmitted back to the calling sequence.

The function Growth can be used in this statement provided it is in scope:

```
Edit1.Text:= FloatToStr(Growth(0.03,2.5));
```

9.10 Recursion

Recursion is a powerful technique, used by mathematicians but also heavily used by professional programmers. The basic idea is simple; a function or procedure calls itself. Programming folklore has it that looking up recursion in a certain dictionary gives 'See recursion'. On the other hand, there must be some mechanism for these calls to stop, otherwise the project will loop indefinitely.

First, we look at a simple mathematical function, and a Pascal function to evaluate it. For a positive integer n its factorial is defined as

$$n! = n (n - 1)(n - 2) \dots 3.2.1$$
$$n! = n(n - 1)!$$

So $n!$ can be found by finding the previous factorial, $(n - 1)!$, and multiplying it by n. The function in Listing 9.8 does this in Object Pascal.

Listing 9.8 Factorial function

```
1: function Factorial(n: Cardinal): Cardinal;
2: {-----------------------------------------------------------}
3: {This function uses recursion to evaluate n!              }
4: {-----------------------------------------------------------}
```

```
 5: begin
 6:    if n=0 then
 7:       Factorial:=0
 8:    else if n=1 then
 9:          Factorial:= 1
10:          else
11:             Factorial:= n*Factorial(n-1);
12: end;
```

- The general case, in line 11 of Listing 9.8, uses the result of the previous factorial.

- Every recursive function or procedure must incorporate a means of stopping that recursion. In the function `Factorial` this is line 9.

- A recursive function must store its parameters, or their addresses, and local variables on the internal stack before making that recursive call. This takes space which, in the case of value parameters which are arrays or records, can be considerable.

Looking back at population growth problems, in Chapter 6 and in this chapter, it is more significant how the population changes over several years, and it is interesting to see if it settles down to a constant value. So we now look at an equation for growth, which incorporates a time parameter. The heading of the corresponding Object Pascal function becomes

```
function NewGrowth
    (const x,Lambda:Double;Year:Cardinal):Double;
```

and now the population at the end of year 5 depends on the population at the end of year 4, and so on, until the population at the end of year 1 is just as calculated in Section 9.9. NewGrowth can be coded using a **for** loop: see Listing 9.9.

Listing 9.9   Iterative NewGrowth

```
 1: function NewGrowth
 2:    (const x,Lambda:Double;Year:Cardinal):Double;
 3: {-----------------------------------------------------------}
 4: {Iterative function to calculate population change.         }
 5: {Sometimes the solutions converge, but not always!          }
 6: {-----------------------------------------------------------}
 7: var ThisYear: Cardinal;
 8: begin
 9:    Result:= x;
10:    for ThisYear:= Year downto 1 do
11:    begin
12:       Result:= Lambda * Result * (1-Result);
13:    end;
14: end;
```

This is quite compact yet reasonably obvious, so it is probably the best method. However it is also easy to code the same algorithm using recursion as in Listing 9.10.

Listing 9.10) Recursive `NewGrowth`

```
 1: function NewGrowth(const x,Lambda: Double;
 2:   const Year: Cardinal): Double;
 3: {-----------------------------------------------------------}
 4: {Recursive function to illustrate the use of recursive     }
 5: {techniques to calculate population change                 }
 6: {-----------------------------------------------------------}
 7: begin
 8:   if Year > 1 then
 9:     Result:= Lambda * NewGrowth(x,Lambda,Year-1)
10:       *(1-NewGrowth(x,Lambda,Year-1))
11:   else
12:     Result:= Lambda * x *(1-x);
13: end;
```

- The iterative version of Listing 9.9 uses a **for** loop, which is not necessary in the recursive version.

- In Listing 9.10, the general case, starting in line 9, uses the result of the previous year twice.

- The recursive version in Listing 9.10 uses an **if** statement to choose between the general case and the starting situation. Without selection in this manner, the recursive function would call itself for ever, theoretically. In practice, within the Delphi environment, you can sometimes stop infinite loops by pressing Ctrl+Alt+SysRq, or the program may run out of stack space, otherwise it will be necessary to reboot. In Windows 95, Ctrl+Alt+Del, then choosing End Task, may allow the user to regain control.

- In Delphi 1 stack space is limited, but the programmer can increase it to allow deeply recursive procedures to run. Choose Options|Project then press the Linker tab.

- Recursion is an elegant method for coding otherwise complex algorithms. Advanced structures such as linked lists and trees are much easier to code in a recursive manner.

9.11) A recursive procedure

Recursion is not limited to functions; the technique is equally useful for procedures. We will now develop a recursive procedure which draws ellipses of varying colours. The ellipses appear one inside the other, then disappear again.

1. Start a new project, then place on the form one main menu component and one large image, placed centrally. The main menu bar has just one option, File, and the submenu choices are Go and Quit.

2. Enter code as shown in Listing 9.11 into the Go1Click event handler. The event handler is in lines 31 to 54; the programmer needs to enter lines 32 to 51 and line 53 in Listing 9.11.

 • The procedure Shapes is recursive. In general it calls itself in line 47, with a larger parameter Space.

 • Before and after calling itself, it draws an ellipse on the canvas of the image.

 • The drawing is done by using the Ellipse method for canvases. An ellipse is drawn just inside a rectangle, and the four coordinates give top left and bottom right corners of the rectangle.

 • Procedure Shape will cease to call itself when Space is large with respect to the Width of Image1. More precisely, action will stop if Space is greater than one-third of the form width or one-third of the height of the form. See line 35.

 • The two calls to ShowMessagePos merely illustrate what is happening. The final two parameters determine the position on the screen, and can be adjusted for best effect.

 • The inner **with** statement starting in line 37 just changes the Color property of the Pen to add interest. Note that a **case** statement cannot be used, because the colour constants are not part of an ordinal type.

The complete unit is shown in Listing 9.11.

(Listing 9.11) Concentric ellipses

```
 1: unit U9_11;
 2:
 3: interface
 4:
 5: uses
 6:    Windows, Messages, SysUtils, Classes, Graphics,
 7:    Controls, Forms, Dialogs, ExtCtrls, Menus;
 8:
 9: type
10:    TForm1 = class(TForm)
11:       MainMenu1: TMainMenu;
12:       File1: TMenuItem;
13:       Go1: TMenuItem;
14:       Quit1: TMenuItem;
15:       Image1: TImage;
16:       procedure Go1Click(Sender: TObject);
17:       procedure Quit1Click(Sender: TObject);
18:    private
19:       { Private declarations }
20:    public
21:       { Public declarations }
22:    end;
23:
24: var
```

```
25:    Form1: TForm1;
26:
27: implementation
28:
29: {$R *.DFM}
30:
31: procedure TForm1.Go1Click(Sender: TObject);
32: procedure Shapes(Space: Integer);
33: begin
34:    with Image1 do
35:      if (Space < Width div 3) and (Space < Height div 3) then
36:      begin
37:        with Canvas.Pen do
38:        begin
39:          if Color = clRed then
40:            Color:= clBlue else
41:            if Color = clBlue then
42:              Color:= clGreen else
43:                Color:= clRed;
44:        end; {with}
45:        ShowMessagePos('going down now!',200,200);
46:        Canvas.Ellipse(Space,Space,Width-Space,Height-Space);
47:        Shapes(Space+10);
48:        ShowMessagePos('going up now!',200,200);
49:        Canvas.Ellipse(Space,Space,Width-Space,Height-Space);
50:      end; {if}
51: end {Shapes};
52: begin
53:    Shapes(0);
54: end;
55:
56: procedure TForm1.Quit1Click(Sender: TObject);
57: begin
58:    Close;
59: end;
60:
61: end.
```

Figure 9.10 shows a typical run. Several concentric ellipses have been drawn, one inside another. New recursive calls have ceased, and now larger and larger ellipses are being drawn, erasing the earlier ellipses. A modal box appears before each ellipse is drawn.

(9.12) List box components

Before embarking on a longer example, a further visual component, the list box, will be discussed, which will then be used to illustrate sorting.

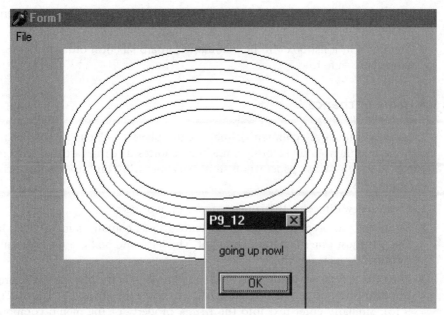

Figure 9.10 Using recursion to draw ellipses.

Edit boxes, which allow the program or user to enter a line of data, and memo components, which allow entry of several lines of text, have already been used; for example

```
Edit1.Text:= IntToStr(Twice);
```

converts `Twice` to **string** type before assigning it to the `Text` property of `Edit1`, and

```
Memo1.Lines.LoadFromFile(SaveDialog1.FileName);
```

copies the contents of a text file, previously specified by the user, into the `Lines` property of `Memo1`.

A list box component is similar to a memo superficially, but differs in these ways:

● A memo component can allow the user to edit in data directly, but a list box component does not. Changes to the contents of a list box are done by using the `Add`, `Insert` and `Delete` methods for `Items`; for example

```
List1.Items.Insert(Count, NewOne);
```

puts `NewOne` in the position `Count`, where the top of the list is number zero, assuming that `List1` is not sorted automatically.

● The user may select from a list box, and multiple selections are possible if the `MultiSelect` property is true.

● A list box can contain graphics as well as text. For this to be so, the `Style` property must be set to `lbOwnerDrawFixed`, indicating that every item's height is given by the `ItemHeight` property of this list box, or `lbOwnerDrawVariable`, indicating that the height of the items can differ: see Help on the OnMeasureItem event for further details.

● The items in a list box will be maintained in alphabetical order if the Sorted property is set to true.

(9.13) A game of chance

This project simulates a children's game. The two players each choose scissors, paper or stone, and then simultaneously mime their choices. The rules are that scissors cut paper (so scissors wins), paper wraps stone (so paper wins) and stone blunts scissors (so stone wins).

1. Create a new directory, then open a new Delphi project.

2. Set up the prototype form shown in Figure 9.11. It contains a main menu item, File, with just one submenu item, Quit. The left-hand box is a list box, but the right-hand one is a memo.

3. Enter the text shown below into the Items property of the list box by clicking on the ellipsis opposite Items (Figure 9.12), to enter the String List Editor (Figure 9.13). Similarly enter text into the Lines property of the memo component. Then set the Enabled property of the memo to False. This stops the user entering data there.

4. Use the Object Inspector or the form itself to access the event handlers FormCreate, Quit1Click and ListBox1Click in turn. Insert code so the project is as shown in Listing 9.12.

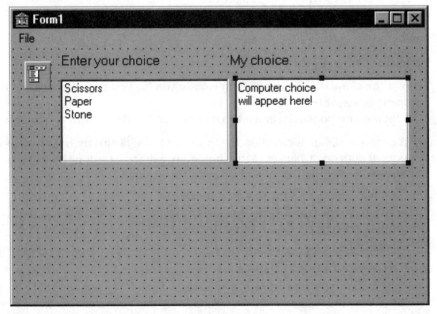

Figure 9.11 Prototype form for 'scissors, paper, stone'.

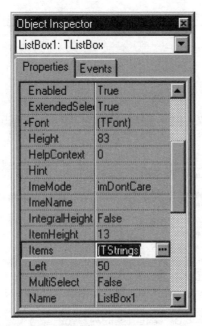

Figure 9.12   Accessing the String List Editor.

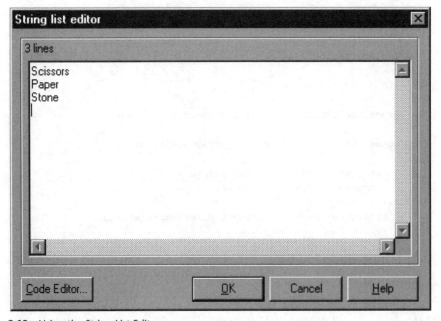

Figure 9.13   Using the String List Editor.

Listing 9.12 Scissors, paper, stone

```
 1: unit U9_12;
 2:
 3: interface
 4:
 5: uses
 6:   Windows, Messages, SysUtils, Classes, Graphics,
 7:   Controls, Forms, Dialogs, StdCtrls, Menus;
 8:
 9: type
10:   TForm1 = class(TForm)
11:     MainMenu1: TMainMenu;
12:     File1: TMenuItem;
13:     Quit1: TMenuItem;
14:     Memo1: TMemo;
15:     ListBox1: TListBox;
16:     Label1: TLabel;
17:     Label2: TLabel;
18:     procedure ListBox1Click(Sender: TObject);
19:     procedure Quit1Click(Sender: TObject);
20:     procedure FormCreate(Sender: TObject);
21:   private
22:     { Private declarations }
23:   public
24:     { Public declarations }
25:   end;
26:
27: var
28:   Form1: TForm1;
29:
30: implementation
31:
32: {$R *.DFM}
33:
34: procedure TForm1.ListBox1Click(Sender: TObject);
35:
36: const No= 3-1;{3 items, but array starts at 0}
37:
38: const List: array [0..No]of string =
39:   ('Scissors','Paper','Stone');
40: var i,Sel: Cardinal;
41:   procedure CheckChoice(const Mine,Yours: string);
42:   {---------------------------------------------------------}
43:   {This procedure checks who has won, and displays an      }
44:   {appropriate message                                     }
45:   {---------------------------------------------------------}
46:   begin
47:     if Mine = Yours then
48:       ShowMessage('we''ve drawn!')
49:     else
```

```
50:          if ((Yours = 'Scissors') and (Mine = 'Paper')) or
51:              ((Yours = 'Paper') and  (Mine = 'Stone')) or
52:              ((Yours = 'Stone') and  (Mine = 'Scissors'))
53:          then
54:              ShowMessage('You win!')
55:          else ShowMessage('I win')
56:    end {CheckChoice};
57:
58: begin {Listbox1Click}
59:    Memo1.Clear;
60:    Memo1.Lines[0]:= List[Trunc(Random(No+1))];
61:    for i:= 0 to No do
62:      with ListBox1 do
63:        if Selected[i] then Sel:= i;
64:      CheckChoice( Memo1.Lines[0],ListBox1.Items[Sel])
65: end { ListBox1Click };
66:
67: procedure TForm1.Quit1Click(Sender: TObject);
68: begin
69:    Close;
70: end;
71:
72: procedure TForm1.FormCreate(Sender: TObject);
73: begin
74:    Randomize;
75: end;
76:
77: end.
```

In Listing 9.12:

- List is a typed constant , whose type is an array of strings. It is initialized to the appropriate strings in lines 38 and 39.

- The next line declares local variables for ListBox1Click.

- Procedure CheckChoice is declared in lines 41 to 56; it has two constant parameters, both of type **string**.

- The body of ListBox1Click starts at line 58.

- Line 59 uses the Clear method of the memo, then the next line uses the in-built random number generator to produce a pseudo-random integer in the range 0 to 2, and assigns a string ('Scissors', 'Paper' or 'Stone') to the first line of the memo.

- The Lines properties of TMemo components and the Items properties of TListBox components are of type TStrings, and the numbering starts at zero.

- Lines 61 to 63 run through the contents of the list box to find the one that has been selected.

- The corresponding string is then compared with the string in the memo using CheckChoice, which is local to ListBox1Click.

9.14 Selection sort

List boxes can sort alphabetically, but not numerically. Frequently an array of records must be sorted, and even with modern computers this can be a time-consuming process, requiring a loop within a loop. Whole books have been written on the subject, and sorting features in almost every book on computing algorithms. First consider a simple sorting algorithm, which is quite adequate where the number and size of the items to be sorted are small.

The general principle of selection sort is as follows:

- Choose the minimum value and put it in the first position.
- Seal that first position from subsequent searches.
- Find the minimum of the remainder, put it in the second position and seal that position.
- Repeat for all but the last position.

The usual refinement is to look for each minimum without shifting the array members, but just remember where that minimum value is stored. Then the minimum value can be swapped with the value in the appropriate position.

The Object Pascal code to sort MyGraph, an array of coordinates, illustrated in Table 9.1, on the value of the first (x) coordinate, is as shown in Listing 9.13, lines 72 to 90.

- In the event handler SelectionSort1Click line 84 assumes that a suitable function LessThanX is in scope to determine the order of two items in the array.
- Line 85 then updates LittleIndex accordingly.
- Line 86 is only within the outer **for** loop. It uses a procedure Swap to interchange the positions of two records. If the records are large, doing this interchange outside the inner loop will be significantly more efficient than other algorithms which do more interchanging.
- Line 87 adds the items to the list box once they are in their final position.

The final unit must naturally include declarations of function LessThanX and of procedure Swap, either in this unit or imported from another unit. To demonstrate the selection sort in event procedure SelectionSort1Click, Generate1Click puts random coordinates into an array of records. The associated form has a pop up menu,

Table 9.1 MyGraph array.

Index	x field	y field
0	1.0	1.0
1	4.0	14.0
2	44.0	23.0
3	18.0	34.0
...		

plus two list boxes to show the original and the sorted array. The main data array is declared in the implementation section so it is in scope for all the event handlers. Listing 9.13 shows the complete unit, and Figure 9.14 shows the project running.

Listing 9.13) Selection sort

```
 1: unit U9_13;
 2:
 3: interface
 4:
 5: uses
 6:    Windows, Messages, SysUtils, Classes, Graphics,
 7:    Controls, Forms, Dialogs, Menus, StdCtrls;
 8:
 9: type
10:    TForm1 = class(TForm)
11:      ListBox1: TListBox;
12:      ListBox2: TListBox;
13:      Label1: TLabel;
14:      Label2: TLabel;
15:      PopupMenu1: TPopupMenu;
16:      File1: TMenuItem;
17:      Generate1: TMenuItem;
18:      Selectionsort1: TMenuItem;
19:      Quit1: TMenuItem;
20:      procedure Generate1Click(Sender: TObject);
21:      procedure FormCreate(Sender: TObject);
22:      procedure SelectionSort1Click(Sender: TObject);
23:      procedure Quit1Click(Sender: TObject);
24:    private
25:      { Private declarations }
26:    public
27:      { Public declarations }
28:    end;
29:
30: var
31:    Form1: TForm1;
32:
33: implementation
34:
35: {$R *.DFM}
36:
37: const MaxP= 50;
38: type TRPoint= record x,y: Single end;
39: type TCoords= array [0..MaxP]of TRPoint;
40: var MyGraph: TCoords;
41:
42: procedure Swap(var One,Other: TRPoint);
43: var Temp: TRPoint;
```

```
44: begin
45:    Temp:= One;
46:    One:= Other;
47:    Other:= Temp;
48: end;
49:
50: function LessThanX(const One,Other: TRPoint):Boolean;
51: begin
52:    LessThanX:= One.X < Other.X;
53: end;
54:
55: procedure TForm1.Generate1Click(Sender: TObject);
56: var i: Integer;
57: begin
58:    for i:= 0 to Maxp do
59:    begin
60:      MyGraph[i].X:= Random(MaxP);
61:      MyGraph[i].Y:= Random(MaxP);
62:      Listbox1.Items.Add ('('+FloatToStr(MyGraph[i].X) +
63:        ','+ FloatToStr(MyGraph[i].Y)+')' );
64:    end;
65: end;
66:
67: procedure TForm1.FormCreate(Sender: TObject);
68: begin
69:    Randomize;
70: end;
71:
72: procedure TForm1.SelectionSort1Click(Sender: TObject);
73: {-----------------------------------------------------------}
74: {Selection sort - a simple method                          }
75: {-----------------------------------------------------------}
76: var j,k,LittleIndex: Integer;
77: begin
78: {Successively find minima }
79:    for k:= Low(MyGraph) to High(MyGraph)-1 do
80:    {invariant assertion - sorted up to MyGraph[ k-1]}
81:    begin
82:      LittleIndex:= k;
83:      for j:= k+1 to  High(MyGraph) do
84:        if LessThanX(MyGraph [j], MyGraph[LittleIndex])
85:        then LittleIndex:= j;
86:      Swap( MyGraph [k] , MyGraph[LittleIndex]);
87:      ListBox2.Items.Add ('(' +FloatToStr(MyGraph[k].X) +
88:        ','+ FloatToStr(MyGraph[k].Y)+')' );
89:    end; {for}
90: end;
91:
92: procedure TForm1.Quit1Click(Sender: TObject);
93: begin
```

```
94:    Close;
95: end;
96:
97: end.
```

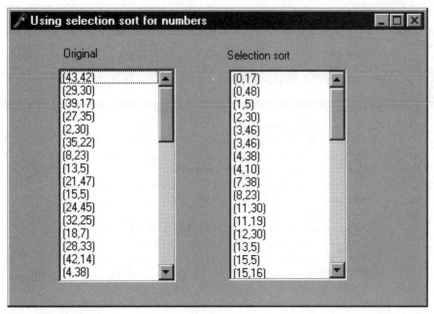

Figure 9.14 Selection sort.

9.15 **Quicksort***

A detailed discussion of sorting techniques is beyond the scope of this text, but one of the best known sorting algorithms, known as Quicksort, attributed to C.A.R. Hoare, is interesting from several points of view:

● On average, it sorts much more efficiently than selection sort.

● Unlike some other sorting algorithms, it does not need an extra array of similar size, nor external files.

● It is easier to implement using recursion.

Listing 9.14 gives an example of a reasonably simple implementation of Quicksort, after the method of Sedgewick (1988).

Listing 9.14 Quicksort

```
1: procedure QSort(Below,Above: Integer);
2: var ThisBelow,ThisAbove: Integer; {Scanning pointers }
```

```
 3:      Pivot: TRpoint; { Value to place}
 4: begin
 5:   if Above > Below then
 6:   begin
 7:     {initialize}
 8:     Pivot:= MyGraph[Above];
 9:     ThisBelow:= Below-1; ThisAbove:= Above;
10:     while ThisBelow < ThisAbove do
11:     begin
12:       repeat
13:         Inc(ThisBelow)
14:       until LessThanEQX(Pivot, MyGraph[ThisBelow]);
15:
16:       repeat
17:         Dec(ThisAbove)
18:       until LessThanEQX(MyGraph [ThisAbove], Pivot);
19:       { Interchange 2 values so each is in correct half}
20:       if ThisBelow< ThisAbove then
21:         Swap( MyGraph [ThisBelow], MyGraph[ThisAbove]);
22:     end {while};
23:
24:     {Place pivot element in correct place}
25:     Swap( MyGraph[ThisBelow] ,MyGraph[Above]);
26:     {sort each subset, by calling this recursively}
27:     QSort(Below,ThisBelow-1);
28:     QSort(ThisBelow+1, Above);
29:   end; {if }
30: end; {QSort}
```

For detailed discussion the reader should refer to Sedgewick (1988) or a similar text on algorithms, but the basic principles are these:

- Choose one value as *pivot*.
- Place this pivot in its final sorted position, by moving the other values such that all values earlier in the list are less than or equal to the pivot, whereas all values later are greater than or equal to the pivot.
- In general, the pivot value itself may move.
- When the pivot is in position, use the same algorithm to sort the two partitions either side of the pivot.
- The array to be sorted gets smaller, until there is no sorting left to do.
- The efficiency comes from the relatively small number of interchanges necessary in most cases.
- In order to illustrate Quicksort in action, incorporate the procedure above in the OnClick event of a further menu item, then call it once:

```
QSort(Low(MyGraph), High(MyGraph));
```

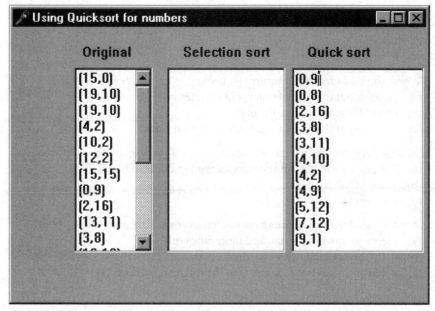

Figure 9.15 Quicksort.

Figure 9.15 shows the result of Quicksort copied into a memo box, but it is much more interesting to use the debugger to watch the algorithm unfold: see Appendix A.

9.16 Summary

This chapter has explored event-handling and programmer-defined procedures. We discussed the various types of parameter, and when to use each. We also introduced the important concept of recursion, and illustrated its use with some simple examples. A sorting example used the list box component, which allows the user to select items.

Quiz

1. What causes a procedure to be executed?
    (a) the declaration of that procedure
    (b) the redeclaration of its identifier
    (c) the occurrence of its identifier in code

2. What is the difference between variable and value parameters?
    (a) Variable parameters are used only for output from the procedure, whereas value parameters are used for input to the procedure.
    (b) Variable parameters are used for output from and input to the procedure, whereas value parameters are used for input to the procedure only.
    (c) Value parameters are used for output from and input to the procedure, whereas variable parameters are used for input to the procedure only.

3. How deeply can procedures be nested?
   (a) nesting is not allowed
   (b) 1 deep
   (c) to any depth

4. Where should a procedure required by just one event handler be declared?
   (a) preferably at the start of that event handler
   (b) preferably at the start of the unit
   (c) preferably at the start of the implementation part

5. What will happen if a procedure attempts to use a variable that is out of scope?
   (a) The project will run but the value of the variable is indeterminate.
   (b) The unit will fail to run.
   (c) The unit will fail to compile.

6. What is the advantage of **const** parameters over value parameters?
   (a) **const** parameters are handled more efficiently.
   (b) Actual **const** parameters are always literals.
   (c) **const** parameters can be changed within the procedure.

7. How many results does a function return?
   (a) as many as in its declaration
   (b) one exactly
   (c) none

8. What is recursion?
   (a) a function or procedure calling itself
   (b) iteration
   (c) a procedure calling a function

9. What difference is there between a memo and a list box?
   (a) Memos can accept user input, but list boxes cannot.
   (b) Memos can accept graphics, but list boxes cannot.
   (c) Memos can use the Add method, but list boxes cannot.

10. Why may recursion use a lot of space?
    (a) Parameters and local variables, or their addresses, must be stored on the stack.
    (b) Global and local variables must be stored on the stack.
    (c) Addresses of value parameters and local variables must be stored in a file.

Exercises

1. Write a function to average numbers of type `single`, held in an open array.

2. Write a procedure to sort real numbers held in an array. Why is it seldom necessary to write code to sort strings alphabetically in Delphi?

3. Write a procedure with appropriate parameters to find the roots of quadratic equations.

4. Write procedures to encrypt and decipher a string, by replacing each letter by the third one following, so *a* becomes *d*, *b* becomes *e*, *x* becomes *a* and so on.

5. Improve Exercise 4 by using a better encrypting algorithm. One simple but effective algorithm is to replace each letter in the string by a letter whose distance from the first in the alphabet is governed by a key word. For example, if the keyword is DELPHI, the first letter of the message is replaced by the fourth letter following (since D is the fourth letter of the alphabet), the second letter is replaced by the fifth letter following (since E is the fifth letter of the alphabet), the third by the twelfth following, and so on, repeating the keyword if necessary. The message is very difficult to decipher without knowing the keyword.

Chapter 10

Objects

10.1 Introduction

Objects are a fundamental building block for software development with Delphi. From the very start of using Delphi, programmers place objects, known as components, on forms and set their properties by using the Object Inspector and define methods using event handlers. In this chapter we will illustrate techniques for creating, using and destroying both non-visual and visual objects. Within object-oriented programming *memory leakage* can cause severe problems. Users are often faced with what should be a relatively small program needing vast amounts of memory. We will show how careful programming can avoid this consumption of resources.

Traditionally, structured programming languages enabled programmers to design data structures and define code to manipulate these structures. Object Pascal offers these facilities in that programmers can use an existing data structure (for example integer) or design their own (for example an array of records) and develop procedures for manipulating these data items. Object-oriented programming (OOP) puts the data and operations together into an object.

10.2 Owner **and** Parent

In Section 8.9 we showed how an instance of an object could be created at run time. The code, repeated here in Listing 10.1, creates a shape object and stores it in pre-declared variable NewShape.

Listing 10.1 Creating NewShape

```
 1: procedure TForm1.FormCreate(Sender: TObject);
 2: begin
 3:   NewShape:= TShape.Create(Self);
 4:   with NewShape do
 5:   begin
 6:     Top:= 25;
 7:     Left:= 25;
 8:     Parent:= Self;
 9:   end;
10: end;
```

The Create at line 3 specifies that Self is the Owner of NewShape; the assignment at line 8 also makes Self the Parent. Recall that Self is an implicit parameter and in this event handler is Form1 (see Section 8.8).

When Delphi component objects are created the programmer must specify the Owner. Once a visual component (control) has been created one of the first properties to be set is the Parent. As with NewShape, Self is often used for both the Owner and the Parent; this is disconcerting for programmers who as a result of this confusion may commit errors. In this section we attempt to clarify the role of each.

The Owner of a component is responsible for freeing the memory of that component, when it is no longer needed, which may be at any time during the life of the Owner. When an Owner component is destroyed all the owned components are also destroyed. The mechanism for destroying objects is explained in Section 10.5.

Visual components (controls) can be placed directly onto the form or grouped together on a panel or other object. When a control appears inside another, then the containing control is called the *Parent*. The Parent property dictates where a component can be seen; the Parent must itself be a visual component. In the previous example the form is Self for the creation of NewShape. Making Self the Parent means that the shape will appear on the form. The Parent does not have to be the same object as the Owner. We could in the example make a previously created panel the Parent of the shape, while the form remained the Owner. This would mean that the shape could only appear inside the panel, but the form had responsibility for claiming back the memory when the shape was no longer required.

All components require owners, but only controls require parents. An OpenDialog is a component that is not a control and does not have a Parent property.

Objects do not have to be components. Later in this chapter we will present an example of such an object that can be used to represent certain numeric values and operations on such numbers. Objects which are not components can inherit directly from TObject, in which case they do not have an Owner or Parent. The programmer is responsible for ensuring that there is some code to release the memory when the object no longer needs it.

(10.3) Creating objects

An object class is declared in a **type** statement and the object is defined in a **var** statement. An instance of an object is created at run time by execution of a Create statement (as seen in Chapter 8). The declaration of the object must include a constructor or inherit a constructor from an ancestor. Constructors are used in programs to create and initialize new objects. A destructor is the opposite of a constructor, destroying objects and releasing the memory. A call to the destructor will release the memory for future use and is essential in cases where objects do not have owners.

In the example shown in Listing 10.2 we use an existing object class, TPanel, as the basis of a programmer-declared *object class* TMyPanel.

Listing 10.2) TMyPanel

```
1: type TMyPanel = class(TPanel)
2: private
3:    {none}
4: public
5:    fNumber: Integer;
6:    constructor Create(Owner: TComponent); override;
7: end;
```

In Listing 10.2:

- Line 1 indicates that the new object TMyPanel is based on the existing object TPanel.

- Lines 2 and 3 show there are no private elements and so these two lines are optional.

- Line 5 declares a new field, fNumber, for TMyPanel objects. Note the keyword **var** is not used here.

- Line 6 declares the constructor that will create and initialize TMyPanel objects, and the word **override** indicates that the new **constructor** takes precedence over the existing TPanel one, but is not replacing it, rather retaining it. The parameter list for the constructor must be identical to the one in the ancestor class (TPanel).

- There is no need specifically to declare a destructor as the inherited one can be used.

- The unit also needs explicitly to include the unit which contains TPanel. This can be done by adding the unit name `ExtCtrls` to the end of the **uses** list at the start of the unit, for example:

```
uses
    Windows, Messages, SysUtils, Classes, Graphics, Controls,
    Forms, Dialogs, ExtCtrls;
```

The role of **uses** will be discussed in detail in Chapter 13.

The code for the constructor is implemented in the implementation part of the unit and Listing 10.3 shows this constructor.

Listing 10.3) The constructor for `TMyPanel`

```
 1: constructor TMyPanel.Create(Owner: TComponent);
 2: const Count: Integer= 1;
 3: begin
 4:    inherited Create(Owner);
 5:    fNumber:= Count;
 6:    Inc(Count);
 7:    Caption:= '# '+ IntToStr(fNumber);
 8:    Height:= 40;
 9:    Width:= 40;
10:    Color:= clWhite;
11:    BorderStyle:= bsSingle;
12: end;
```

In Listing 10.3:

- In line 1 the word **constructor** is used to indicate that this is a special sort of procedure. The formal parameter `Owner` is declared. The component passed as the actual parameter when the constructor is called will be the `Owner` of this newly created component.

- Line 2 declares a static variable `Count` that is accessed and updated each time the constructor is called. `Count` will be 1 when the first panel is created, 2 when the second is created and 3 when the third is created.

- Line 4 initializes all the inherited parts of the object to their default values. The `Create` constructor referred to here is the one that belongs to the ancestor class (`TPanel`). So the defaults are those of `TPanel`.

- Line 5 sets the field `fNumber` to the value of the static variable.

- Line 6 increments the static variable, `Count`, ready for the next time it is used.

- The remaining lines set inherited properties to new values, to produce the personalized object.

A `TMyPanel` object can be defined in a **var** statement:

```
var NewPanel: TMyPanel;
```

Alternatively the programmer can declare an array type and then use it to define an array of these new objects:

```
type TArrayPanels= array[1..10] of TMyPanel;
var MyPanel: TArrayPanels;
```

These declarations and definitions do not actually create any TMyPanel objects. An object is created when the constructor code runs. For example the event handler in Listing 10.4 will create an array of TMyPanel objects.

(Listing 10.4) Creating an array of panels

```
 1: procedure TForm1.FormCreate(Sender: TObject);
 2: var i: Integer;
 3: begin
 4:   for i:= 1 to 10 do
 5:   begin
 6:     MyPanel[i]:= TMyPanel.Create(Self);
 7:     MyPanel[i].Parent:= Self;
 8:     MyPanel[i].Left:= (i-1)*(MyPanel[i].Width+1);
 9:     {spread the panels across the form}
10:   end;
11: end;
```

When FormCreate runs, it will produce a form like the one shown in Figure 10.1.

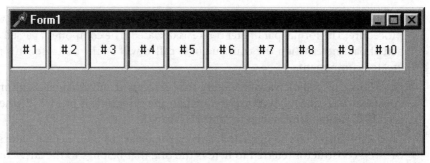

Figure 10.1   A form with objects created at run time.

- Lines 1, 3 and 11 of Listing 10.4 are the template automatically generated for the OnCreate event.
- Line 6 creates a TMyPanel component with its Owner set as Self. Within this event handler Self is Form1.
- Line 7 sets the Parent property to Self (that is Form1).
- Line 8 ensures the spread of panels across the form.

10.4 Defining methods for objects

Programmers can define methods for any object. A method is defined as a procedure. The declaration line, starting with the word **procedure**, is placed within the object's declaration, while the procedure's full definition is placed within the implementation part of the unit. The implementation part of a unit starts after the word **implementation** in the unit listing. See Chapter 13 for more details.

To add a method Disappear to the class TMyPanel the programmer would first add line 7 of Listing 10.5 to the declaration of TMyPanel.

Listing 10.5 Adding the method Disappear

```
1: type TMyPanel = class(TPanel)
2: private
3:   {none}
4: public
5:   fNumber: Integer;
6:   constructor Create(Owner: TComponent); override;
7:   procedure Disappear(Sender: TObject);
8: end;
```

The second stage is to add the full code of this procedure to the implementation part of the unit. The implementation part will also include the constructor and any event handlers coded for events associated with the form or other components declared. The name of the object type must be included in front of the procedure's name as shown in Listing 10.6.

Listing 10.6 Code for the method Disappear

```
1: procedure TMyPanel.Disappear(Sender: TObject);
2: begin
3:   if (Sender is TMyPanel) then
4:   with (Sender as TMyPanel) do
5:     Visible:= False;
6: end;
```

In Listing 10.6:

- Line 3 checks that Sender is of type TMyPanel.
- Line 4 then casts Sender as TMyPanel for the **with** statement.
- Line 5 sets the panel's visibility to False.

The method Disappear is a procedure definition and may be called in code like any other procedure. It can also be associated with an event. For example, within the

constructor code of an object of type TMyPanel, the OnDblClick event could be
assigned the method Disappear. This can be done for the constructor shown in
Listing 10.3 by adding the following assignment after line 11:

```
OnDblClick:= Disappear;
```

This would have the effect that if the user double clicked one of the objects, of the
type TMyPanel, it would disappear.

Although the panels disappear they continue to exist. Other code could be written
that would make them reappear. Disappearing is not the same as destroying.
Destroying objects is the topic of the next section.

(10.5) Destroying objects

When an object created by the programmer is no longer required it should be
destroyed. Destroying an object releases the memory allocated to that object and
makes it available for other use. When a program terminates, all objects associated
with it are automatically destroyed, freeing the computer's memory for other purposes. However, the programmer should not rely on this mechanism. Even small
programs can suffer from memory leakage. For example, a program may create an
object, finish with it and then recreate a new version of the object without releasing
the memory used in the original version. Such objects can consume all the memory
available in the computer. This can result in the program stopping and most likely
the computer will have to be rebooted. It is the programmer's responsibility to indicate where an object is no longer required and its space can be freed.

Destroying objects must be done carefully, but it is often essential. Delphi recom-
mends that programmers call the Free method and this will be explained below.

A destructor provides the mechanism for destroying objects. A destructor can be
considered to be the mirror image of a constructor. The destructor must be programmed to destroy any embedded objects and release any other resources allocated
(for example, a file open for writing) and finally call the inherited Destroy destructor to destroy inherited fields. If the created object neither contains objects nor
otherwise allocates space (for example, by using pointers) then the inherited destructor can be used directly and there is no need to declare a new destructor and override
the inherited one.

If the creation of an object fails, the space already allocated is released and the variable name associated with it is set to **nil**, to indicate it is empty. **nil** is a reserved
word, used to indicate that nothing is pointed to; it will be discussed again in
Chapter 14. The Free method checks if the object is **nil** before calling the relevant
Destroy destructor. This prevents attempts to destroy non-existent objects which
otherwise lead to execution errors. Care is still needed with using Free, in particular:

- once the Free method for an object has been executed, set its variable to **nil** to
  prevent further attempts to destroy it which might cause execution errors;

- never Free an object from within its own methods or from within objects inheriting from it.

We illustrate the definition of destructors and the use of `Free` by extending the object `TMyPanel` used earlier in this chapter. An image will be associated with the panel object and a `Destroy` destructor added, as indicated in Listing 10.7.

Listing 10.7 The amended class `TMyPanel`

```
1: type TMyPanel = class (TPanel)
2: private
3:    {none}
4: public
5:    fNumber: Integer;
6:    fImage: TImage;
7:    constructor Create(Owner: TComponent); override;
8:    destructor Destroy; override;
9: end;
```

In Listing 10.7:

● Line 6 declares an additional field, called `fImage`, in an object of type `TMyPanel`.

● Line 8 declares the inherited `Destroy` destructor which will be overridden, that is, it will have its functionality amended.

Now amend the `Create` constructor to create the field `fImage`, to initialize its values, and to define the destructor: see Listing 10.8.

Listing 10.8 The constructor for `TMyPanel`

```
1: constructor TMyPanel.Create(Owner: TComponent);
2: const Count: Integer= 1;
3: begin
4:    inherited Create(Owner);      { Initialize inherited parts }
5:    fImage:= TImage.Create(Self);
6:    fImage.Parent:= Self;
7:    fImage.Picture.LoadFromFile('hat.bmp');
8:    fNumber:= Count;
9:    Inc(Count);
10:   Caption:= '# '+ IntToStr(fNumber);
11:   Height:= 40;
12:   Width:= 40;
13:   Color:= clWhite;
14:   BorderStyle:= bsSingle;
15: end;
16:
17: destructor TMyPanel.Destroy;
18: begin
19:    fImage.Free;
```

```
20:    FImage:= nil;
21:    inherited Destroy;
22: end;
```

In Listing 10.8:

- Lines 4 to 7 create the new TImage object.
- Within this constructor Self is the object of type TMyPanel, used for calling this constructor. Self will be both Owner and Parent of the image created.
- Line 7 initializes the image contents to a bitmap file 'hat.bmp'. The lack of path name indicates that this is stored in the current directory; another available bitmap could be used here. The rest of the construction is as before (lines 8 to 14).
- Line 19 destroys the field fImage.
- fNumber is not an object, it is an integer, and so needs neither to create nor destroy.
- Line 21 calls the inherited Destroy from TPanel and initiates destruction of all inherited fields.

The event handlers for buttons named Creator and Terminator, shown in Listing 10.9, will create a previously declared object MySinglePanel of type TMyPanel.

Listing 10.9) An event handler for the button Creator

```
 1: procedure TForm1.CreatorClick(Sender: TObject);
 2: begin
 3:    if MySinglePanel<>nil then
 4:        MySinglePanel.Free;
 5:    MySinglePanel:= TMyPanel.Create(Self);
 6:    MySinglePanel.Parent:= Self;
 7: end;
 8:
 9: procedure TForm1.TerminatorClick(Sender: TObject);
10: begin
11:    MySinglePanel.Free;
12:    MySinglePanel:= nil;
13: end;
```

In Listing 10.9:

- Line 3 checks if the object already exists and if so releases it at line 4.
- Line 5 creates the panel and assigns it to MySinglePanel.
- Line 6 sets the Parent property, so that the panel will be displayed on the form.
- Line 11 calls Free which will in turn cause the destructor to be executed.

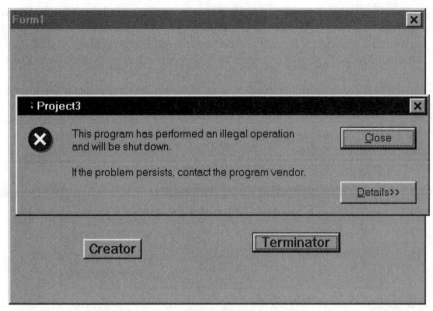

Figure 10.2 A possible consequence of destroying a non-existent object.

● Line 12 sets `MySinglePanel` to **nil**, to prevent further inadvertent attempts to destroy it.

● `Self` in this example is `Form1`.

This project can now be run. The user can click either of the buttons, in any order. Experimentation with the clicking of buttons will show the creation and destruction of the object.

Omitting line 12 in Listing 10.9 will lead to error conditions if attempts are made to repeatedly destroy a previously destroyed object. This can lead to error conditions such as that shown in Figure 10.2 or it may freeze your computer, forcing a reboot. This reinforces the point that it is necessary to be careful when destroying objects. If you choose to conduct this experiment, make sure all other work is saved.

Further experimentation with lines 3 and 4 omitted, and repeated creation of objects, will give rise to memory leakage as indicated by the run time exception error in Figure 10.3.

Figure 10.3 The consequence of memory leakage.

Within Windows there is usually a resource meter available (under Accessories| Systems Tool) which shows the percentage of resources available. Watch this meter as run time objects are created and not destroyed. The percentage of resources available will decline as shown in Figure 10.4. One more `Create` will cause an error.

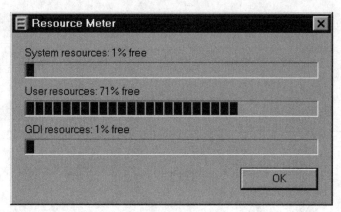

Figure 10.4   Resource meter.

This emphasizes the point that it is essential to destroy unwanted objects or all the available memory will leak away.

The constant creation of images has also consumed the Graphical Device Interface (GDI) resources, used by Windows to control what appears on the screen.

10.6 Object types

The briefest format for declaring an object type is

```
type NewObjectType = class (ExistingObjectType);
```

This declares a new object type, inheriting all the fields, methods and properties of an existing object type. Most newly defined object types do more than simply rename an existing type. New fields, methods and properties can be defined, while inherited ones can be altered.

Object types can only be declared in the outermost scope of a unit. Unlike other types, objects cannot be declared within procedures.

Delphi has a predefined object type (or class) TObject that is considered to be the ultimate ancestor of all objects. TObject includes methods for creating and destroying objects, along with other methods that are applicable to all objects. The class TComponent is the common ancestor of all components. TComponent itself is a descendant of TObject. TComponent encapsulates the fundamental behaviour common to all components, including creation which for a component includes an Owner parameter. All components must have an Owner; the Owner is responsible for disposing of the object when it is no longer required.

Table 10.1	Visibility specifiers of objects.
public	Things declared in this section are in scope in the current unit and in all units that use the current unit.
private	Things declared in this section are in scope for the current unit but not accessible from beyond it.
protected	A cross between public and private. Things declared in this section are in scope in the current unit and to any objects that inherit from the object declared here.
published	Essentially the same as public, only used when creating components. When a published property is inherited by a new object that property may be promoted to public. Advanced users can add their own components to the Component Palette; published properties of such components can be manipulated at design time using the Object Inspector.

The availability of an object's fields, methods and properties to other parts of the program is dictated by the use of the reserved words **public**, **private**, **protected** and **published**, to delineate a section declaring fields, methods and properties. The meanings of these sections are summarized in Table 10.1.

On starting a new application Delphi creates a unit code with an object type TForm1 declared as shown in Listing 10.10.

Listing 10.10 The initial declaration of TForm1

```
1: type
2:   TForm1 = class(TForm)
3:   private
4:     { Private declarations }
5:   public
6:     { Public declarations }
7:   end;
```

All this code is generated automatically:

- Line 3 is a visibility specifier for the private section, as indicated by the comment on line 4.
- Line 5 is a visibility specifier for the public section, as indicated by the comment on line 6.

This object type inherits from the class TForm, without altering or adding any fields, methods or properties.

The class is personalized as the programmer adds components and event handlers. For example adding a button, with an OnClick event handler, will make the class declaration become the code shown in Listing 10.11.

Listing 10.11 The declaration of TForm1 with a button and an event handler

```
1: type
2:   TForm1 = class(TForm)
3:     Button1: TButton;
4:     procedure Button1Click(Sender: TObject);
5:   private
6:     { Private declarations }
7:   public
8:     { Public declarations }
9:   end;
```

In Listing 10.11:

- Line 3 shows the field Button1 added and this is of type TButton.
- Line 4 shows the method Button1Click also added. The event handler TForm1.Button1Click is a procedure definition in the implementation part of the unit. Delphi has provided the template (see Listing 10.12); the programmer must add the code.
- There is no visibility specifier before the declaration of Button1 at line 3. This means that fields, methods and properties in this section take the default visibility: **public**. After a visibility specifier appears, all declarations follow the scope rules associated with that most recent specifier.
- The **end** at line 9 of Listing 10.11 marks the completion of the object's type declaration.

Listing 10.12 Template

```
procedure TForm1.Button1Click(Sender: TObject);
begin

end;
```

Suppose the programmer wants to associate an integer variable with this form. If only this unit needs to access that variable then it should be put in the private section, while if other units need to access this variable it must go in the public section. See Listing 10.13.

Listing 10.13

```
1: type
2:   TForm1 = class(TForm)
3:     Button1: TButton;
4:     procedure Button1Click(Sender: TObject);
5:   private
```

```
 6:       { Private declarations }
 7:       SecretInt: Integer;
 8:     public
 9:       { Public declarations }
10:       KnownInt: Integer;
11:     end;
```

In Listing 10.13:

- Line 7 declares an integer, SecretInt, that can be used only in this unit.
- Line 10 declares an integer, KnownInt, that can be used by other units.

Declaring a variable private to the form has a similar effect to declaring the variable in the implementation section. The difference is that for access by procedures within the unit, but not belonging to the form, it is necessary to qualify the variable with the encapsulating object's name. For example:

```
Form1.SecretInt
```

would be used within the current unit to access the integer declared at line 7 in Listing 10.13, whereas a variable declared within the implementation part can be referred to by its unqualified name throughout the unit.

A publicly declared variable must also be qualified by its object name whenever it is used outside that object and this access may be from other units too. Indeed all fields, methods and properties declared within an object must be qualified when used outside that object.

10.7 Non-visual objects

Objects do not have to be based on visual components. Any data type and its associated operations can be encapsulated into an object. Here we will present an example based on integer complex numbers and the associated operations.

10.7.1 Brief introduction to complex numbers

A complex number can be considered as a two-dimensional number as shown in Figure 10.5. The x-axis (the horizontal axis) represents the range of *real* whole numbers from -10 to 10, while the y-axis (vertical) represents the *imaginary* range, going from $-10 \times \sqrt{-1}$ to $10 \times \sqrt{-1}$. Note that *real* here is used in the sense of 'opposite to imaginary', not a floating-point number.

The number at A could be written as

$$4 + 7i$$

where $i^2 = -1$. Similarly the number at B can be written

$$-6 - 3i$$

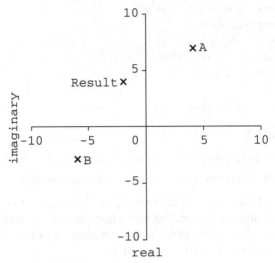

Figure 10.5 Example of complex numbers.

The result of adding the numbers A and B is calculated by adding the individual real parts (4 add −6) and imaginary parts (7 add −3) to give

$$-2 + 4i$$

which is the number shown at Result.

The general form of adding and multiplying imaginary numbers can be written as:

$$(a + bi) + (c + di) = (a + c) + (b + d)i$$
$$(a + bi) \times (c + di) = (ac - bd) + (ad + bc)i$$

An object TComplex can be defined that will have fields for representing the parts of a complex number and methods for adding and multiplying them.

10.7.2   The object TComplex

The object type TComplex can be declared as shown in Listing 10.14.

Listing 10.14 TComplex

```
1: type
2:    TComplex = class(TObject)
3:    private
4:       FRealPart: Integer;
5:       FImagPart: Integer;
6:    public
7:       procedure Add (const First, Second: TComplex);
8:       procedure Multiply (const First, Second: TComplex);
9:       function ToStr: string;
```

```
10:     procedure ToComplex (AString: string);
11:     end;
```

In Listing 10.14:

- Line 2 indicates that TComplex inherits from TObject, the ultimate ancestor of all objects.
- Lines 4 and 5 define fields for the real and imaginary parts of the complex number. These are declared to be private to the object type TComplex and its implementation unit. In a multi-unit project this would prevent other units accessing these values. They could be written as a single definition:

```
    FRealPart, FImagPart: Integer;
```

- Lines 7 and 8 are the definitions of methods that can be applied to an object of type TComplex. Both have two parameters that are themselves of type TComplex. These parameters are constant parameters as they are not altered by the method.
- Line 9 defines a function ToStr. When this is applied to an object of TComplex it will return a string representation of the complex number, in a similar manner to the functions IntToStr and FloatToStr.
- Line 10 defines a method that takes a string and stores it in an object of TComplex as the real and imaginary parts of the complex number.
- There is no need to define a constructor or destructor. TComplex does not itself create other objects or otherwise allocate resources. So the constructor and destructor inherited from TObject will be sufficient to create and destroy objects of type TComplex.

The methods are public so they can be accessed by other units in a project with more than one unit (see Chapter 13). They are declared in the implementation part of the unit (Listing 10.15).

Listing 10.15 Implementation of TComplex

```
1: procedure TComplex.Add (const First,Second: TComplex);
2: begin
3:    FRealPart:= First.FRealPart+Second.FRealPart;
4:    FImagPart:= First.FImagPart+Second.FImagPart;
5: end;
6:
7: procedure TComplex.Multiply (const First,Second: TComplex);
8: begin
9:    FRealPart:= (First.FRealPart*Second.FRealPart)
10:                   -(First.FImagPart*Second.FImagPart);
11:    FImagPart:= (First.FRealPart*Second.FImagPart)
12:                   +(First.FImagPart*Second.FRealPart);
13: end;
```

```
14:
15: function TComplex.ToStr: string;
16: begin
17:    Result:= IntToStr(FRealPart);
18:    if FImagPart>=0 then Result:= Result+'+';
19:    Result:= Result+IntToStr(FImagPart)+'i';
20: end;
21:
22: procedure TComplex.ToComplex (AString: string);
23: var Position,Positioni: Integer; var Temp: string;
24: begin
25:    Position:= Pos('+',AString);
26:    if Position=0 then
27:      Position:= Pos('-', AString);
28:    if Position=1 then {starts with a + or - }
29:    begin
30:      Temp:= Copy(AString,2,Length(AString)-1);
31:      Position:= Pos('+',Temp);
32:      if Position=0 then
33:         Position:= Pos('-', Temp);
34:      Inc(Position);
35:    end;
36:    Positioni:= Pos('i',AString);
37:    { error checking should be added to cope with incorrectly
38:      presented numbers}
39:    FRealPart:= StrToInt(Copy(AString,0,Position-1));
40:    FImagPart:= StrToInt(Copy(AString,Position,
41:                              Positioni-Position));
42: end;
```

In Listing 10.15:

- Each method definition (lines 1, 7, 15 and 22) is preceded by the TComplex to indicate that these methods are for use by instances of objects of the type TComplex.
- The implementations of the Add and Multiply methods match the description given earlier in the mathematical presentation.
- The function method ToStr (lines 15 to 20) is based on the existing IntToStr function.

The result string is constructed by

- creating a string representation of the real part (line 17);

● if the imaginary part is positive, forcing the inclusion of a plus sign (line 18), otherwise a minus sign is automatically included in the next step;

● adding imaginary part to the string followed by the symbol 'i' (line 19).

The method ToComplex (lines 22 to 42) converts a string into the object's complex number. This is much more complicated than the function ToStr to allow for picking out the plus and minus signs that may appear at the front of the number and between the real and imaginary parts:

● The function Pos is used to find the position of a specified character in a string; zero is returned if that character is not in the string. Pos is found in the Delphi system unit, which is available by default.

● The function Copy copies a specified range of a string.

● The code extracts any leading plus or minus (lines 25 to 35); then for all strings sets the local variable Position to the position of the sign separating the real and imaginary parts.

● Positioni is used to indicate the presence of the letter i.

● The string can then be divided up and assigned to the real part (line 39) and the imaginary part (lines 40 and 41).

● This method does not handle incorrectly presented numbers but more code could be added at lines 37 and 38 to deal with errors.

When the methods are called they will be preceded by the name of an instance of this object not the object type. For instance variables AComplex, BComplex and CComplex can be declared as public on a form:

```
type
  TForm1 = class(TForm)
{ other definitions and declarations }
  public
    AComplex,BComplex,CComplex: TComplex;
  end;
```

Then the OnCreate of the form can create instances of the object:

```
procedure TForm1.FormCreate(Sender: TObject);
begin
  AComplex:= TComplex.Create;
  BComplex:= TComplex.Create;
  CComplex:= TComplex.Create;
end;
```

Note there is no Parent property as TComplex is not a visual component. The rudimentary Create that TComplex inherits from TObject does not have an Owner. To ensure the memory allocated is returned the objects should be destroyed at the same time as the form:

```
procedure TForm1.FormDestroy(Sender: TObject);
begin
  AComplex.Free;
  BComplex.Free;
  CComplex.Free;
end;
```

Strictly this is not necessary as the form will be destroyed only at the end of the application when all allocated memory will be reclaimed. However, as indicated earlier, it is good practice to free unwanted memory.

In order to add the values of BComplex to CComplex, giving a value in AComplex, the Add method of AComplex should be called:

```
AComplex.Add(BComplex,CComplex);
```

Likewise to multiply the values of AComplex and BComplex, giving a value in CComplex, the multiply method of CComplex should be called:

```
CComplex.Multiply(AComplex,BComplex);
```

Values can be written and read using the methods ToStr and ToComplex.

10.7.3 A project using TComplex

Here the object TComplex is used to make a simple calculator for adding and multiplying complex numbers.

1. Create a form as shown in Figure 10.6.
2. Use the Object Inspector to make the bottom edit box read only, so the user cannot enter values here.

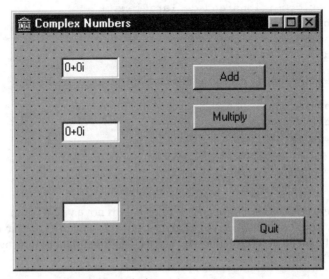

Figure 10.6   A complex number calculator.

3. Using the code developed above, a complete unit can be composed, as shown in Listing 10.16.

Listing 10.16 A unit illustrating the use of TComplex

```
 1: unit U10_16;
 2:
 3: interface
 4:
 5: uses
 6:   Windows, Messages, SysUtils, Classes, Graphics, Controls,
 7:   Forms, Dialogs, StdCtrls;
 8:
 9: type
10:    TComplex = class(TObject)
11: {-----------------------------------------------------------}
12: { Objects of TComplex represent Complex numbers and their  }
13: { operations                                               }
14: {-----------------------------------------------------------}
15:    private
16:       FRealPart: Integer;
17:       FImagPart: Integer;
18:    public
19:       procedure Add(const First,Second: TComplex);
20:       procedure Multiply (const First,Second: TComplex);
21:       function ToStr: string;
22:       procedure ToComplex(AString: string);
23:    end;
24:
25: type
26:    TForm1 = class(TForm)
27:       Edit1: TEdit;
28:       Edit2: TEdit;
29:       Edit3: TEdit;
30:       AddButton: TButton;
31:       MultiplyButton: TButton;
32:       QuitButton: TButton;
33:       procedure FormCreate(Sender: TObject);
34:       procedure FormDestroy(Sender: TObject);
35:       procedure AddButtonClick(Sender: TObject);
36:       procedure MultiplyButtonClick(Sender: TObject);
37:       procedure QuitButtonClick(Sender: TObject);
38:    public
39:       AComplex, BComplex, CComplex: TComplex;
40:    end;
41:
```

```
42: var
43:    Form1: TForm1;
44:
45: implementation
46:
47: {$R *.DFM}
48: procedure TComplex.Add(const First,Second: TComplex);
49: begin
50:    FRealPart:= First.FRealPart+Second.FRealPart;
51:    FImagPart:= First.FImagPart+Second.FImagPart;
52: end;
53:
54: procedure TComplex.Multiply (const First,Second: TComplex);
55: begin
56:    FRealPart:= (First.FRealPart*Second.FRealPart)
57:                     -(First.FImagPart*Second.FImagPart);
58:    FImagPart:= (First.FRealPart*Second.FImagPart)
59:                     +(First.FImagPart*Second.FRealPart);
60: end;
61:
62: function TComplex.ToStr: string;
63: {----------------------------------------------------------}
64: { Converts a complex number to a string                    }
65: {----------------------------------------------------------}
66: begin
67:    Result:= IntToStr(FRealPart);
68:    if FImagPart>=0 then Result:= Result+'+';
69:    Result:= Result+IntToStr(FImagPart)+'i';
70: end;
71:
72: procedure TComplex.ToComplex(AString: string);
73: {----------------------------------------------------------}
74: { Converts a string to a complex number                    }
75: {----------------------------------------------------------}
76: var Position,Positioni: Integer; var Temp: string;
77: begin
78:    Position:= Pos('+',AString);
79:    if Position=0 then
80:      Position:= Pos('-', AString);
81:    if Position=1 then {starts with a + or - }
82:    begin
83:      Temp:= Copy(AString,2,Length(AString)-1);
84:      Position:= Pos('+',Temp);
85:      if Position=0 then
86:        Position:= Pos('-', Temp);
87:      Inc(Position);
```

```
88:     end;
89:     Positioni:= Pos('i',AString);
90:     { error checking should be added to cope with
91:       incorrectly presented numbers}
92:     FRealPart:= StrToInt(Copy(AString,0,Position-1));
93:     FImagPart:= StrToInt(Copy(AString,Position,
94:                             Positioni-Position));
95:   end;
96:
97: procedure TForm1.FormCreate(Sender: TObject);
98: {------------------------------------------------------------}
99: { Create instances of complex numbers                       }
100: {------------------------------------------------------------}
101: begin
102:   AComplex:= TComplex.Create;
103:   BComplex:= TComplex.Create;
104:   CComplex:= TComplex.Create;
105: end;
106:
107: procedure TForm1.FormDestroy(Sender: TObject);
108: {------------------------------------------------------------}
109: { Release the memory allocated for complex numbers          }
110: {------------------------------------------------------------}
111: begin
112:   AComplex.Free;
113:   BComplex.Free;
114:   CComplex.Free;
115: end;
116:
117: procedure TForm1.AddButtonClick(Sender: TObject);
118: {------------------------------------------------------------}
119: { Get the values of two complex numbers, add them and       }
120: { display the result                                        }
121: {------------------------------------------------------------}
122: begin
123:   BComplex.ToComplex(Edit1.Text);
124:   CComplex.ToComplex(Edit2.Text);
125:   AComplex.Add(BComplex,CComplex);
126:   Edit3.Text:= AComplex.ToStr;
127: end;
128:
129: procedure TForm1.MultiplyButtonClick(Sender: TObject);
130: {------------------------------------------------------------}
131: { Get the values of two complex numbers, multiply them and }
132: { display the result                                        }
133: {------------------------------------------------------------}
```

```
134: begin
135:    BComplex.ToComplex(Edit1.Text);
136:    CComplex.ToComplex(Edit2.Text);
137:    AComplex.Multiply(BComplex,CComplex);
138:    Edit3.Text:= AComplex.ToStr;
139: end;
140:
141: procedure TForm1.QuitButtonClick(Sender: TObject);
142: begin
143:    Close;
144: end;
145:
146: end.
```

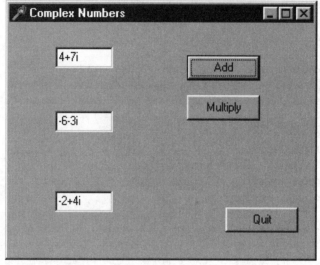

Figure 10.7   Running the complex number calculator.

4. This code can then be used for calculating the result of adding or multiplying two complex numbers: see Figure 10.7.

(10.8) Polymorphism*

Polymorphism literally means having many shapes. In object-oriented programming it means that different objects may respond to the same message in different ways. By default, Delphi methods are static. This means that a reference to a particular method denotes a call to a specific procedure. Polymorphism means that the binding of methods to procedures occurs, dynamically, at run time. The same method can be bound to different procedures depending on the object. We have already seen polymorphism in use when we call constructors, which differ between objects. In this section we will discuss four of the mechanisms Object Pascal supplies that facilitate polymorphism.

10.8.1   Virtual methods

Virtual methods greatly enhance the power of inheritance. It is this mechanism that introduces polymorphism into Delphi. Virtual methods allow the same method to have different code for different objects descended from the same ancestor class. At run time the version of the method that is to be invoked will depend on the object doing the calling.

Each object that inherits a virtual method can override the ancestor's code to enhance or redefine the capabilities, while maintaining the name and parameter list. The type of the object calling will determine which version of the code is executed.

Inheritance is often explained in terms of the animal kingdom and here we provide a simple example of a virtual method.

An object can be declared to define all mammals and methods that are common to all. This object will be based on a class TAnimal that we assume is previously declared. The basic methods of all mammals might include these declarations:

```
type TMammal = class(TAnimal)
public
  procedure Eat(var Food: TFood); virtual;
  procedure Sleep(Time: TTime);
  { other declarations }
end;
```

All mammals sleep in the same way and the method can be defined in the implementation part associated with TMammal. The method by which mammals eat has some basic commonality – the food goes in the mouth – and that can be defined in the implementation part of TMammal.

```
procedure TMammal.Eat(var Food: TFood);
begin
  FoodGoesInMouth;
end;
```

FoodGoesInMouth calls a procedure which defines the general actions of a mammal eating.

However, different animals eat in different ways; for example cows chew the cud, while dogs gnaw bones. Declarations of different animal types could all override the Eat method to include details of the particular species. For example:

```
type TCow = class(TMammal)
public
  procedure Eat(var Food: TFood); override;
end;
```

In the implementation the procedure would be defined as in Listing 10.17.

Listing 10.17 Implementation of TCow.Eat

```
1: procedure TCow.Eat(var Food: TFood);
2: begin
3:   inherited Eat(Food);
4:   ChewCud;
5: end;
```

In Listing 10.17:

- Line 3 calls the method for eating from the ancestor class TAnimal. If this was omitted, an instance of a cow would not have any of the actions for eating associated with TAnimal.

- Line 4 calls a procedure ChewCud, which would define what it is that a cow does. Other lines could be added as appropriate.

In the above example the correct way of eating is chosen depending on the animal.

The constructors for most controls (visual components) are virtual, allowing the correct version of Create to be chosen depending on the object to be created (for example, see the override used in Section 10.3).

10.8.2   Dynamic methods

A dynamic method looks to the programmer identical to a virtual method, with only the word **virtual** replaced by **dynamic**. The run time system handles the two in different ways. A virtual method produces an efficient link while a dynamic method produces slightly less code. Most of the differences are slight and the virtual method is recommended, though if an object has a large number of virtual methods and only a small number of these are overridden by inheriting objects the dynamic method is recommended.

10.8.3   Abstract methods

Sometimes when an object class defines a virtual method there is no generic code that can be provided, the ancestor class merely requiring to mark the name and parameters. The method can be defined as abstract and there is no need to provide any code for the method in the implementation. For example, the object type TAnimal may have a method Grow, for which there is no general statement applicable to the animal kingdom. Adding the following line to the **type** declaration would indicate that inheriting objects could declare an override on a method Grow with a single parameter of type TTime.

```
procedure Grow(Time: TTime); virtual; abstract;
```

There would be no need for any code to appear in the implementation part of TAnimal declaring the actions of Grow.

Only virtual or dynamic methods can be abstract.

10.8.4   Redeclaring methods

Object types can redeclare methods defined in ancestor objects. Redeclaration means that the ancestor method goes out of scope and the new declaration becomes the current one. This follows the same rules of scope as all declarations and is consistent with the Pascal programming model.

In general it is better that, within a family of objects, all methods with the same name take the same number and type of parameters; using virtual methods and overriding them ensures this.

The Create constructor is an example where Delphi does redeclare a method. TObject.Create is virtual and takes no parameters; inheriting objects can override this Create. TComponent inherits from TObject but redeclares Create so as to take the parameter Owner. Note TComponent.Create is defined to be virtual, so that inheriting components can override its actions.

10.9   Summary

In this chapter we have introduced the vocabulary of object-oriented programming, paying particular attention to the definition of objects and the inheritance from one object to another. A customized version of the panel component was defined and later refined to illustrate the creation and destruction of objects. A non-component object was defined that could be used to represent simple complex numbers. A number of methods were defined that would allow operations on complex numbers. In some cases methods were declared to be virtual so as to introduce polymorphism, whereby the version of code used would be chosen at run time depending on the object calling.

Quiz

1. What is an object?
    (a) data
    (b) operations
    (c) data and related operations

2. What is the Owner responsible for?
    (a) displaying a control
    (b) creating an object
    (c) destroying an object

3. What is the Parent responsible for?
    (a) displaying a control
    (b) creating an object
    (c) destroying an object

4. What is the role of a **constructor**?
    (a) destroying objects and freeing their space
    (b) replacing one object with another
    (c) creating and initializing new objects

5. Why when an object is destroyed should its variable be set to **nil**?
    (a) to prevent further attempts to destroy it via `Free`
    (b) so all its contents are set to zero
    (c) to make it disappear from the form

6. What is the scope of things declared private?
    (a) in this unit and in all units using this units
    (b) in this unit but not beyond
    (c) in all units and accessible via the Object Inspector

7. Where in a unit can the **type** statement for an object occur?
    (a) locally in a procedure
    (b) inside another object
    (c) only at the outermost level of scope

8. Consider the expression

    ```
    TOL = class(TOR)
    ```

    What best describes the relationship between TOL and TOR?
    (a) TOR is the `Owner` of TOL
    (b) TOR is the `Parent` of TOL
    (c) TOL inherits from TOR

9. What does overriding a method do?
    (a) extends and refines it
    (b) replaces it
    (c) changes the number of parameters

10. An abstract method is best described as:
    (a) fully defined
    (b) showing a message
    (c) containing no generic code

Exercises

1. Define an object inheriting from `TPanel` that will display a bitmap and a string describing it. Be sure to include a destructor that will be responsible for freeing the memory allocated to the bitmap.

2. Write a program that uses your object and allows the user to place several such objects on a form.

3. Extend the complex number example in Section 10.7.3 so that a graph similar to the one in Figure 10.5 is created for each arithmetic operation performed. Graphs no longer visible should be destroyed.

4. Define an object suitable for representing data on animals (similar to that in Section 8.5) and develop associated operations (for example to amend a name).

5. Define a die object that works like a normal die. Develop a game using the die.

Chapter 11

Exceptions handling

11.1 Introduction

From the earliest chapters we have addressed how to deal with compile time and logical errors. In Appendix A we explain how to use the integrated debugger to track down the elusive bugs. In this chapter we will concentrate on errors that occur at run time.

Most computer users have come across run time errors in some of their applications. Often this is quite dramatic, with the computer freezing and the only way to revive it being to reboot the machine with the loss of any unsaved data.

This chapter explains how Delphi uses exceptions to trap run time errors; this enables them to be fixed or at least allows some clean-up actions before a crash. We will show how programmers can include their own exceptions and handling routines. The use of exception handling will be demonstrated with a project that creates on-screen shapes; the user can drag and drop the shapes into position.

11.2 The `try … except` construct

Earlier chapters have made much use of the function `StrToInt` to convert a text string entered by the user into an integer. If the user has not entered a whole number then an error occurs. When running with integrated debugging turned on, the user is taken into the debugger and an error such as that in Figure 11.1 shows. Beyond the debugger, or when running without it, an error such as the one shown in Figure 11.2 is displayed.

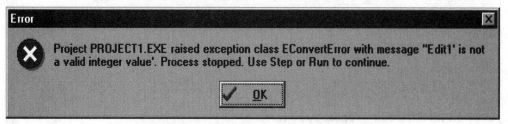

Figure 11.1   A `StrToInt` exception in the debugger.

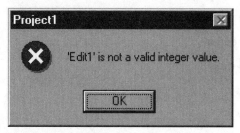

Figure 11.2   A `StrToInt` exception beyond the debugger.

Instead of relying on the exception handling supplied by Delphi, the programmer can write code that will handle such exceptions. In Section 4.10 we developed code that specifically stopped the user entering anything other than a digit. Here we do not dictate what the user can type. If whatever is typed causes an error our exception handler will deal with it, rather than passing it to the Delphi exception handling routines. The example in Listing 11.1 shows how the programmer can incorporate code for dealing with the exception raised when `StrToInt` tries to convert a non-integer.

1. Turn the debugger's exception handling off, as its messages will obscure the programmer's exception handling. This is done in the environment option by ensuring in the Debugging panel (Figure A.4) that Break On Exception is not checked. Alternatively turn the whole of the debugger off, remembering to turn it back on as needed. Appendix A describes the use of the debugger, Figure A.4 shows the page where both Break On Exception and debugging can be turned off.

2. Construct a form with a button (`Button1`) and an edit box (`Edit1`).

3. Create an OnClick event for the button as shown in Listing 11.1.

The **try** ... **except** construct is used to trap an exception that may occur in the **try** clause (from lines 5 and 6) and provides code that deals with any exceptions in the **except** clause (lines 8 and 9). Run this program and enter an integer, say 4, in the edit box, then click the button; the message shown in Figure 11.3 will be displayed. If, on the other hand, an incorrect input is made, an error message such as Figure 11.4 will be displayed.

Listing 11.1) A **try** ... **except** statement

```
 1: procedure TForm1.Button1Click(Sender: TObject);
 2: var Number: Integer;
 3: begin
 4:   try
 5:     Number:= StrToInt(Edit1.Text);
 6:     ShowMessage('that''s: '+IntToStr(Number));
 7:   except
 8:     ShowMessage('that''s not an integer');
 9:     Edit1.Text:= '0';
10:   end;
11: end;
```

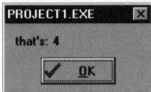
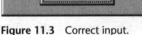

Figure 11.3   Correct input.

Figure 11.4   Erroneous input.

The **except** clause is called as soon as an exception is met. So in Listing 11.1, line 6 is executed only if the edit box contains an integer. Any exception raised in the **try** clause will immediately pass execution to the **except** clause without further execution of the **try** part.

In general when an **except** catches an exception it will be resolved. However, if required, the programmer can *re-raise* the exception, indicating that further action is needed. It is often wiser to specifically list the exceptions that are to be resolved, and raise all others to be dealt with elsewhere, as in Listing 11.2.

Listing 11.2) Re-raising an exception

```
 1: procedure TForm1.Button1Click(Sender: TObject);
 2: var Number: Integer;
 3: begin
 4:   try
 5:     Number:= StrToInt(Edit1.Text);
 6:     ShowMessage('that''s: '+IntToStr(Number));
 7:   except
 8:   on EConvertError do
 9:   begin
10:     ShowMessage('that''s not an integer');
11:     Edit1.Text:= '0';
```

```
12:    end { on EConvertError }
13:    else
14:      raise;
15:    end; { try...except }
16: end;
```

In Listing 11.2:

- Line 8 checks if the exception is an EConvertError and if so handles it.

- Delphi raises an EConvertError when there is a string conversion error: see the online help for more details.

- The **else** at line 13 causes the exception to be re-raised to be dealt with by another exception handler. This may be by the global handler that Delphi supplies or in code provided by the programmer. Section 11.3 will illustrate nested **try** statements.

- Between lines 12 and 13 other conditions can be included to deal with a variety of exceptions.

- The **on ... do** clause allows the programmer to specify which errors are to be handled. Within the **except** clause the structure is as shown in Listing 11.3. If the exception matches *E1* then statement *S1* is executed; if the exception matches *E2* then statement *S2* is executed. All other exceptions are dealt with by the catch-all statement associated with the **else** clause. Where there is no **on** all exceptions are dealt with in the same way, as was the case in Listing 11.1.

(Listing 11.3) Pseudocode for the **on ... do** clause

```
1: except
2: on E1 do statement S1
3: on E2 do statement S2
4: else
5:   catchall statement
6: end {try . . . except}
```

(11.3) The **try ... finally** construct

Sometimes it is impossible for the programmer to deal with the exception. However, it is usually possible to do a final clean-up before the exception is handled elsewhere. For instance, when a program is operating on a file an error may occur with the underlying operating system. By trapping such an error the Delphi programmer can ensure that open files are closed before other error handling occurs. Files that are not properly closed can cause lots of problems for users.

Listing 11.4) A **try ... finally** statement

```
 1: type TRain= array [1..10] of Double;
 2: var RainFile: file of TRain;
 3:     RainGrid: TRain;
 4: procedure TForm1.Button2Click(Sender: TObject);
 5: begin
 6:   if OpenDialog1.Execute then
 7:   begin
 8:     AssignFile(RainFile,OpenDialog1.FileName);
 9:     try
10:       Reset(RainFile);
11:       Read(RainFile,RainGrid);
12:     finally
13:       CloseFile(RainFile);
14:     end;
15:   end;
16: end;
```

The code shown in Listing 11.4 shows the use of **try ... finally** to protect the reading of a file of data.

● Line 1 declares an array type TRain.

● Line 2 declares a file that can hold data of type TRain; this is a binary file, as opposed to the text files we used in Chapter 6.

● Line 6 displays the OpenDialog box. If the user does not select a valid file name, this condition is false and control passes to the end of the procedure (line 16).

● Line 8 assigns the chosen file name to RainFile.

● Lines 9 to 14 are the **try ... finally** statement.

● Line 10 prepares the file for reading and line 11 reads the contents of the file into RainGrid.

● After successfully reading, control passes to the **finally** clause and the file is closed.

● If an exception is raised during the execution of the **try** clause, control passes immediately to the **finally** clause and the CloseFile is executed. This may be because the file that is read has insufficient data. It will not be that the data is of the wrong format, which would require the programmer to perform validation on the binary file.

● Once raised, the exception remains and is passed up to the first level that can handle it, which may well involve terminating the application and may even require the machine to be restarted.

The key difference between the **try ... finally** construct and the **try ... except** construct is that:

● the **finally** clause is always executed, whether there is an exception or not;

● the **except** clause is executed only if an exception occurs.

Delphi allows the nesting of **try** statements. Exceptions are always caught by the nearest (in scope) **finally** or **except** and the associated code executed. The **finally** then passes the exception up to the next level of nesting. An **except** resolves the exception, unless it specifically raises it to the next level. This can be illustrated by the pseudo code in Listing 11.5.

Listing 11.5   Pseudocode for **try** statements

```
 1: try
 2:    statements A
 3:    try
 4:      statements B
 5:      try
 6:        statements C
 7:      except
 8:        statements D
 9:      end
10:    finally
11:      statements E
12:    end
13: except
14:    statements F
15: end
```

In Listing 11.5:

● If an exception is raised during the statements *A* in line 2, the nearest **except** in scope is at line 13 and the statements *F* at line 14 will be executed.

● If no exception happens in line 2, control will pass to the **try** at line 3 and statements *B* will be executed.

● If an exception occurs during line 4, control will pass to the **finally** at line 10 and the statements *E* at line 11 will be executed. A **finally** cannot resolve an exception and it will be raised again and caught by the **except** at line 13, so the statements *F* at line 14 will be executed.

● If no exception happens at line 4, control will pass to the **try** at line 5 and statements *C* will be executed.

● If an exception is raised during statements *C* this will be caught by the **except** at line 7 and statements *D* will be executed.

● Whether or not there are exceptions during statements *B* and *C* the execution will always be followed by the **finally** at line 10 and statements *E*.

- Once an exception occurs in a **try** clause the rest of the statements are not executed, neither are they returned to after the exception is dealt with.
- The **except** clauses may include **on** … **do** clauses (see Listing 11.3).

11.4 Raising an exception

All exceptions descend from the generic Exception object. There are dozens of predefined exceptions inheriting from Exception; see the online help for details. The programmer can write code to raise an exception by using the reserved word **raise** followed by an instance of an exception object. For example:

```
raise EConvertError.Create('Bogus error');
```

will raise an EConvertError, which if not caught by an **except** will display a message similar to the one in Figure 11.5.

Figure 11.5   Bogus error.

Note the following points:

- When an exception handler resolves an exception it then destroys the exception instance. The programmer does not have to destroy an exception instance. Likewise there is no need for the programmer to create an instance variable.
- There are several other constructors defined for exceptions. These provide information that is useful for debuggers and help systems, and which the advanced programmer may wish to interact with. See the online help for more details.

11.5 User-defined exceptions

As with any Delphi object the programmer can define objects that inherit from the class Exception. These exception objects can then be raised within the code.
Consider the declaration:

```
type EMyErr= class(Exception);
```

This inherits all the characteristics of the base type Exception. Following standard practice, this exception identifier starts with a capital E. This exception is raised in code by the following statement:

```
raise EMyErr.Create('err');
```

This will display a message similar to the one in Figure 11.6, which will be provided by the Delphi exception handling. If the programmer calls this statement within a **try** ... **except** statement then the way in which the error is dealt with is at the programmer's discretion.

Figure 11.6 EMyErr.

As with all objects it is possible to modify the methods of the object. Consider the fragment of code in Listing 11.6.

(Listing 11.6) An inherited constructor

```
 1: type EMyErr= class(Exception)
 2:    constructor Create(const Msg: string);
 3: end;
 4:
 5:
 6: implementation
 7:
 8: {$R *.DFM}
 9:
10: constructor EMyErr.Create(const Msg: string);
11: const MyErrCode: Integer=1;
12: begin
13:    inherited Create(Msg);
14:    ShowMessage('this error has occurred '
15:      +IntToStr(MyErrCode)+' times.');
16:    Inc(MyErrCode);
17: end;
```

In Listing 11.6:

● Lines 1 to 3 declare a new object EMyErr based on the existing object Exception.

● Line 2 indicates it has a new constructor Create. The Create inherited from Exception is static and so this is a new declaration rather than an override (see Section 10.8).

- Lines 10 to 17 are the definition of the constructor.
- Line 11 declares a static variable, initially 1, that is incremented in line 16 every time this constructor is called.
- Line 13 inherits Create from the parent Exception.
- Lines 14 and 15 force a message to be shown each time this constructor is called. The message indicates how many times this particular exception has occurred. The message is shown even if the exception is caught by an **except** (more realistically a message would be written to a text file).

11.6 Silent exceptions

All the exceptions seen above will, by default, display a message box. This is not always convenient. A beginner may be frightened by a software package that booms out exceptions; on the other hand an expert user may understand what is happening and see no need for acknowledging a message box.

The exception EAbort is silently handled by the global exception handler. Consider the code in Listing 11.7.

Listing 11.7) A silent exception

```
1: procedure TForm1.Button5Click(Sender: TObject);
2: begin
3:    ShowMessage('1');
4:    raise EAbort.Create('');
5:    ShowMessage('2');
6: end;
```

When the button is clicked by the user, the statement at line 3 will be executed, then the exception at line 4 will be raised, exiting this block of code. The statement at line 5 is not executed.

The EAbort can be nested inside **try** constructs. An **except** or **finally** clause can deal with an EAbort and may not be silent.

A call to the Abort procedure can be used in place of line 4 in Listing 11.7. This has exactly the same effect.

Like all other exceptions, aborts are usually protected by a conditional statement, otherwise the statements after the abort, such as line 5, will never be executed and so may as well not have been written.

11.7 Drag and drop*

The Delphi programmer can write programs that allow the user to create objects, move them around the form, delete selected objects, save the current state of the form or read a previously saved state. There is plenty of scope within this list for exceptions to occur. We will conclude this chapter with an example that performs these operations and provides exception handling where necessary. Before presenting the example we will explain how to program the drag and drop operations.

To see how drag and drop works, create a prototype form with a TShape object on it.

1. Set the name property of the TShape to Circle. Set the shape property of Circle to stCircle, and the brush colour to clBlue, to create a blue circle that can be moved around the form.

2. Set the DragCursor property of Circle to dmAutomatic. If it remains as dmManual then the programmer will have to add extra code to deal with the start and end of the drag.

3. Now ensure the form accepts the dragging of a TShape over it. This is done by creating the OnDragOver event shown in Listing 11.8.

Listing 11.8 OnDragOver

```
1: procedure TForm1.FormDragOver(Sender, Source: TObject;
2:    X, Y: Integer; State: TDragState; var Accept: Boolean);
3: begin
4:    Accept:= (Source is TShape);
5: end;
```

The programmer has merely added line 4. The expression

    (Source is TShape)

evaluates to True if the Source object, that is the one being dragged, is a TShape, otherwise it is False. Recall, from Section 8.8, that the is operator will return True only when the object Source is of type TShape.

4. The Sender object is the form. If several forms were being dragged over, the programmer would have to set the Parent property to the appropriate form for the shape to be displayed.

5. The form must also be prepared to have a TShape dropped on it: see Listing 11.9.

    The programmer adds lines 4 to 9. The conditional at 4 ensures the remaining statements are only performed if the source object is a TShape. Line 5 casts the Source as a TShape and makes it the subject of the **with**. Lines 7 and 8 make the Left and Top of the Source (which is of type TShape) equal to the point (X,Y) where the drop occurred.

6. Save and run the project.

7. Click on the circle and drag it along. Note the following:

    ● The circle does not move with the drag. Instead, a drag cursor appears; when the mouse button is released the circle appears at the drop point.

Listing 11.9 OnDragDrop

```
 1: procedure TForm1.FormDragDrop(Sender, Source: TObject;
 2:   X, Y: Integer);
 3: begin
 4:   if (Source is TShape) then
 5:     with (Source as TShape) do
 6:     begin
 7:       Left:= X;
 8:       Top:= Y;
 9:     end;
10: end;
```

● If the cursor rests on the circle it will change to a prohibited cursor. This is because the code does not have any statements allowing a TShape to be dragged over any TShape (not even itself).

The shape can be made to move with the cursor by amending the form's OnDragOver event to the version shown in Listing 11.10.

Listing 11.10 Moving the shape with the cursor

```
 1: procedure TForm1.FormDragOver(Sender, Source: TObject;
 2:   X, Y: Integer; State: TDragState; var Accept: Boolean);
 3: begin
 4:   Accept:=(Source is TShape);
 5:   if (Source is TShape) then
 6:     with (Source as TShape) do
 7:     begin
 8:       Left:= X;
 9:       Top:= Y;
10:     end;
11: end;
```

The code in lines 5 to 10 is the same as the code that was used in the earlier OnDrop event. The OnDrop event will no longer be needed for this example as the drag moves the shape into position.

The shape can be made to accept its dragging over itself by adding the OnDragOver event shown in Listing 11.11.

Note the following:

● This code accepts movement of a TShape over any visible control (TControl), line 4.

● Sender is what is being moved over; Source is what is moving.

Listing 11.11 Moving the shape over any control

```
 1: procedure TForm1.CircleDragOver(Sender, Source: TObject;
 2:   X, Y: Integer; State: TDragState; var Accept: Boolean);
 3: begin
 4:   Accept:=(Source is TShape) and (Sender is TControl);
 5:   if (Source is TShape) and (Sender is TControl) then
 6:     with (Source as TShape) do
 7:     begin
 8:       Left:=(Sender as TControl).Left+X;
 9:       Top:=(Sender as TControl).Top+Y;
10:     end;
11: end;
```

- Lines 8 and 9 align the `Left` and `Top` of what is being moved in relation to what it is moved over. These will need to be refined if controls (visual components) are nested, to ensure correct positioning with respect to the whole form.

Commercial drawing packages do not always move the whole shape along as the user drags. They often drag along an outline of the shape, only moving the shape when the user drops it. To do this the programmer needs to set the drag mode property to `dmManual` and write special code for starting and finishing dragging.

All controls have methods:

```
BeginDrag
EndDrag
```

which must be called when dragging is required for a control in `dmManual` drag mode. Later versions of Delphi also have an `OnStartDrag` event for controls matching the `OnEndDrag`, which is available in all versions. Full details of the available properties and methods are given in the Delphi help pages. Using combinations of the available commands the Delphi programmer can produce sophisticated object manipulation packages.

11.8 An example*

This example illustrates the creation and destruction of shape objects. The shapes can be dragged around the form. The state of the form can be written to a file and read later. Exception handling is included to prevent the user from adding too many shapes and to deal with any input/output errors.

1. Create a prototype form as shown in Figure 11.7 with a MainMenu, OpenDialog, SaveDialog and ColorDialog. The main menu should have options File and Piece. Suboptions under File include New, Open, Save and Exit. The option under Piece is Add.

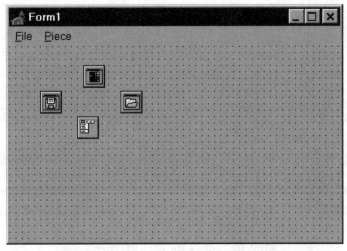

Figure 11.7   Prototype form.

2. In the interface part declare two constants:

```
const MaxShape= 10; {maximum number on the form}
      Sides= 50; {length of side of each shape}
```

to be used throughout the declarations and code.

3. Declare a new object, below the constants:

```
type TCustomShape = class(TShape)
  public
    constructor Create (Owner:TComponent); override;
  private
    fNumber: Cardinal;
end;
```

The field fNumber will be useful if a 'delete piece' procedure is added later (see Exercise 5 at the end of this chapter).

Make sure that the **uses** statement in the interface section includes

```
ExtCtrls
```

so that the project has access to the object TShape (see Section 8.8).

4. Add the constructor for TCustomShape to the implementation part: see Listing 11.12.

Listing 11.12

```
1: constructor TCustomShape.Create (Owner:TComponent);
2: begin
3:    inherited Create(Owner);
4:    DragMode:= dmAutomatic;
```

```
 5:   OnDragOver:= Form1.Shape1DragOver;
 6:   DragCursor:= crDefault;
 7:   Height:= Sides;
 8:   Width:= Sides;
 9:   fNumber:= Form1.Count; {which shape in the order of creation}
10: end;
```

In Listing 11.12:

- Line 3 inherits the `Create` from `TShape`; the lines following customize it.
- Line 4 sets the drag mode, so there is no need to initiate the dragging movement.
- Line 5 sets the `OnDragOver` event to an event associated with `Form1`; this event will be presented below.
- Line 6 makes the drag cursor the default arrow.
- Lines 7 and 8 set the size of the shape.
- Line 9 sets `fNumber`.

5. Declare two record types to be used for reading and writing the data on how the shapes appear: see Listing 11.13.

Listing 11.13

```
 1: type TInfo= record
 2: { vital elements of each shape, its colour,
 3:   position and number }
 4:   IColour: TColor;
 5:   ITop,ILeft: Cardinal;
 6:   INum: Cardinal;
 7: end;
 8:
 9: type TShBank= record
10: { an echo of Shapes on the form used for
11:  reading and writing files }
12:   ShCount: Cardinal;
13:   ShArray: array[1..MaxShape] of TInfo;
14: end;
```

6. Add four declarations to the private section of `TForm`:

```
private
      ShapeArray: array[1..MaxShape] of TCustomShape;
      Count: Cardinal; {number of shapes on form}
      ShBank: TShBank;
      ShapeFile: file of TShBank;
```

Note the following:

- ShapeArray elements will be created and destroyed as shapes appear and are removed from the form.
- Count will keep track of how many shapes are on the form and where in ShapeArray the next one should be created.
- ShBank is a copy of the vital information for each shape, providing input/output data.
- ShapeFile is the file type that is read and written; it is a binary file.

7. Now create the code that allows a shape to be dragged over the form, as shown in Listing 11.14.

Listing 11.14 OnDragOver for form and shape

```
 1: procedure TForm1.FormDragOver(Sender, Source: TObject;
 2:   X, Y: Integer; State: TDragState; var Accept: Boolean);
 3: begin
 4:   Accept:=(Source is TCustomShape);
 5:   if (Source is TCustomShape) then
 6:     with (Source as TCustomShape) do
 7:     begin
 8:       Left:= X;
 9:       Top:= Y;
10:     end;
11: end;
12:
13: procedure TForm1.Shape1DragOver(Sender, Source: TObject;
14:   X, Y: Integer; State: TDragState; var Accept: Boolean);
15: begin
16:   Accept:=(Source is TCustomShape) and (Sender is TControl);
17:   if (Source is TCustomShape) and (Sender is TControl) then
18:     with (Source as TCustomShape) do
19:     begin
20:       Left:=(Sender as TControl).Left+X;
21:       Top:=(Sender as TControl).Top+Y;
22:     end;
23: end;
```

These procedures are similar to those discussed in Section 11.7. Shape1DragOver is not associated with a component on the form and so the programmer must manually add its definition to the declaration of the TForm object. An appropriate place may be the public section at the end of the declaration:

```
public
    procedure Shape1DragOver(Sender, Source: TObject;
        X, Y: Integer; State: TDragState; var Accept: Boolean);
```

8. Add a `Close` statement to the exit option event on the File submenu and initialize `Count` to zero in the Form's `OnCreate` event, see Listing 11.15.

(Listing 11.15) Exit and initialization code

```
1: procedure TForm1.Exit1Click(Sender: TObject);
2: begin
3:   Close;
4: end;
5:
6: procedure TForm1.FormCreate(Sender: TObject);
7: begin
8:   Count:= 0; {no shapes on blank form}
9: end;
```

9. The code for adding shapes to the form can now be entered, see Listing 11.16.

(Listing 11.16) Adding shapes

```
1: procedure TForm1.Add1Click(Sender: TObject);
2: begin
3:   if Count>= MaxShape then
4:     raise Exception.Create('Shape Bank size limit reached');
5:   Inc(Count);
6:   ShapeArray[Count]:= TCustomShape.Create(Self);
7:   with ShapeArray[Count] do
8:   begin
9:     Parent:= Self;
10:    Visible:= False;
11:    {choose a colour then make shape visible}
12:    if ColorDialog1.Execute then
13:      Brush.Color:= ColorDialog1.Color;
14:    Visible:= True;
15:   end {with ShapeArray[Count]}
16: end;
```

In Listing 11.16:

- Line 3 checks if the maximum number of shapes has already been created, and if so raises an exception.
- Line 6 creates a new shape and stores it in the first vacant element of `ShapeArray`. The constructor performs most of the initialization.

- Line 9 sets the parent.
- Line 10 makes the shape invisible while the user chooses the colour (lines 12 and 13); it becomes visible at line 14.

10. Now add the code for saving a file (Listing 11.17).

(Listing 11.17) Saving a file

```
 1: procedure TForm1.Save1Click(Sender: TObject);
 2: var i: Cardinal;
 3: begin
 4:   if SaveDialog1.Execute then
 5:   try
 6:     Assignfile(ShapeFile,SaveDialog1.FileName);
 7:     Rewrite(ShapeFile);
 8:     for i:= 1 to Count do
 9:     begin
10:       ShBank.ShArray[i].IColour:=ShapeArray[i].Brush.Color;
11:       ShBank.ShArray[i].ITop:=ShapeArray[i].Top;
12:       ShBank.ShArray[i].ILeft:=ShapeArray[i].Left;
13:       ShBank.ShArray[i].INum:=ShapeArray[i].fNumber;
14:     end;
15:     ShBank.ShCount:= Count;
16:     Write(ShapeFile,ShBank);
17:   finally
18:     CloseFile(ShapeFile);
19:   end;
20: end;
```

Note the following:

- At design time the programmer could set the filter for SaveDialog1 to a suitable file type for storing shape information, and select the option of OverWriteProtect, so when the user tries to overwrite an existing file, the write must be verified.
- Line 4 of Listing 11.17 causes the SaveDialog box to be open. The other lines of the procedure are executed only if the user selects a file.
- The writing to the file is protected by the **try** ... **finally** clause.
- Lines 6 and 7 ready the file for writing.
- Lines 8 to 15 copy all the vital data into ShBank.
- Line 16 writes the information.
- Line 18 closes the file at the end of a successful write, or if an error occurs.

11. The code for opening a previously written file is given in Listing 11.18.

Listing 11.18 Opening a previously written file

```
 1: procedure TForm1.Open1Click(Sender: TObject);
 2: var i: Cardinal;
 3: begin
 4:   if OpenDialog1.Execute then
 5:   try
 6:     { free the previously assigned shapes }
 7:     for i:= 1 to Count do
 8:       ShapeArray[i].Free;
 9:     Assignfile(ShapeFile,OpenDialog1.FileName);
10:     Reset(ShapeFile);
11:     Read(ShapeFile,ShBank);
12:     {assign the newly read shapes}
13:     Count:=ShBank.ShCount;
14:     for i:=1 to Count do
15:     begin
16:       ShapeArray[i]:=TCustomShape.Create(Self);
17:       ShapeArray[i].Parent:=Self;
18:       ShapeArray[i].Brush.Color:=ShBank.Sharray[i].IColour;
19:       ShapeArray[i].Top:=ShBank.Sharray[i].ITop;
20:       ShapeArray[i].Left:=ShBank.Sharray[i].ILeft;
21:       ShapeArray[i].fNumber:=ShBank.Sharray[i].INum;
22:     end;
23:   finally
24:     CloseFile(ShapeFile);
25:   end;
26: end;
```

In Listing 11.18:

- Line 4 causes the OpenDialog box to be displayed. The other lines of the procedure are executed only if the user selects a file. As with the SaveDialog the programmer could set the filter and other properties at design time.

- Lines 7 and 8 destroy all existing shapes. It may be prudent to add code here that asks if the user wants to save this pattern before destroying it.

- The reading from the file is protected by the **try ... finally** clause.

- Lines 9 and 10 prepare the file for reading at line 11.

- Lines 13 to 22 copy all the vital data from ShBank, with line 16 creating a new object for each shape.

- Line 24 closes the file, whether reading has been successful or not.

12. The code for the option New is a subset of the above, see Listing 11.19.

13. Save and run the program.

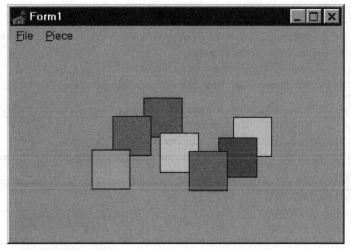

Figure 11.8 The running program.

Listing 11.19 Complete unit to demonstrate **for** loops

```
1: procedure TForm1.New1Click(Sender: TObject);
2: var i: Cardinal;
3: begin
4:    for i:= 1 to Count do
5:        ShapeArray[i].Free;
6:    Count:= 0;
7: end;
```

The user can create a variety of patterns, such as the one shown in Figure 11.8.

This program can be refined in a number of ways, including adding facilities to delete shapes, change their colour, texture and outline (see Exercise 5 at the end of this chapter).

11.9 Summary

In this chapter we have shown how Delphi uses exceptions to trap run time errors. By trapping these errors the programmer is sometimes able to fix them and let processing continue. In other cases the programmer can only perform clean-up actions before the program closes down.

We have shown the programmer how to drag and drop objects around the form. The final example in this chapter includes dragging shapes around the form and incorporates exception handling to produce a robust piece of software.

Quiz

1. Which of the following causes the **finally** clause of a **try** statement to be executed?
    (a) only an exception in the **try** clause
    (b) only successful completion of the **try** clause
    (c) either an exception in the **try** clause or successful completion of the **try** clause

2. Which of the following causes the **except** clause of a **try** statement to be executed?
    (a) only an exception in the **try** clause
    (b) only successful completion of the **try** clause
    (c) either an exception in the **try** clause or successful completion of the **try** clause

3. By default all exceptions, except one, display a message box. Which exception does not display a message box?
    (a) EDivByZero
    (b) EIntOverflow
    (c) EAbort

4. How can the debugger be prevented from intercepting exceptions?
    (a) by turning the debugger off
    (b) by ensuring the environment option Break On Exception is not checked
    (c) by using a **try** statement

5. What does the statement:

    ```
    raise EDivByZero.Create('Divide by zero error');
    ```

    do?
    (a) If the program attempts to execute a divide by zero it shows the message 'Divide by zero error'.
    (b) If the program attempts to execute a divide by zero it raises the error to be handled by the first in scope EDivByZero exception handler.
    (c) It raises the error to be handled by the first in scope EDivByZero exception handler.

6. Why is it not necessary to protect the creation of an object with a **try** statement?
    (a) If the creation of an object fails, Free is automatically called.
    (b) Object creation never fails.
    (c) A partly created object never consumes any resources.

7. For an object to be dragged, which of the following must be true?
    (a) The object must be in drag mode dmAutomatic.
    (b) The object must be in drag mode dmManual, and BeginDrag executed.
    (c) The DragCursor must be crDefault.

8. Which of the following can an object of type TShape be dragged over?
    (a) any object
    (b) only the form
    (c) any object that accepts (Source **is** TShape)

9. What does the OnDragDrop event do?
    (a) It moves the object to the final resting place.

(b)   It specifies what happens when the user drops the object.

(c)   It does nothing.

10.   Why should the writing of a file be protected by a **try** statement?

(a)   in case the user opens the wrong file

(b)   because an error may occur in the underlying hardware

(c)   because an error might occur in the operating system

Exercises

1.   Write an exception handler that catches range check errors and displays a suitable message. All other exceptions should be passed to the global event handlers.

2.   In Section 6.9 we developed a project that merged two files and wrote to a third. Add exception handling to this to make it more robust.

3.   Put a button and a panel on a form, allow both of them to be dragged over the form, and raise an exception if the user attempts to drag the button over the panel.

4.   Develop a project with two forms which allows an object initially on the second form to be dragged onto the first form.

5.   Refine the program in Section 11.8 to include facilities to delete shapes or to change their colour, texture and outline.

6.   The function TComplex.ToStr presented in Section 10.7.2 does not deal with incorrectly entered numbers; add an exception handler to deal with such errors.

Chapter 12

Enumerated types and sets

12.1 Introduction

In this chapter we introduce the related topics of enumerated types and sets. We will illustrate their use with two Delphi components: check boxes and radio buttons. An enumerated type is an ordered list of elements, while a set is an unordered collection of elements. The set concept is based on the mathematical set and Pascal provides a set type for defining sets and operations for manipulating them. Delphi check boxes provide a suitable interface when a user has to choose some options from a set, while radio buttons are useful when selecting one and only one option from a set. Windows users will be familiar with both radio buttons and check boxes, as they are used by many applications. For example, the print dialog box in Figure 12.1 uses radio buttons to allow the user to select the page range, and check boxes to choose the options of printing to file and collating.

12.2 Enumerated types

Pascal enables the programmer to create user-defined types. We have seen a number of user-defined types in earlier chapters, including subranges, arrays and records. An

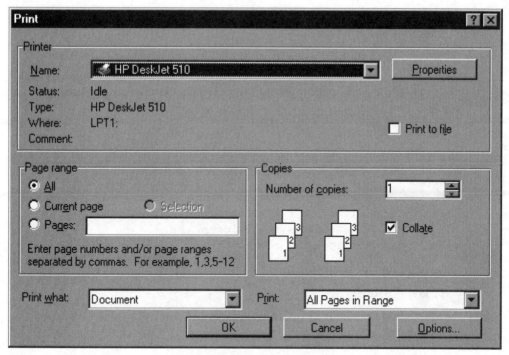

Figure 12.1   A Windows print box with radio buttons and check boxes.

enumerated type is defined by an ordered list of names representing constant values of that type. For example, a type to represent days of the week can be defined as:

```
type TDays = (Monday,Tuesday,Wednesday,Thursday,
                    Friday,Saturday,Sunday);
```

It is important to realize that the enumeration constant Monday is neither a string nor a variable. An enumeration is more like a literal value such as True or 72. The order in which the enumeration is presented is important as this dictates the underlying ordinal value. An enumerated type is an example of an *ordinal type*.

An ordinal type is one where each value (except the first) has a unique predecessor and each value (except the last) has a unique successor. Integer, Char and Boolean are all examples of predefined ordinal types, but real types and strings are not ordinal. For example, the character 'D' is preceded by 'C' and followed by 'E'. However, it is not possible to say definitively what real number immediately precedes or follows the number 1.123.

The function Ord can be applied to any ordinal type, including enumerations. For example, with the type TDays

- Ord(Monday) returns 0

- Ord(Tuesday) returns 1

- Ord(Wednesday) returns 2

- Ord(Thursday) returns 3

- `Ord(Friday)` returns 4
- `Ord(Saturday)` returns 5
- `Ord(Sunday)` returns 6

the value returned is a `LongInt` in all versions of Delphi. The range of `LongInt` (up to 2,147,483,647) provides the only limitation on the number of elements in an enumeration.

```
var Today: TDays;
```

declares a variable of the enumerated type `TDays`. Values can be assigned to such variables, which can be incremented and decremented:

```
Today:= Tuesday;
Inc(Today); {Today is now Wednesday}
Inc(Today,2); {Today is now Friday}
Dec(Today,4); {Today is now Monday}
```

Values and variables can also be used in relational expressions such as:

```
Today > Wednesday
```

which would be false if the value of `Today` was `Monday`.

A statement such as

```
Dec(Today,9);
```

will compile but will raise an exception at run time, if range checking is turned on (see Chapter 7).

Arrays can be indexed by an enumerated type. For example, given a record type containing meteorological data:

```
type TWeather= record
                 Rain: Single;
                 Wind: 0..15;
               end;
```

an array type for a whole week can be declared as

```
type TWeek= array[TDays]of TWeather;
```

The range `Monday..Sunday` could replace `TDays` in the above.

A variable of type `TWeek` can be declared as

```
var WeekWeather: TWeek;
```

All items in `WeekWeather` can be initialized using a **for** statement, such as this:

```
for Today:= Monday to Sunday do
  with WeekWeather[Today] do
  begin
    Rain:= 0;
    Wind:= 0;
  end;
```

The programmer can develop other operations to be used with variables of types TDays, TWeek and TWeather which could be encapsulated with the type to make a new object.

12.3 A brief introduction to sets and set operations

The set of activities offered at a leisure centre is an example of a set, assuming that the term *activities* is sufficiently defined. The set of activities undertaken by a lazy person may be an example of an empty set. A leisure centre user may wish to construct a set of all his or her activities in the last year. The set does not distinguish if an activity has been undertaken more than once, merely whether or not the user has participated in it. For example the set may be

[Judo, Badminton, Fencing]

The sportsman in this example may wish to compare his set of activities with a friend's. Her set may be

[Badminton, Aerobics, Tennis, Judo, Trampolining]

The *intersection* of the sets is those elements they have in common:

[Badminton, Judo]

The *union* of the sets is all the elements:

[Badminton, Aerobics, Fencing, Tennis, Judo, Trampolining]

The order of elements within a set is unimportant; this is quite different from structures such as arrays and records where order is important.

In mathematics, curly braces are usually used to denote sets, but Delphi uses curly braces to enclose comments. So here we have used square brackets to hold elements of a set.

12.4 The set type

The order of elements in a set is of no significance. However, Pascal requires the set to be defined on a base type. The general form of a declaration of a set type is

```
set type = set of base ordinal type;
```

where *base ordinal type* may be any type including an enumerated one. So it is possible to declare a set based on the days of the week:

```
type TSetDays = set of TDays;
```

It is important to remember that variables of type TSetDays are not ordered.

In all versions of Delphi the number of elements in the *base ordinal type* can be up to 256. If it is a subrange of integers the largest number must not exceed 256.

It is possible to use an anonymous type; for example a type for a set of activities might be

```
type TSetExample = set of (Badminton, Aerobics, Fencing, Tennis,
                    Volleyball, Judo, Karate, Trampolining,
                    Basketball, Dance);
```

the round brackets delimiting the possible literal values of the set. An anonymous type is inflexible in its use, so it is better practice to create an enumeration and then base the set type on that. Replacing the above TSetExample with

```
type TActivities = (Badminton, Aerobics, Fencing, Tennis,
                    Volleyball, Judo, Karate, Trampolining,
                    Basketball, Dance);

type TSetActivities = set of TActivities;
```

provides a more flexible type.

Within code, values can be assigned to variables of types TSetActivities and TSetDays. For example, if the following variables are now declared:

```
var HisActivities, HerActivities, OurActivities: TSetActivities;
    HerBusyDays, HisBusyDays, OurBusyDays, OurFreeDays: TSetDays;
```

then the statements

```
OurActivities:= [];
OurFreeDays:= [];
```

assign the empty set to the variables OurActivities and OurFreeDays. Note that empty square brackets are used to denote the empty set. Then the assignments

```
HisActivities:= [Judo, Badminton, Fencing];
HerActivities:= [Badminton, Aerobics, Tennis, Judo, Trampolining];
HerBusyDays:= [Monday];
HisBusyDays:= [Saturday, Sunday];
```

assign the sets of activities undertaken and the days on which the pair are busy. The set elements are enclosed in square brackets.

Set operations can be defined on these variables. The activities in which both have participated are found using the intersection operation, represented by the * symbol:

```
OurActivities:= HisActivities * HerActivities;
```

The days that one or other is busy are found using the union operator (+):

```
OurBusyDays:= HisBusyDays + HerBusyDays;
```

It is not possible to perform set operations between HisActivities and HisBusyDays because they are of incompatible base types.

There is also a difference operation (−) which removes elements from a set:

```
[Monday,Tuesday,Saturday] - [Wednesday,Tuesday]
```

will evaluate to [Monday, Saturday].

The **in** operator tests if the left operand is a member of the set to the right. The following code will show an appropriate message as to whether he is busy or not on Monday.

```
if Monday in HisBusyDays then
    ShowMessage('not Monday')
else
    ShowMessage('Monday ok');
```

The operand on the left of the **in** is not a set; it is an element of the set.

Consider the fragment of code in Listing 12.1.

Listing 12.1) Code fragment

```
1: for Today:= Monday to Sunday do
2:    if not(Today in OurBusyDays) then
3:       OurFreeDays:= OurFreeDays + [Today];
```

- The variable Today is of the enumerated type TDays.
- The variables OurBusyDays and OurFreeDays are of type TSetDays which is based on the enumeration TDays.
- As TDays is ordinal it is acceptable to use a variable of that type as the control variable in a **for** loop, at line 1. A variable of type TSetDays could not be used.
- The variable Today is made into a one-element set by putting square brackets round it in line 3. It can then be used in the union operation.

Relational operators can also be used with sets, as outlined below:

=	(equality)	Returns true if the sets are equal, i.e. their members are the same.
<>	(not equal)	Returns true if the sets differ (even by a single element).
<=	(subset)	Returns true if all the elements of the first set are in the second.
>=	(superset)	Returns true if all the elements of the second set are in the first.

(12.5) The radio group

Delphi provides a RadioButton component on the Standard page. A radio button is used to represent Yes/No or True/False options. Only one radio button can be selected at a time within the parent. Radio buttons are usually grouped together on a parent group box or panel. Alternatively the programmer can choose the RadioGroup component, which encapsulates both group and radio buttons.

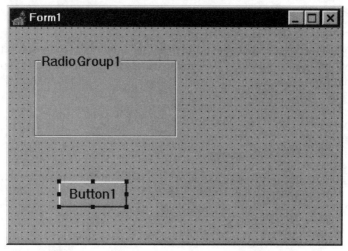

Figure 12.2   Prototype form.

The following steps place a RadioGroup on a form and list the options as days of the week.

1. Put a button and a RadioGroup onto a prototype form, see Figure 12.2.
2. With the RadioGroup selected, double click on the Items property in the Object Inspector to produce the String List Editor. Enter seven strings corresponding to the names of the days of the week, then press OK. This is a similar process to that used in Section 9.13 for setting lines of memo box.
3. Set the ItemIndex property for the RadioGroup to 0, so the first radio button is the default selected.
4. The project can now be run. When the user clicks one radio button it turns on and the other turns off. As no other code is implemented, that is all the project does.
5. Code can be associated with the OnClick event of Button1 to illustrate the use of radio buttons: see Listing 12.2.

(**Listing 12.2**) Example of the use of radio buttons
_____

```
1: procedure TForm1.Button1Click(Sender: TObject);
2: begin
3:   case RadioGroup1.ItemIndex of
4:   0: ShowMessage('Today''s Monday');
5:   1: ShowMessage('Today''s Tuesday');
6:   2: ShowMessage('Today''s Wednesday');
7:   3: ShowMessage('Today''s Thursday');
8:   4: ShowMessage('Today''s Friday');
9:   5: ShowMessage('Today''s Saturday');
```

```
10:    6: ShowMessage ('Today''s Sunday');
11:    else
12:       ShowMessage ('invalid');
13:    end;
14:
15:    if RadioGroup1.Items.Strings[RadioGroup1.ItemIndex]
16:                   = 'Monday' then
17:       ShowMessage ('Today''s Monday')
18:    else
19:       ShowMessage ('some other day');
20: end;
```

In Listing 12.2:

- Line 3 is a **case** on the index to the radio buttons.

- The numbers could be replaced by a call on the function Ord, for example by replacing line 4 with:

  ```
  Ord(Monday): ShowMessage('Today''s Monday');
  ```

- The radio buttons can be moved around within the box but there is a danger that the programmer will make a mistake with matching the index to the enumeration. The code at line 15 examines the string associated with the radio button to ensure the correct button is on. However, a case statement cannot be used here as a string is not an ordinal type.

- A **with** statement around the conditional at line 15 would save having to repeat RadioGroup1.

6. Definition of a function StrToDay, as in Listing 12.3, will make it easier to deal with this enumerated type.

Listing 12.3) StrToDay

```
1: function StrToDay(DayStr:string): TDays;
2: begin
3:    if CompareText(DayStr,'Monday')=0 then
4:       StrToDay:= Monday
5:    else if CompareText(DayStr,'Tuesday')=0 then
6:       StrToDay:= Tuesday
7:    else if CompareText(DayStr,'Wednesday')=0 then
8:       StrToDay:= Wednesday
9:    else if CompareText(DayStr,'Thursday')=0 then
10:       StrToDay:= Thursday
11:    else if CompareText(DayStr,'Friday')=0 then
12:       StrToDay:= Friday
13:    else if CompareText(DayStr,'Saturday')=0 then
14:       StrToDay:= Saturday
```

```
15:   else if CompareText(DayStr,'Sunday')=0 then
16:      StrToDay:= Sunday
17:   else
18:      raise EConvertError.Create(DayStr+ ' is not a day');
19: end;
```

In Listing 12.3:

- The function `CompareText` performs a non-case-sensitive string comparison. This allows the user to enter the day of the week with or without capital letters.

- The exception `EConvertError` is the one used with `IntToStr` errors.

7. This new function will then allow the **case** statement in Listing 12.2 to be replaced by the more meaningful statement in Listing 12.4.

(Listing 12.4) Revised **case** statement

```
1: case StrToDay(RadioGroup1.Items.Strings
2:         [RadioGroup1.ItemIndex])of
3: Monday:    ShowMessage('Today''s Monday');
4: Tuesday:   ShowMessage('Today''s Tuesday');
5: Wednesday: ShowMessage('Today''s Wednesday');
6: Thursday:  ShowMessage('Today''s Thursday');
7: Friday:    ShowMessage('Today''s Friday');
8: Saturday:  ShowMessage('Today''s Saturday');
9: Sunday:    ShowMessage('Today''s Sunday');
10: else
11:   ShowMessage ('invalid');
12: end;
```

We will add to this example in the next section.

(12.6) Check boxes

The CheckBox component represents a Windows check box and allows the programmer to offer the user options to select or not. Unlike radio buttons the user can select several check boxes within a parent or none at all. Check boxes can be grouped together on a group box or panel; alternatively they can be placed directly on the form. On the Additional page of newer versions of Delphi there is a CheckListBox component that works in the same manner as the RadioGroupBox. Here we will illustrate how check boxes can be created and placed on a panel at run time, a technique particularly useful with earlier versions of Delphi, or where check boxes are to be grouped with other controls on the same parent, such as in the print box shown in Figure 12.1.

1. This can be added to the earlier project illustrating the use of radio buttons.

2. Add a scroll box from the Additional page of the Component Palette. This will allow the user to scroll up and down the list of check boxes created, saving having to resize the box if the list becomes too long.

3. Add the type definitions for activities below the implementation part:

```
type TActivities= (Badminton, Aerobics, Fencing, Tennis,
                   Volleyball, Judo, Karate, Trampolining,
                   Basketball, Dance);
type TSetActivities= set of TActivities;
```

and a variable declaration for an array of check boxes:

```
var ArrayChecks: array [Badminton..Dance] of TCheckBox;
```

This array will be indexed using the enumeration of TActivities. So the first element will be

```
ArrayChecks [Badminton]
```

and the tenth element will be

```
ArrayChecks [Dance]
```

4. The enumerations are not strings and cannot be used for captions, so a function needs to be developed that will convert the enumeration to the corresponding string: see Listing 12.5.

   Because variables of the type TActivities are ordinal, a **case** statement can be used to match the string to the enumeration. This is neater than Listing 12.3

Listing 12.5) SportToStr

```
 1: function SportToStr (Sport: TActivities):string;
 2: begin
 3:   case Sport of
 4:   Badminton:    SportToStr:= 'Badminton';
 5:   Aerobics:     SportToStr:= 'Aerobics';
 6:   Fencing:      SportToStr:= 'Fencing';
 7:   Tennis:       SportToStr:= 'Tennis';
 8:   Volleyball:   SportToStr:= 'Volleyball';
 9:   Judo:         SportToStr:= 'Judo';
10:   Karate:       SportToStr:= 'Karate';
11:   Trampolining:SportToStr:= 'Trampolining';
12:   Basketball:   SportToStr:= 'Basketball';
13:   else
14:      SportToStr:= 'Dance'
15:   end;
16: end;
```

where nested **if** statements were needed because the choice was based on the string DayStr.

5. The array of check boxes can be created at the same time as the form by using the OnCreate event of the form: see Listing 12.6.

Listing 12.6) Creating check boxes

```
 1: procedure TForm1.FormCreate(Sender: TObject);
 2: const Count:Integer=5; Gap=5;
 3: var Activity:TActivities;
 4: begin
 5:   for Activity:= Badminton to Dance do
 6:   begin
 7:     ArrayChecks[Activity]:= TCheckBox.Create(Self);
 8:     with ArrayChecks[Activity] do
 9:     begin
10:       Parent:= ScrollBox1;
11:       Top:= Count;
12:       Inc (Count,20);
13:       Left:= Gap;
14:       Caption:= SportToStr(Activity);
15:       Width:= 100;
16:     end;
17:   end;
18: end;
```

In Listing 12.6:

- Lines 1, 4 and 18 are automatically generated for the event handler.

- The static constant Count is used to spread the check boxes down the parent and the constant Gap is used to move the check boxes slightly to the left of the parent.

- The variable Activity of type TActivities is used as an enumerated type control variable, taking values from Badminton to Dance in the **for** loop from lines 5 to 17.

- Line 7 creates the check boxes with Self (the form) as the Owner.

- The **with** construct from lines 8 to 16 is a convenience to save repeated typing of ArrayChecks [Activity].

- Line 10 sets the parent to the scroll box, so the check boxes will only appear within the scroll box.

- Lines 11 and 12 spread the check boxes out.

- Line 13 ensures the check box is not flush with the edge of the parent.

- Line 14 uses the `SportToStr` function to set the caption to a string equivalent of the activity.

- Line 15 sets the width of the caption to be wider than the default, in order to accommodate the longer names of some sports.

6. When the program is run, the user can check the boxes associated with the activities listed. These values can then be manipulated. Adding a second button and the code in Listing 12.7 will illustrate this.

Listing 12.7 Count of number of activities

```
 1: procedure TForm1.Button2Click(Sender: TObject);
 2: var Activity:TActivities; MyActivities:TSetActivities;
 3:     Sum: Integer;
 4: begin
 5:   MyActivities:= [];
 6:   for Activity:= Badminton to Dance do
 7:   begin
 8:     if ArrayChecks[Activity].Checked then
 9:       MyActivities:= MyActivities+ [Activity];
10:   end;
11:   Sum:= 0;
12:   for Activity:=Badminton to Dance do
13:     if Activity in MyActivities then
14:       Inc(Sum);
15:   ShowMessage ('You do: '+IntToStr(Sum)+ ' Activities');
16: end;
```

In Listing 12.7:

- Lines 1, 4 and 16 are automatically generated for the event handler.

- The variable `Activity` is used as a control variable for the two **for** loops in lines 6 to 10 and 12 to 14.

- The set variable `MyActivities` is initialized to the empty set at line 5.

- The variable `Sum` is initialized to 0 at line 11.

- Lines 8 and 9 test if the check property of the check box is true, and if it is, add it to the set of `MyActivities`. Square brackets have to be put around the variable `Activity` in line 9 to convert it into a one-element set. These have a different purpose from the square brackets in line 8, which indicate an array index.

- Lines 12 to 14 iterate round all the activities.

- Line 13 checks if the current activity is in the set `MyActivities`, and if so `Sum` is incremented in line 14.

- Line 15 causes a simple message to be displayed indicating the number of sports played.

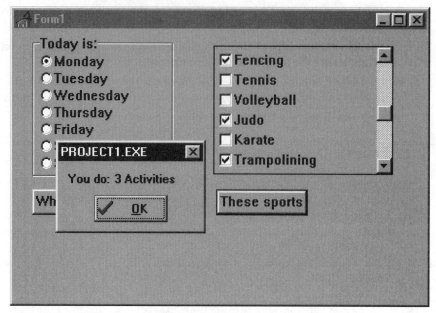

Figure 12.3 Radio buttons and check boxes.

The running form illustrating radio buttons and check boxes is shown in Figure 12.3.

12.7 Variant records*

In Chapter 8 we introduced the concept of records. Pascal offers the programmer the opportunity to construct variant records, whereby records of the same type can have different fields. To use these it is usual to access the variant part via an enumerated type and so we have delayed explanation until this chapter.

Variant records are of less use in an object-oriented language as programmers often find the use of inheritance (see Chapter 10) a better way to present slightly different articles. A variant record should not be confused with a variant type; the latter is a type introduced in Delphi 2 that can be used when the programmer does not know the type of a variable at run time (normally due to interactions with other systems).

The code in Listing 12.8 shows an extension to the Animal record developed in Chapter 8, whereby different data is stored depending on the sex of the animal.

Listing 12.8 A variant record

```
1: type
2:    TAnimalRec = record
3:      Name: string;
```

```
 4:        Species: string;
 5:        DoB: TDate;
 6:        case Sex:TSex of
 7:          Male:    (Mate: ShortString);
 8:          Female: (OffSpring: Integer);
 9:          Unknown:(CheckAgain: Boolean);
10:    end;
```

Lines 6 to 9 are the variant part of the record. Note the following:

- A record can have only one variant part.
- The variant declaration must be at the end of the record.
- The tag field (Sex above) cannot be a long string or of type variant and is normally an enumerated type. In this example TSex is an enumerated type, declared as

  ```
  type TSex = (Male, Female, Unknown);
  ```

- A field within the variant cannot be a long string or of type variant, although short strings are acceptable as shown in line 7. Delphi 1 does not offer long strings or variant types and so this is not a problem for Delphi 1 programmers.

The variant fields of a record AAnimal, which is of type TAnimalRec, can be set using assignment statements:

```
AAnimal.Sex:= Unknown;
AAnimal.CheckAgain:= False;
```

Code can also be developed to access the variant fields: for example, see Listing 12.9.

When the code is executed, depending on the value of Sex various messages will be displayed.

Listing 12.9 Accessing variant fields

```
 1: with AAnimal do
 2: begin
 3:   case Sex of
 4:   Male:    Edit1.Text:= Mate;
 5:   Female: Edit1.Text:= IntToStr(OffSpring);
 6:   Unknown:
 7:           if CheckAgain then
 8:              Edit1.Text:= 'Check again'
 9:           else
10:              Edit1.Text:= 'not known';
11:   end;
12: end;
```

12.8 Summary

In this chapter we have introduced the concepts of enumerated types and sets. The use of these concepts in Delphi has been explained. The `RadioButton` and `CheckBox` components have been introduced along with their grouped counterparts. We have shown how enumerated types can be used to access the fields of variant records.

Quiz

1. Which of the following types are ordinal?
   (a) sets
   (b) enumerations
   (c) real numbers

2. The intersection of two sets gives:
   (a) the elements that appear in both the first and the second set
   (b) all elements that appear in either set
   (c) the elements that appear in only one of the two sets

3. What is the maximum number of elements in a variable of enumerated type?
   (a) 16
   (b) 256
   (c) 2,147,483,647

4. What is the maximum number of elements in a variable of set type?
   (a) 16
   (b) 256
   (c) 2,147,483,647

5. Within a group of radio buttons how many buttons can be selected?
   (a) 0
   (b) 1
   (c) any number

6. Within a group of check boxes how many buttons can be selected?
   (a) 0
   (b) 1
   (c) any number

7. In Object Pascal what is the representation of the empty set?
   (a) `nil`
   (b) { }, curly brackets
   (c) [ ], square brackets

8. Which of the following types can the tag field of a variant record be?
   (a) variant
   (b) string
   (c) enumerated

9. What programming concept may be preferable to the use of variant records?
    (a) inheritance
    (b) strings
    (c) arrays

10. Which operator is used to check if an element belongs to a set?
    (a) `in`
    (b) `as`
    (c) `is`

Exercises

1. Define an enumerated type for months of the year, allow the user to enter a month name via an edit box and display it in a message box.

2. Extend the previous exercise so that the month names can be entered in both full and abbreviated forms or as a number (for example January, Jan or 1).

3. Define a set of Greek islands, and write a program that uses check boxes for the user to indicate islands a tourist would like to visit.

4. Within a team of programmers various skills may be required (for example Delphi, networks and databases). Define a set type that will be used to indicate which skills a team member has. Create a suitable data structure for storing records of team members.

5. Using enumerated types define an object that can be used to represent playing cards. Include a procedure `Shuffle` that will list all 52 cards in random order.

Chapter 13

Units and modular programming

13.1 Introduction

Within a Delphi project each form has an associated unit, but a unit need not have a form. In Chapter 8 we showed how additional forms and their associated units could be added to a project. In this chapter we will demonstrate how Delphi units are used to provide libraries of useful objects and operations. Units allow modular programming and we show how a large unit can be divided into smaller logically related units. We describe how objects can be used within a modular programming environment.

13.2 The structure of a unit

Units are the building blocks of modular programming. The concept is seen across a number of high-level programming languages, under a number of different names. In Modula-2 they are called modules, while in Ada they are called packages. Common to all is the division of the module into two sections, that is perhaps best presented by analogy. In a restaurant the menu is available for all to inspect; those who like what is on offer can buy and eat the food. The recipes are a closely guarded secret and made available only to the staff of the restaurant. Likewise with modular programming a module has a *Menu* part that can be inspected and those with the wherewithal can use the module, but the way in which the module is implemented is not generally available.

A Delphi unit has two distinct sections: the interface part and the implementation part. Consider two units called AUnit and BUnit; anything listed in the interface part of AUnit is available to BUnit, if BUnit includes AUnit in its uses list. BUnit does not have access to the implementation part of AUnit. So the interface part can be seen as the public side of AUnit while the implementation part is private, hidden from all others.

All Delphi units have the same basic structure, as summarized in Listing 13.1.

Listing 13.1 The basic structure of a unit

```
 1: unit identifier;
 2: interface
 3: uses list of units;
 4: public declarations
 5: implementation
 6: uses list of units used locally;
 7: private declarations
 8: implementation of procedures and functions
 9: initialization
10: initialization code
11: finalization
12: final code
13: end.
```

In Listing 13.1:

- Line 1 is the unit header, which contains the reserved word **unit** followed by the unit's name. Normally the unit name matches the file name where the Pascal code is kept (the .pas file).

- Line 2 contains the reserved word **interface**. The interface part of a unit is in scope to other units or applications that use this unit.

- The **uses** statement can appear in two places: immediately after **interface**, line 3 in Listing 13.1, or immediately after **implementation**, line 6 in the listing. It indicates the other units that this unit needs to access. These may be systems units, such as SysUtils, which Delphi automatically includes in the uses lists for most Delphi programs. Alternatively these may be units a programmer has written, as part of this or another project. The **uses** in line 6 (within the implementation part) lists units used just by this unit. Anything that will be needed by other units as a result of importing from this unit must be listed in the interface part of this unit.

- The remainder of the interface part consists of declarations. These declarations include constants, data types, objects, variables, procedures and functions. All things declared in the interface part are available to other units that use this one. The code for procedures and functions declared in the interface part is defined (or implemented) in the implementation part.

- The interface part finishes at the word **implementation**, line 5, which also marks the start of the implementation part.

- Everything declared in the interface part is accessible in the implementation part.

- Anything declared in the implementation part is available throughout the current unit (unit wide), but not beyond.

- The full code (implementation) of routines declared in the interface part appears in the implementation part.

- The header of every routine defined in the implementation part either must exactly match the declaration in the interface part, or can take a *short form*, where parameters and return values are omitted. Use of the short form can lead to confusion when debugging code, and the short form should be used with caution. Procedures declared in the implementation part must use the long form of the declaration.

- Following the implementation part there are two optional sections: the initialization part and the finalization part.

- The optional initialization part can be used to initialize data used within the unit. Where several units are used the initializing takes place according to the order in which the units appear in the **uses** statement.

- The finalization part is not available in Delphi 1 and can only be used by later versions if there is an initialization part. However, it is useful for cleaning up at the end of an application, for example freeing resources allocated in the initialization part. A finalization part is executed in the reverse order to the initialization. Delphi 1 users can use `ExitProc` to act in a similar manner to finalization but it involves advanced programming techniques, beyond the scope of this book. Details are available in the online help.

- A unit terminates with the reserved word **end** followed by a full stop (period).

13.3 uses list

On opening a new project the project source (accessed via View from the Delphi tool bar) contains two items in its uses list:

```
uses
  Forms,
  Unit1 in 'Unit1.pas' {Form1};
```

This list ensures the Forms library unit is included; this is essential so that the application starts. The Forms library unit contains the definition of the type `TApplication`, of which the program's application is an instance. The second item is the name of the unit that is associated with the default form. This line is automatically generated by the Delphi system. The unit name is the name under which the programmer saved the unit. The **in** clause is only available within the project source indicating the file in which the unit is saved, and should not be confused with the **in** operator used with sets. If the unit is in a subdirectory the path will be added, for example:

```
Unit1 in 'temp\Unit1.pas' {Form1};
```

If the unit is in a completely different directory the full path name, including drive if necessary, will be given. The commented `Form1` reminds the programmer of the form with which this unit is associated. The project manager (accessed via View) can also be used to see what units are associated with a project and to verify the path names.

On starting a new Delphi 3 application the unit associated with the blank form has this **uses** list:

```
uses
    Windows, Messages, SysUtils, Classes, Graphics, Controls,
    Forms, Dialogs;
```

while the Delphi 1 **uses** list is

```
uses
    SysUtils, WinTypes, WinProcs, Messages, Classes, Graphics,
    Controls, Forms, Dialogs;
```

The `Windows` unit defines the Delphi implementation of the Windows API. The `WinTypes` and `WinProcs` serve the same purpose in Delphi 1; Delphi 3 aliases `WinTypes` and `WinProcs` to `Windows` to ensure that most Delphi 1 projects will work in the Delphi 3 environment. However, Delphi 3 projects do not work in Delphi 1.

The `Messages` unit provides types for all the standard Windows messages.

The `SysUtils` unit contains the declarations for exception classes, string routines, date and time routines as well as other routines. It is automatically added to the **uses** statement whenever a new form is created.

The unit `System` is not included in any **uses** clause but is always available. It contains low-level routines for such things as string handling and dynamic memory allocation.

The `Classes` unit contains the declarations for most of the base object classes that are used by Delphi.

The `Graphics` unit contains the Delphi implementation of the Windows GDI (Graphics Device Interface) unit. It enables the use of fonts, bitmaps, metafiles, and pictures in applications.

The `Controls` unit contains the declaration of the basic controls (visible components).

As well as containing the definition of `TApplication` the `Forms` unit contains the declarations for `TForm` and its associated objects, types and routines.

The `Dialogs` unit contains the declarations for the common dialog boxes from the Dialogs page of the Component Palette and routines for displaying message boxes.

When designing the form the programmer may use components that are contained in other units. For example, when a shape component is added to a form and the unit is compiled Delphi will add another unit, ExtCtrls, to the **uses** list. If shapes are to be created at run time then it is the programmer's responsibility to ensure this unit is included. The ExtCtrls unit contains declarations for some of the components that appear on the Standard, Additional and Systems pages of the Component Palette and their associated objects, types and constants. Many other frequently used components are found in StdCtrls. However, there is no obvious way to predict what component is in what unit; the easiest way to find out is to place the component on the form of a new project, compile it and see what units are added to the **uses** list.

The appearance of a unit in the **uses** list does not mean that all its code is added to the current project. Only the code that is needed is linked in; the **uses** list ensures the compiler knows where to search for the required objects.

13.4 Programmer-defined units

The predefined Delphi units can be supplemented by individual programmers or teams of programmers developing their own units for private use or wider distribution. The same mechanism can be used to allow a single program to be developed as a number of units, rather than a single mammoth unit. Delphi forces some modularization onto the programmer as a separate unit is required for each form in the program, as was seen in Chapter 8.

A unit consists of the two basic parts, the interface and the implementation. The interface part is available to other units, advertising what is available from this unit. The implementation part is the hidden partner, not directly accessible from other units, but providing the code for the procedures plus any local definitions not available to the outside world.

The correct approach to program development is to design the interface part first and then to consider the implementation. During the development stage the usual approach is to put procedure headers in the implementation part with code issuing a simple message as in Listing 13.2. This is known as a procedure stub.

Listing 13.2

```
1: unit U13_2;
2: interface
3: procedure Test(var First: Integer; Second: Single);
4: {this is a test procedure to illustrate the development
5:   process}
6: implementation
7: uses Dialogs;
8: procedure Test(var First: Integer; Second: Single);
```

```
 9: begin
10:    ShowMessage('procedure Test not yet available');
11: end;
12: end.
```

In Listing 13.2:

- Line 3 defines the procedure Test.
- The comments at lines 4 and 5 describe the action of the procedure.
- Line 7 in the implementation part indicates that Dialogs is used in the implementation of this unit (it makes ShowMessage available).
- Line 8 matches line 3.
- The message at line 10 indicates the code has not yet been written.

A programmer-defined unit would be a useful way of encapsulating the types TDays and TSetDays defined in Chapter 12 and associated functions and procedures: see Listing 13.3.

Listing 13.3

```
 1: unit U13_3;
 2: {----------------------------------------------------------}
 3: {This unit offers a number of facilities for calculations  }
 4: {associated with the days of the week.                      }
 5: {----------------------------------------------------------}
 6:
 7: interface
 8: type TDays = (Monday,Tuesday,Wednesday,Thursday,
 9:                 Friday,Saturday,Sunday);
10: {----------------------------------------------------------}
11: {TDays is an enumerated type that can be used by other      }
12: {units, its use is not restricted to the functions and      }
13: {procedures of this unit                                    }
14: {----------------------------------------------------------}
15:
16: type TSetDays = set of TDays;
17: {----------------------------------------------------------}
18: {TSetDays is a set type for days of the week,               }
19: {it is not used in this unit, but is provided as a useful    }
20: {type                                                       }
21: {----------------------------------------------------------}
22:
23: function StrToDay(DayStr: string): TDays;
24: {----------------------------------------------------------}
25: {Converts the string DayStr to the corresponding            }
```

```
26: {enumeration of TDays. The conversion is not case      }
27: {sensitive, but DayStr must be the complete day name,   }
28: {abbreviations such as Wed are not recognized.          }
29: {An EConvertError is raised for any invalid values of   }
30: {DayStr                                                  }
31: {-----------------------------------------------------------}
32:
33: function DayToStr(Day: TDays): string;
34: {-----------------------------------------------------------}
35: {Converts the enumeration Day to the corresponding       }
36: {string.  The first letter is capitalized, the rest are  }
37: {lower case, e.g. 'Wednesday'                            }
38: {-----------------------------------------------------------}
39:
40: procedure AddDays(var Day: TDays; More: Integer);
41: {-----------------------------------------------------------}
42: {Sets the value of Day to More days beyond its current   }
43: {value, if More is negative then days before are calculated}
44: {-----------------------------------------------------------}
45:
46: implementation
47: uses SysUtils;
48:
49: function StrToDay(DayStr: string): TDays;
50: {-----------------------------------------------------------}
51: {Converts the string DayStr to the corresponding         }
52: {enumeration of TDays.                                    }
53: {An EConvertError is raised for any invalid values of    }
54: {DayStr                                                   }
55: {-----------------------------------------------------------}
56: begin
57:   if CompareText(DayStr,'Monday')=0 then
58:     StrToDay:= Monday
59:   else if CompareText(DayStr,'Tuesday')=0 then
60:     StrToDay:= Tuesday
61:   else if CompareText(DayStr,'Wednesday')=0 then
62:     StrToDay:= Wednesday
63:   else if CompareText(DayStr,'Thursday')=0 then
64:     StrToDay:= Thursday
65:   else if CompareText(DayStr,'Friday')=0 then
66:     StrToDay:= Friday
67:   else if CompareText(DayStr,'Saturday')=0 then
68:     StrToDay:= Saturday
69:   else if CompareText(DayStr,'Sunday')=0 then
70:     StrToDay:= Sunday
71:   else
```

```
72:      raise EConvertError.create(DayStr+' is not a day');
73: end;
74:
75: function DayToStr(Day: TDays): string;
76: {-----------------------------------------------------------}
77: {Converts the enumeration Day to the corresponding          }
78: {string.                                                    }
79: {-----------------------------------------------------------}
80: begin
81:   case Day of
82:     Monday:    DayToStr:= 'Monday';
83:     Tuesday:   DayToStr:= 'Tuesday';
84:     Wednesday:DayToStr:= 'Wednesday';
85:     Thursday: DayToStr:= 'Thursday';
86:     Friday:    DayToStr:= 'Friday';
87:     Saturday: DayToStr:= 'Saturday';
88:     Sunday:    DayToStr:= 'Sunday';
89:   end;
90: end;
91:
92: procedure AddDays(var Day: TDays; More: Integer);
93: {-----------------------------------------------------------}
94: {Sets the value of Day to More days after its current value}
95: {if More is negative then days before is calculated         }
96: {The calculation adjusts the number of days more to less    }
97: {than 7, then increments or decrements the value of Day     }
98: {to arrive at the correct new value.  If the code needs     }
99: {altering check carefully the correct Inc and Dec are used }
100: {-----------------------------------------------------------}
101: var More7: Integer;
102: begin
103:   More7:= More mod 7; {remove excess weeks}
104:   {More7 will be negative if More is negative}
105:   if More<0 then      {days before Day}
106:   begin
107:     More7:= Abs(More7);
108:     if More7<=Ord(Day) then {this week}
109:       Dec(Day,More7)
110:     else                {week before}
111:       Inc(Day,7-More7)
112:   end
113:   else               {days after Day}
114:   begin
115:     if More7+Ord(Day)<7 then {this week}
116:       Inc(Day,More7)
117:     else               {week after}
```

```
118:        Dec(Day,7-More7)
119:    end;
120: end;
121:
122: end.
```

In Listing 13.3:

- Lines 7 to 45 are the interface part.

- Lines 46 to 121 are the implementation part.

- Lines 8 and 9 declare the type TDays.

- Line 16 declares the corresponding set type and it is described in the subsequent comment lines.

- Line 23 declares the function StrToDay.

- Lines 24 to 31 describe the function in terms suited to another programmer who wants to use this function.

- Line 33 declares the function DayToStr and lines 34 to 38 describe its use.

- Line 40 declares the procedure AddDays and lines 41 to 44 describe its use.

- The **uses** statement at line 47 ensures CompareText (from SysUtils) is available within this unit.

- Lines 49 to 73 are the implementation of StrToDay.

- The comment at lines 50 to 55 is a brief description of the functionality. These comments will only usually be read by another programmer who wants to adapt this function. For this function, part of the comment from the interface part is used.

- Lines 75 to 90 are the implementation of DayToStr, with a brief descriptive comment at lines 77 and 78.

- Lines 92 to 120 are the implementation of AddDays.

- The comment in lines 93 to 100 is specifically aimed at a programmer who may need to adapt this code, explaining the modulo 7 and warning about confusions with Dec and Inc.

(13.5) Unit testing

Testing programs is an important part of the programmer's job. Although a program may compile and run, this is not necessarily a sign that it is functioning correctly. The programmer needs to verify that the program works correctly. The simplest tests are those where the programmer runs the program a few times and sees if the results look right. This approach is applicable only to the simplest of programs, such as those in the first chapter of this book. Programs must be tested in a logical manner. The programmer must ensure all paths through the program are tested within the range of values of data. As programs become larger the opportunity for bugs increases proportionally; unfortunately the amount of testing needed increases exponentially. However, the effort of testing can be reduced by thoroughly testing individual units. When these have all been proved to work satisfactorily individually, the parts of a program can be integrated and tested as a whole.

To test a unit, that is itself not a whole program, it is necessary to develop a test harness. The test harness will allow the programmer to exercise the unit's operation. The harness will not be part of the final program but will allow:

- testing of input and output, for both the expected range of values and unexpected values (for example, if an edit box is supposed to contain an integer, what happens if it is blank);

- testing all the procedures and functions, with expected and unexpected values for parameters.

Within Delphi it is possible to use watch variables (see Appendix A) to establish the values of variables part way through execution, and so the tests can establish the values of variables within procedures without the need for output. However, the debugger does interfere with exception handling and the programmer will need to make sure that the Break On Exceptions is switched off (see Section 11.2).

Before commencing testing it is normal practice to list what functionality is being tested, what values it is intended to supply and what the expected results will be. Table 13.1 contains a testing plan for the function `StrToDay` from Listing 13.3.

Table 13.1 Testing plan for `StrToDay`.

DayStr	Result expected to be returned by `StrToDay`	Result actually returned
`'Monday'`	Monday of type TDay	
`'Tuesday'`	Tuesday of type TDay	
`'Wednesday'`	Wednesday of type TDay	
`'Thursday'`	Thursday of type TDay	
`'Friday'`	Friday of type TDay	
`'Saturday'`	Saturday of type TDay	
`'Sunday'`	Sunday of type TDay	
`'monday'`	Monday of type TDay	
`'TUESDAY'`	Tuesday of type TDay	
`'wEDNESDAY'`	Wednesday of type TDay	
`'SUNday'`	Sunday of type TDay	
blank	exception raised	
`'MON'`	exception raised	
`'Monda'`	exception raised	
`'Wedesday'`	exception raised	
1	exception raised	

Commercial organizations will have their own standards for testing that should be adhered to by members of those organizations.

We can now develop a harness to test the unit in Listing 13.3. This will allow testing of the function StrToDay and all other functionality.

1. Create a prototype form as shown in Figure 13.1.

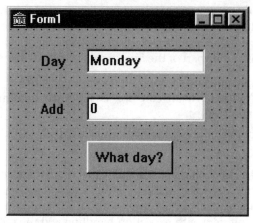

Figure 13.1 Prototype form.

2. Add the unit from Listing 13.3 to the project, by selecting File|Add to project, and then negotiating the file structure to find the unit code. Alternatively the unit can be added using the Project Manager.

3. Add

   uses U13_3;

   to the implementation part of the unit associated with the prototype form: see line 29 of Listing 13.4.

Listing 13.4

```
 1: unit U13_4;
 2:
 3: interface
 4:
 5: uses
 6:   Windows, Messages, SysUtils, Classes, Graphics, Controls,
 7:   Forms, Dialogs, StdCtrls;
 8:
 9: type
10:   TForm1 = class(TForm)
11:     Edit1: TEdit;
12:     Label1: TLabel;
13:     Button1: TButton;
```

```
14:      Edit2: TEdit;
15:      Label2: TLabel;
16:      procedure Button1Click(Sender: TObject);
17:   private
18:      { Private declarations }
19:   public
20:      { Public declarations }
21:   end;
22:
23: var
24:   Form1: TForm1;
25:
26: implementation
27:
28: {$R *.DFM}
29: uses U13_3;
30: procedure TForm1.Button1Click(Sender: TObject);
31: {-------------------------------------------------------------}
32: {Provides a test harness for U13_3                           }
33: {-------------------------------------------------------------}
34: var Today: TDays; Later: Integer;
35: begin
36:   Today:= StrToDay(Edit1.Text);
37:   Later:= StrToInt(Edit2.Text);
38:   AddDays(Today,Later);
39:   ShowMessage('Today is: '+DayToStr(Today));
40: end;
```

4. Add line 34 and the code from lines 36 to 39 to the event handler for the button.

5. The test harness is complete and we will need to test the function StrToDay. Place a breakpoint at line 37 and run the program. Enter strings in Edit1 and place Today in a watch variable to see the value returned by StrToDay. The values in Today should match those in Table 13.1. If there is a mismatch the program has failed the test and will need to be revised.

6. Test the other function and procedure in a similar fashion.

7. Having tested the functions and procedure independently it is also necessary to test that they operate correctly together. This is done by running the test harness: entering days of the week into the first edit box and numbers into the second allows the programmer to exercise all procedures and functions – see Figure 13.2.

The more functionality there is within a unit the more complicated the testing will become.

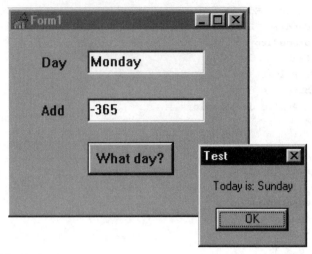

Figure 13.2   Testing.

13.6 Initialization and finalization

The initialization part of a unit is executed when the project starts. If there is more than one unit with an initialization part, they are executed in the order in which the units appear in the uses clauses.

The finalization part is not available in Delphi 1; in later versions it can only be used if the unit has an initialization part. Finalization parts are executed in the reverse order of initialization.

The final **end** at line 122 in Listing 13.3 can be replaced by the code in Listing 13.5.

Listing 13.5) Initialization and finalization

```
122: var Recording: TextFile;
123: initialization
124:   try
125:     AssignFile(Recording,'log.txt');
126:     Rewrite(Recording);
127:     WriteLn(Recording,'started using Week at '
128:            +TimeToStr(Time));
129:   except
130:     CloseFile(Recording);
131:     raise;
132:   end;
133: finalization
134:   try
135:     WriteLn(Recording,'finished using Week at '
```

```
136:                    +TimeToStr(Time));
137:    finally
138:      CloseFile(Recording);
139:    end;
140: end.
```

In Listing 13.5:

● Line 122 declares a `TextFile` that will be used for output. This is a unit-wide variable.

● Lines 123 to 132 are the initialization part.

● The **try...except** protects the opening of the file for writing and in case of exception closes it and then re-raises the error.

● The `TimeToStr` and `Time` functions are both from `SysUtils` that are already in the **uses** statement of this unit.

● Lines 133 to 139 are the finalization part, which completes the writing to the file and closes it.

● Line 140 is the end of the unit.

These changes to `U13_3` do not alter the interface part of the unit. So any units that use `U13_3` do not themselves need to be recompiled, although `U13_3` must itself be recompiled and the projects that include it must be re-linked. The Delphi environment automatically does all this when the Compile option is chosen.

Running the test harness developed in Listing 13.4 will have the same appearance as before. However, in the background a file `log.txt` will be recorded, detailing how long the programmer spent using `U13_3`: see Figure 13.3.

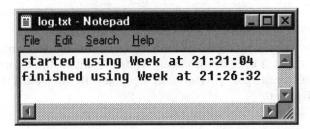

Figure 13.3 `log.txt`.

13.7 Objects and units

As seen in Chapter 10 an object is an encapsulation of data and related operations. In this chapter programmer-defined units have been introduced as a way of encapsulating data and related operations. In this section we will show the relationship between these two concepts and how they can be used to complement each other.

A unit is a *physical* collection of data and operations stored together in a file, whereas an object is an instance of a *logical* collection of data and related operations.

Programmers new to the concepts of object-oriented and modular programming sometimes believe they have a choice of using either objects or units. With Delphi, objects and units can and should be used together.

When developing a Delphi application the programmer must decide:

1. Should this data type and its related operations be implemented as an object?
2. How should this project be split into units?
3. Can objects be grouped together into library units?

To expand on these points:

1. Should this data type and its related operations be implemented as an object? Objects can often be recognized in a problem's description. For example, if a program is to be developed to play cards then the deck of cards may be an obvious object. If there does not appear to be an obvious candidate on which to base a class, it is better to continue development and define types and operations. Once these exist it is usually relatively easy to transform them into a class definition.

2. How should this project be split into units? Delphi insists that there is a separate unit for each form, so a program with more than one form will be modular. Where objects are developed that are independent of a particular form they should normally be placed in a separate unit. Some programmers use a separate unit for each of their objects. Others group everything that does not belong to a specific form into a single unit. Both approaches have their place but neither should be followed blindly. Two guidelines might help:

   - Once a unit is more than several pages long it should be examined to see if it can naturally be divided into a number of units. Otherwise the testing will become very complicated within this unit.

   - Where a unit listing is less than a page, examine those units that use it and those that it uses; if it is closely related to any of these consider if the units should be merged. This includes merging with those units that are associated with forms.

   Where a team of programmers is working together on a project, they are likely to divide the work so that each programmer is developing separate units. With team work it is essential that good software engineering principles are followed. With a Delphi project this will involve agreeing on the interface parts of all units. The implementation parts need only match the interface part for success.

3. Can objects be grouped together into library units? When objects have been developed that will be useful to the programmer for other projects they should be put into one or more units so they can be used again. Such library units may be considerably larger than those in a typical project, in order to keep related operations together. The interface part that others will need to consult must remain of a manageable size.

If objects are judged to be very useful the programmer may wish to add them to the Component Palette. Section 15.6 outlines how this can be done.

Sometimes the programmer will be unable to establish any objects amongst the types and operations defined, for example in a project to develop a number of statistical operations. In this case units can still be used, with the definition of types and operations placed in the interface part and the code in the implementation part.

(13.8) An example

In this section we demonstrate how the class developed in Section 10.7 for representing and manipulating complex numbers could be made into the unit shown in Listing 13.6.

(Listing 13.6)

```
 1: unit Complex;
 2:
 3: interface
 4:
 5: type
 6:    TComplex = class(TObject)
 7: {-----------------------------------------------------------}
 8: { Objects of TComplex represent Complex numbers and their  }
 9: { operations                                               }
10: {-----------------------------------------------------------}
11:
12:    private
13:       FRealPart: Integer;
14:       FImagPart: Integer;
15:    public
16:       constructor Create;
17:       procedure Add(const First, Second: TComplex);
18:       procedure Multiply (const First, Second: TComplex);
19:       function ToStr: string;
20:       procedure ToComplex(AString: string);
21: end;
22:
23: implementation
24:
25: uses SysUtils;
26:
27: constructor TComplex.Create;
28: begin
29:    inherited Create;
30: end;
```

```
31:
32: procedure TComplex.Add(const First, Second: TComplex);
33: begin
34:    FRealPart:= First.FRealPart+Second.FRealPart;
35:    FImagPart:= First.FImagPart+Second.FImagPart;
36: end;
37:
38: procedure TComplex.Multiply(const First, Second: TComplex);
39: begin
40:    FRealPart:= (First.FRealPart*Second.FRealPart)
41:                   -(First.FImagPart*Second.FImagPart);
42:    FImagPart:= (First.FRealPart*Second.FImagPart)
43:                   +(First.FImagPart*Second.FRealPart);
44: end;
45:
46: function TComplex.ToStr: string;
47: {----------------------------------------------------------}
48: { converts a complex number to a string                    }
49: {----------------------------------------------------------}
50: begin
51:    Result:= IntToStr(FRealPart);
52:    if FImagPart>=0 then Result:= Result+'+';
53:    Result:= Result+IntToStr(FImagPart)+'i';
54: end;
55:
56: procedure TComplex.ToComplex(AString: string);
57: {----------------------------------------------------------}
58: { converts a string to a complex number                    }
59: {----------------------------------------------------------}
60: var Position,Positioni: Integer; var Temp: string;
61: begin
62:    Position:=Pos('+',AString);
63:    if Position=0 then
64:       Position:= Pos('-', AString);
65:    if Position=1 then {starts with a + or - }
66:    begin
67:       Temp:= Copy(AString,2,Length(AString)-1);
68:       Position:= Pos('+',Temp);
69:       if Position=0 then
70:          Position:= Pos('-', Temp);
71:       Inc(Position);
72:    end;
73:    Positioni:= Pos('i',AString);
74:    { error checking should be added to cope with incorrectly
75:      presented numbers}
76:    FRealPart:= StrToInt(Copy(AString,0,Position-1));
```

```
77:    FImagPart:= StrToInt
78:               (Copy(AString,Position,Positioni-Position));
79: end;
80:
81: end.
```

In Listing 13.6:

● Lines 3 to 22 are the interface part containing the definition of the object class TComplex.

● Lines 23 to 80 are the implementation part.

● The **uses** statement at line 25 is necessary to make IntToStr available to the implementation.

This unit is close to our lower limit on the suggested size of a unit. Other complex operations may be found desirable so the unit may expand in size. Alternatively the programmer may define a Maths unit as a library of useful mathematical functions developed over a number of projects. This unit could contain a variety of statistical and trigonometric routines as well as class definition for objects such as TComplex.

Later versions of Delphi provide a unit called Math that offers some mathematical functionality to supplement the basics offered by Delphi and the Systems unit. A listing of the Math unit can be found in the Delphi directory Source\Rtl\Sys in a file Math.pas, assuming that a full Delphi installation is available. At over 20 pages this is what we would consider a large unit. The user of this unit should need to consult only the interface part, which is considerably smaller, some 200 lines. Testing would not have been overcomplicated by the size of the unit as much of the functionality is completely independent.

13.9 Summary

Within this chapter we have shown how units can be used to facilitate modular programming and develop libraries. We have examined the anatomy of units, describing the roles of the interface and implementation parts; the initialization and finalization parts; and the role of the **uses** statements. We have also examined the relationship between units and objects. The final section presented an example of an object in a unit.

Quiz

1. Within a unit which part occurs first?
    (a) implementation
    (b) initialization
    (c) interface

2. Where can a **uses** statement occur?
    (a) at the start of the implementation part
    (b) at the start of the initialization part
    (c) at the start of the interface part

3. What is a procedure stub?
    (a) a parameter
    (b) the procedure header
    (c) a procedure that is not yet fully implemented, but shows a simple message

4. In what order are initialization statements executed?
    (a) the order in which they appear in the uses list
    (b) alphabetically
    (c) Delphi units initializations first, then programmer-defined initializations

5. Finalization parts are available in
    (a) Delphi 1
    (b) Delphi 2
    (c) Delphi 3

6. A unit is best described as which of the following?
    (a) a logical collection of data and operations
    (b) a physical collection of data and operations
    (c) an object

7. What unit is available to all units, but does not need to be in the **uses** lists?
    (a) System
    (b) SysUtils
    (c) Windows

8. What does the Math unit contain?
    (a) the standard mathematical routines available in Delphi
    (b) mathematical routines that supplement the standard routines in Delphi
    (c) the object TComplex

9. With a large project it is essential that programmers agree on which of the following?
    (a) the interface parts of their units
    (b) variable names within their individual implementation parts
    (c) the use of comments

10. Each time a form is added to a project, how many units are added?
    (a) 0
    (b) 1
    (c) 2

Exercises

1. Write a unit that supplies trigonometric functions: sine and cosine, expecting input in degrees rather than radians.

Hint: the easiest way is to start with degrees, multiply by $\pi/180$ to convert to radians, then use the standard sine and cosine functions. Alternatively, use a suitable formula and work from first principles, being careful about accuracy.

2. Amend the function `StrToDay` in the unit in Listing 13.3, so that input is case sensitive. Indicate how you would test this revised function.

3. Develop an object for representing weights in pounds and ounces. Operations offered should include conversions to and from metric.

4. Write a test harness to ensure the weight conversion works correctly.

5. Develop a unit called Translation that will convert a small number of words between several languages. For example, the user may supply a string representing the name of a day of the week in English and expect the corresponding French name to be returned.

Pointers

14.1 Introduction

Assembler programmers are aware that the computer stores the data they manipulate in locations within their computer. Each location has a unique *address*, commonly given as a hexadecimal number. Object Pascal, in common with other high-level languages, protects the programmer from handling addresses for the most part. It does so fundamentally by using identifiers for variables instead. The Delphi environment incorporates features such as list boxes which the environment can maintain in a sorted order, thus the programmer will not need to write so many sorting procedures. The **class** structure in Delphi's Object Pascal is an improvement on the **object** structure in earlier versions of Object Pascal in that it lessens the need for pointers (see Reference model online help). However, the use of advanced programming structures, necessary for many larger projects, requires the programmer to understand addresses. The concept of a *pointer*, which is a variable holding an address, makes the actual coding easier. Pointers are necessary to exploit the full power of Object Pascal, but in languages such as C they play a much more central role.

We will first examine the idea and simple uses of pointers; then we discuss some of the useful structures that can be built using pointers.

14.2 Pointer types

The variables we have used so far have been essentially blocks of memory with a label or identifier attached. Declarations of such variables are

```
var Index: Cardinal;
```

and the statement

```
Index:= 5;
```

accesses the memory labelled `Index`, and puts the value 5 into it in a binary format. We can declare a further type

```
type TPCard= ^Cardinal;
```

and a variable of that new pointer type

```
var PIndex: TPCard;
```

This declares a variable `PIndex` which is a pointer to a `Cardinal`, that is it can hold the address of a `Cardinal` variable. Then the statement

```
PIndex:= @Index;
```

assigns the address in memory of `Index` to `PIndex`, as illustrated in Figure 14.1.

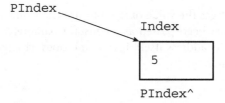

Figure 14.1 Pointer variables and simple variables.

Further, the statement

```
PIndex^:= 7;
```

dereferences the variable `PIndex`, that is, finds the address in memory that `PIndex` contains, then assigns the value of the expression on the right-hand side (7) to that address. Thus, it will alter the value of the memory labelled `Index` from 5 to binary 7. So `PIndex^` is currently another name or an alias for `Index`.

14.3 Variable parameters

In Chapter 9 we said that Pascal passed variable parameters using pointers. We showed then that

```
procedure Third(var D: Char; E: Char);
begin
  D:= 'D';
  E:= 'E';
end {procedure Third};
```

when called in the statement

```
Third(MyD,MyE);
```

changed the value of MyD but not the value of MyE.

The inner workings of variable parameters can be illustrated by another procedure which uses pointers and addresses explicitly to do the same task.

Assume that this type definition has been made, and is in scope

```
type TPChar = ^Char;
```

and this procedure is defined:

```
procedure Fourth(const D: TPChar; E: Char);
begin
  D^:= 'd';
  E:= 'e';
end {procedure Fourth};
```

The corresponding call is now

```
Fourth(@MyD,MyE);
```

which again changes the value of MyD but not the value of MyE. This is because the address of MyD has been passed as a constant parameter. Although the procedure cannot change the address itself, it can, and does, change the value stored at that address in the statement

```
D^:= 'd';.
```

This is because D^ *dereferences* D, that is, it finds the value to which D points.

This use of pointers and addresses in place of a 'proper' variable parameter is interesting because the same technique is regularly used by C programmers, as ANSI C lacks a variable parameter facility. It was one of the new features added to C++, thus making it easier to use than ANSI C.

(14.4) Pointers and the global heap

The pointers we have used so far have merely given us a different (and indirect) way of accessing a part of standard memory. It is much more useful to be able to access a part of memory hitherto inaccessible; it is called the global heap. The named variables used so far are allocated space in the local heap, which is limited in size particularly in Delphi 1. The global heap does have limits, but they are generous, and determined by Windows rather than Delphi.

Pointers on the global heap enable the programmer to book and release memory as it is needed, in contrast to arrays which are fixed in size at compile time. They also make it possible to build complex structures, such as linked lists and trees, most of which are outside the scope of this book. For further information on linked lists and trees, and algorithms to manipulate them, consult a specialized text such as that by Wirth (1976).

Before embarking on a discussion of linked lists, let us see how to use space on the global heap for a single `Cardinal` value. Assume the type declaration

```
type TPCard= ^Cardinal;
```

and a variable declaration

```
var PIndex: TPCard;
```

then the statement

```
New(PIndex);
```

uses the in-built procedure `New` to grab space on the global heap. Further, it makes `PIndex` 'point' to the newly booked space.

So far, space has been booked, but that space has not been initialized. The statement

```
PIndex^:= 10;
```

dereferences `PIndex` (finds the location at the address in `PIndex`) then assigns the constant 10 to that location, as shown in Figure 14.2.

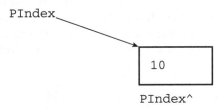

Figure 14.2 Anonymous variables.

`PIndex^` can be used in any position in code where a variable of type `Cardinal` could be used. This is because the dereferencing operator ^ delivers a `Cardinal`. So for instance

```
PIndex^:= PIndex^ + 15;
```

● finds the value to which `PIndex` points (10),

● adds 15 to that value (25), and

● puts 25 back wherever `PIndex` points.

The address in `PIndex` is unchanged; the value at that address has been changed. Figure 14.3 indicates the result.

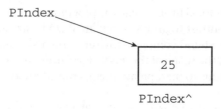

PIndex^

Figure 14.3   Change in anonymous variable.

We have already seen that it is possible to assign one address to another address. The only operations that can be performed on PIndex are dereferencing (^), equality (=) and inequality (<>). Assignment is also allowed, but strictly speaking assignment in Pascal is not an operation, although it is in some languages like C. In Object Pascal it is possible neither to perform arithmetic on addresses, nor to assign an address to an integer type. Either addresses to be compared must be pointers to the same type, or an address may be compared with a special constant **nil**, which is the pointer equivalent of zero. **nil** is a pointer that points nowhere; it is compatible with any pointer type.

Variables like PIndex^ are known as anonymous variables, as they do not have a name of their own.

Once space on the heap is no longer required, it should be released back into the available heap. The statement

```
Dispose(PIndex);
```

does just this, and the value to which PIndex pointed will be lost. There is a likeness to the destructors for objects. In Chapter 10 we recommended that the programmer set objects to **nil** after using Free. Similarly, in the case of pointer type variables, the programmer should usually then set the pointer to **nil** by means of a statement like

```
PIndex:= nil;
```

after the Dispose. Reversing the order of these two statements may give rise to an error from the debugger such as that shown in Figure 14.4 in Delphi 1.

It is not possible to use Free or Destroy with pointers.

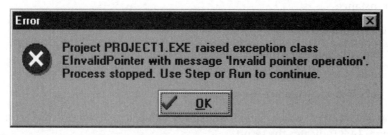

Figure 14.4   Result of attempting to dispose of a nil pointer in Delphi 1.

(14.5) Linked structures

As mentioned already, the power of pointers is seen with the use of different structures. The simplest of such structures are linked lists, see Figure 14.5.

Each cell must contain at least two parts: one is the data to be manipulated, the other contains the address of the next cell in the chain. The address of the very first item must be available too, in order to find the chain at all. Also, the end of the chain must be recognizable. The usual way is to put **nil** in the address field of the last cell, but alternatively a count of the number of cells can be maintained. This is similar to the counting objects discussed in Chapter 10.

If the data consists of just one letter, then a suitable type definition for a cell is

```
type
  TPCell = ^TCell;
  TCell = record
            Letter: Char;
            Next: TPCell;
          end;
```

TPCell is defined to be a pointer to a variable of type TCell before TCell has been defined. The forward reference

```
  TPCell = ^TCell;
```

is permitted for pointers to deal with cases of this kind where each type requires the other. In this case the Letter field contains the data, here just one character; the Next field is of an appropriate pointer type to hold the address of the next complete cell, which in turn contains both data and an address.

Then a suitable variable declaration for the first item is

```
var ChainTop: TPCell; {pointer to top of chain}
```

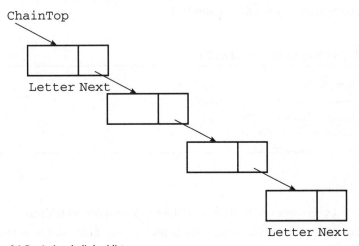

Figure 14.5 A simple linked list.

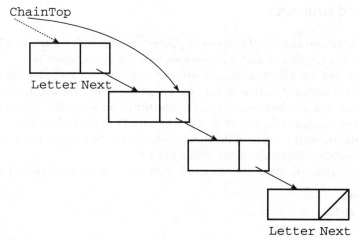

Figure 14.6   Walking down a linked list.

It is now possible to find the address of the second item by moving the pointer down the list with code like

```
ChainTop:= ChainTop^.Next;
```

as shown in Figure 14.6. This dereferences `ChainTop`, and finds the field called `Next`. This is a pointer of type `TPCell` so it can be assigned to `ChainTop`, thus walking down the chain.

The chain must first be built up, and this can be done by creating a new cell, then attaching it to the chain. If the declaration

```
var NewCell: TPCell; ThisChar: Char;
```

is in scope, and some of the chain exists, the code shown in Listing 14.1 adds a new cell to the start, as shown in Figure 14.7.

(**Listing 14.1**)   Adding a cell to a linked list

```
1:  New(NewCell);
2:  NewCell^.Letter:= ThisChar;
3:  NewCell^.Next:= ChainTop;
4:  ChainTop:= NewCell;
```

In Listing 14.1:

● Line 1 gets space on the heap, and `NewCell` contains its address.

● Line 2 dereferences `NewCell`, finds the `Letter` field, and puts the data proper into it.

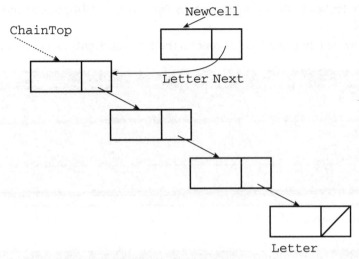

Figure 14.7   Adding a new cell to the start of the chain.

- Line 3 again dereferences NewCell, finds the Next field, of pointer type, and copies the address held in ChainTop into there.
- The chain is now linked together again.
- Line 4 assigns the address in NewCell to ChainTop, thus resetting the start point.

These algorithms can be used to simulate a common structure in computing, a stack. For more complex structures cells can be added to the middle of a chain, or removed from the middle of a chain. Trees are recursive structures in which each cell can have more than one link to other similar cells; they are usually programmed using both pointers and recursion, and details can again be found in many standard Pascal texts such as Wirth (1976).

14.6   Stacks

Stacks are a simple but effective structure, used by operating systems to store calls to procedures and the associated data. Compilers also use stacks, and they can be useful in simulations. A pile of trays in a canteen is a more mundane example of a stack. Trays are added to the top one by one, and also taken off one by one, so it is a 'last in first out' *(LIFO)* structure.

It is quite possible to program a stack using arrays. In some languages this is the only option, but in Pascal, C and related languages a linked structure using pointers is much better, because the addition and removal of items is straightforward. The operation to add an item is called a push, and the opposite is a pop.

1. Open a new project and add a main menu as shown in Figure 14.8 with two main menu items, File and Stack.
2. Add just one submenu option, Exit under File.

3. Under Stack add submenu options Pop, Push and Dispose, as shown in Figure 14.9.

4. Now add the event handler code for the OnClick event of Push1 – see Listing 14.2.

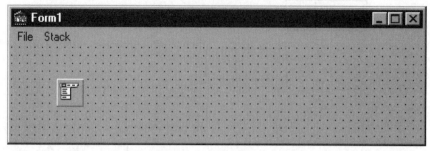

Figure 14.8   Stack project.

Figure 14.9   Main menu for stack project.

Listing 14.2   Pushing a new cell item onto a stack

```
 1: procedure TForm1.Push1Click(Sender: TObject);
 2: {------------------------------------------------------------}
 3: {Uses InputQuery to obtain a new character                   }
 4: {then adds it to the stack                                   }
 5: {------------------------------------------------------------}
 6: var NewCell: TPCell; ThisLetter: string;
 7: begin
 8:   ThisLetter:= '?';
 9:   repeat until
10:     InputQuery('Push onto stack',
11:     'Enter your letter',ThisLetter);
12:   New(NewCell);
13:   NewCell^.Letter:= ThisLetter[1];
14:   NewCell^.Next:= StackTop;
15:   StackTop:= NewCell;
16: end;
```

Listing 14.2 is very similar to Listing 14.1, which added a new cell to the top of a chain, then adjusted the pointer so that new cell was included in the chain. The new feature is obtaining the new data via an input box. ThisLetter is a string type, but only one letter is required in this case, so ThisLetter[1] is used on the right-hand side of line 13. Lines 14 and 15 reference StackTop, which is a pointer type bound to the type TCell. Most of the event handlers will use StackTop, so the programmer must define it globally. That definition can be either in the interface part if it is to be available to other units, or in the implementation part if it is preferred to restrict access to the current unit. For the present we will define both types and the variable StackTop in the implementation part.

5. Add these declarations to the implementation part:

```
type
    TPCell= ^TCell;
    TCell= record
                Letter:Char;
                Next:TPCell;
           end;
var StackTop:TPCell; {pointer to top of stack}
```

6. Next, code for the opposite event, that of popping a cell of the stack, is required. In order to perform this action safely, it is essential to check whether the stack structure has cells in it or not. The event handler that disposes of the whole stack can use the same procedure if it is placed so it is in scope for both. So put the short function

```
function IsEmpty: Boolean;
begin
   IsEmpty:= StackTop= nil;
end;
```

at the start of the implementation part of the unit, after the variable and type declarations, but before the event handlers. Alternatively it could be made private to the form: see Chapter 10 on Objects and later in this chapter.

7. Now add code to the event handler TForm1.Pop1Click as shown in Listing 14.3.

(Listing 14.3) Removing the top item from a stack

```
1:  procedure TForm1.Pop1Click(Sender: TObject);
2:  {-----------------------------------------------------------}
3:  {Obtains a new Character from stack,                        }
4:  {displays it, removes it from stack                         }
5:  {-----------------------------------------------------------}
6:  var Rubbish :TPCell;
7:  begin
8:     if IsEmpty then
9:        ShowMessage('Empty stack')
```

```
10:    else
11:    begin
12:      ShowMessage(' Top item: '+ StackTop^.Letter +
13:        ' has been removed');
14:      Rubbish:= StackTop;
15:      StackTop:= StackTop^.Next;
16:      Dispose(Rubbish);
17:      Rubbish:= nil;
18:    end;
19: end;
```

In Listing 14.3:

- Line 6 declares a new local variable, to be used for tidying up heap space after removing one item.
- Lines 8 to 10 deal with the case when the stack is empty.
- Line 12 uses a message box to display the value of the top item on the stack.
- Line 14 records the address of the old top of the stack.
- Line 15 steps down the stack, making a new top.
- Lines 16 and 17 tidy up by returning space to the heap and then setting a pointer to nil.

The Dispose1Click event handler is rather similar to that for TForm1.Pop1Click, except that it uses a **while** loop to work its way down the stack, as long as IsEmpty is true. It is detailed in Listing 14.4.

Listing 14.4

```
1: procedure TForm1.Dispose1Click(Sender: TObject);
2: {---------------------------------------------------------}
3: {Removes items on stack silently, starting from top       }
4: {---------------------------------------------------------}
5: var Rubbish: TPCell;
6: begin
7:   Rubbish:= nil;
8:   while not IsEmpty do
9:   begin
10:     Rubbish:= StackTop;
11:     StackTop:= StackTop^.Next;
12:     Dispose(Rubbish);
13:     Rubbish:= nil
14:   end;
15:   StackTop:= nil;
16: end;
```

8. Finally add `Close` to the `TForm1.Quit1Click` event handler.

The finished unit is shown in Listing 14.5.

(Listing 14.5) Stack stored as a linked list
_____

```
 1: unit U14_5;
 2:
 3: interface
 4:
 5: uses
 6:    Windows, Messages, SysUtils, Classes, Graphics,
 7:    Controls, Forms, Dialogs, Menus;
 8:
 9: type
10:    TForm1 = class(TForm)
11:      MainMenu1: TMainMenu;
12:      File1: TMenuItem;
13:      Exit1: TMenuItem;
14:      Stack2: TMenuItem;
15:      Pop1: TMenuItem;
16:      Push1: TMenuItem;
17:      Dispose1: TMenuItem;
18:      procedure Push1Click(Sender: TObject);
19:      procedure Pop1Click(Sender: TObject);
20:      procedure Dispose1Click(Sender: TObject);
21:      procedure Exit1Click(Sender: TObject);
22:    private
23:      { Private declarations }
24:    public
25:      { Public declarations }
26:    end;
27:
28: var
29:    Form1: TForm1;
30:
31: implementation
32:
33: {$R *.DFM}
34:
35: type
36:      TPCell= ^TCell;
37:      TCell= record
38:              Letter: Char;
39:              Next: TPCell;
40:            end;
```

```
41:
42: var StackTop:TPCell= nil; {pointer to top of stack}
43:
44: function IsEmpty: Boolean;
45: begin
46:   IsEmpty:= StackTop= nil;
47: end;
48:
49: procedure TForm1.Push1Click(Sender: TObject);
50: {------------------------------------------------------------}
51: {Uses InputQuery to obtain a new character                   }
52: {then adds it to the stack                                   }
53: {------------------------------------------------------------}
54: var NewCell:TPCell;ThisLetter:string;
55: begin
56:   ThisLetter:='?';
57:   repeat until
58:     InputQuery('Push onto stack',
59:     'Enter your letter',ThisLetter);
60:   New(NewCell);
61:   NewCell^.Letter:= ThisLetter[1];
62:   NewCell^.Next:= StackTop;
63:   StackTop:= NewCell;
64: end;
65:
66: procedure TForm1.Pop1Click(Sender: TObject);
67: {------------------------------------------------------------}
68: {Obtains a new character from stack,                         }
69: {displays it, removes it from stack                          }
70: {------------------------------------------------------------}
71: var Rubbish :TPCell;
72: begin
73:   if IsEmpty then
74:     ShowMessage('Empty stack')
75:   else
76:   begin
77:     ShowMessage(' Top item: '+ StackTop^.Letter +
78:       ' has been removed');
79:     Rubbish:= StackTop;
80:     StackTop:= StackTop^.Next;
81:     Dispose(Rubbish);
82:     Rubbish:= nil;
83:   end;
84: end;
85:
86: procedure TForm1.Dispose1Click(Sender: TObject);
```

```
 87: {---------------------------------------------------------}
 88: {Removes items on stack silently, starting from top      }
 89: {---------------------------------------------------------}
 90: var Rubbish: TPCell;
 91: begin
 92:    Rubbish:= nil;
 93:    while not IsEmpty do
 94:    begin
 95:      Rubbish:= StackTop;
 96:      StackTop:= StackTop^.Next;
 97:      Dispose(Rubbish);
 98:      Rubbish:= nil
 99:    end;
100:    StackTop:= nil;
101: end;
102:
103: procedure TForm1.Exit1Click(Sender: TObject);
104: begin
105:    Close;
106: end;
107:
108: end.
```

(14.7) Linked lists as objects*

Within Listing 14.5 the event handlers are written in standard Pascal. Chapter 10 demonstrated that Delphi's Object Pascal has facilities to encapsulate data and methods, which make code more robust yet extensible. An object-oriented version of the stacks project, shown in Listing 14.6, offers just the same functionality as Listing 14.5. The operations such as pop and push and the data structure itself are now bound into one class, TStack.

(Listing 14.6) Stacks using objects

```
1: unit U14_6;
2:
3: interface
4:
5: uses
6:    Windows, Messages, SysUtils, Classes, Graphics,
7:    Controls, Forms, Dialogs, Menus;
8: type
```

```
 9:    TPCell = ^TCell;
10:    TCell = record
11:                Letter: Char;
12:                Next: TPCell;
13:           end;
14:
15: type
16:    TStack = class(TObject)
17:    public
18:      function Pop:Char;
19:      procedure Push;
20:      procedure Clear;
21:      constructor Create;
22:      destructor Destroy; override;
23:    private
24:      StackTop: TPCell;
25:      function IsEmpty: Boolean;
26:
27:    end;
28: type
29:    TForm1 = class(TForm)
30:      MainMenu1: TMainMenu;
31:      File1: TMenuItem;
32:      Exit1: TMenuItem;
33:      Pop1: TMenuItem;
34:      Push1: TMenuItem;
35:      Dispose1: TMenuItem;
36:      procedure Pop1Click(Sender: TObject);
37:      procedure Push1Click(Sender: TObject);
38:      procedure Exit1Click(Sender: TObject);
39:      procedure FormCreate(Sender: TObject);
40:      procedure Dispose1Click(Sender: TObject);
41:      procedure FormDestroy(Sender: TObject);
42:    private
43:      { Private declarations }
44:    public
45:      { Public declarations }
46:    end;
47:
48: var
49:    Form1: TForm1;
50:
51: implementation
52:
53: {$R *.DFM}
```

```
54:
55: var StackA: TStack; ThisOne: Char;
56:
57: constructor TStack.Create;
58: begin
59:   inherited Create;
60:   StackTop:= nil;
61: end;
62:
63: destructor TStack.Destroy;
64: begin
65:   Clear;
66:   inherited Destroy;
67: end;
68:
69: function TStack.IsEmpty: Boolean;
70: begin
71:   IsEmpty:= StackTop= nil;
72: end;
73:
74: procedure TStack.Clear;
75: {----------------------------------------------------------}
76: {Works down the stack, calling dispose as it goes         }
77: {----------------------------------------------------------}
78: var Rubbish: TPCell;
79: begin
80:   Rubbish:= nil;
81:   while not IsEmpty do
82:   begin
83:     Rubbish:= StackTop;
84:     StackTop:= StackTop^.Next;
85:     Dispose(Rubbish);
86:     Rubbish:= nil;
87:   end;
88:   StackTop:= nil;
89: end;
90:
91: function TStack.Pop:Char;
92: {----------------------------------------------------------}
93: {Obtains a new character from stack,                      }
94: {displays it, removes it from stack                       }
95: {----------------------------------------------------------}
96:
97: var Rubbish: TPCell;
98: begin
```

```
 99:   if IsEmpty then
100:     ShowMessage('Empty stack')
101:   else
102:   begin
103:     ShowMessage(' Top item: ' + StackTop^.Letter +
104:       ' has been removed');
105:     Rubbish:= StackTop;
106:     StackTop:= StackTop^.Next;
107:     Dispose(Rubbish);
108:     Rubbish:= nil;
109:   end;
110: end;
111:
112: procedure TStack.Push;
113: {-----------------------------------------------------------}
114: {Uses InputQuery to obtain a new character                 }
115: {then adds it to the stack                                 }
116: {-----------------------------------------------------------}
117:
118: var NewCell: TPCell; ThisLetter :string;
119: begin
120:   ThisLetter:= '?';
121:   repeat until
122:     InputQuery('Push onto stack',
123:     'Enter your letter',ThisLetter);
124:   New(NewCell);
125:   NewCell^.Letter:= ThisLetter[1];
126:   NewCell^.Next:= StackTop;
127:   StackTop:= NewCell;
128: end;
129:
130: procedure TForm1.Pop1Click(Sender: TObject);
131: begin
132:   ThisOne:= StackA.Pop;
133: end;
134:
135: procedure TForm1.Push1Click(Sender: TObject);
136: begin
137:   StackA.Push;
138: end;
139:
140: procedure TForm1.Exit1Click(Sender: TObject);
141: begin
142:   Close;
143: end;
```

```
144:
145: procedure TForm1.Dispose1Click(Sender: TObject);
146: begin
147:    StackA.Clear;
148: end;
149:
150: procedure TForm1.FormCreate(Sender: TObject);
151: begin
152:    StackA:= TStack.Create;
153: end;
154:
155: procedure TForm1.FormDestroy(Sender: TObject);
156: begin
157:    StackA.Free;
158: end;
159:
160: end.
```

Comparing Listings 14.5 and 14.6:

● The type declarations for TPCell and TCell are the same in each, but in Listing 14.6 the declaration has moved up to the interface part, lines 8–13. This ensures it is within scope for TStack.

● TStack in Listing 14.6 is the object which includes the structure of a stack of characters, and methods to perform operations on such stacks. The procedure and function headers appear in lines 18–22 and 25, as well as a constructor and a destructor. The methods, apart from IsEmpty, are public, so they could be accessed from another unit.

● IsEmpty is private to the unit, but if the programmer decides to make it available to other units then it just needs to be moved to the public part.

● Line 24 of Listing 14.6 declares StackTop which is a property of TStack; it is the address of the top of a stack. It is private to this unit, as it is part of the inner mechanism of the TStack object.

● Line 55 of Listing 14.6 instantiates an object StackA, which is used in the very simple event handlers that appear near the end of this listing. Essentially each event handler uses a method of TStack. For instance in line 137 TForm1.Push1Click calls the Push method of TStack to manipulate StackA.

● The class TStack has a Clear method, which is similar in its action to Dispose1Click near the end of Listing 14.5. It is also used in the destructor in line 65 of Listing 14.6, to clear all the pointers and the space allocated for the individual cells that make up the stack.

● The constructor and destructor are used in lines 152 and 157 to create an object when the form is created, and destroy it when the form itself is destroyed.

14.8 Summary

This chapter introduced the powerful concept of pointers. Pointers are used in many complex structures, and this was illustrated by programming a stack. Initially this was done in classical Pascal, and finally in an object-oriented manner.

Quiz

1. A pointer is
    (a) a variable that holds an address
    (b) a constant that holds an address
    (c) essential for program structures such as stacks and queues

2. The statement `A^ := B;`
    (a) assigns the address of `B` to `A`
    (b) assigns the value in `B` to `A`
    (c) assigns the value in `B` to the address to which `A` points

3. Parameters passed by pointers are
    (a) variable or constant
    (b) value or constant
    (c) value or variable

4. Pointers make it possible
    (a) to use bigger structures
    (b) to determine structure size at compile time
    (c) to determine structure size at run time

5. The procedure `New`
    (a) must be called at least once for each pointer type variable
    (b) gets space from the heap
    (c) is only used for objects

6. Pointers in object Pascal can be
    (a) assigned
    (b) compared
    (c) added

7. **Nil** is a pointer type constant that is
    (a) compatible with any other pointer type
    (b) assigned to every pointer variable by default
    (c) analogous to zero

8. `Dispose` is an in-built procedure
    (a) which is unnecessary in small applications
    (b) which should be used after the appropriate pointer has been assigned **nil**
    (c) which releases heap space

9. A linked list
    (a) is always preferable to an array
    (b) takes more space than the corresponding array
    (c) has exactly one pointer to it

10. A stack is
    (a) a first in first out structure
    (b) a last in last out structure
    (c) a tree structure

Exercises

1. Write an event handler to create a new linked list by reversing the elements in a given list.

2. A queue is a first in first out structure. Write a program to manipulate queues using a linked list structure.

3. Use an array as the underlying structure to write a program to manipulate stacks.

4. Write a delphi program, using linked lists, to simulate the following:

    n people are in a giant hot air balloon. It runs out of ballast and half the people aboard must be thrown overboard. There is no time for debating, so they arrange themselves around the edge of the basket, and every ninth person is thrown overboard, until only $n/2$ people remain. Add suitable graphics to illustrate people plummeting from the balloon.

5. Extend the program to associate suitable random weights with each person, and continue to jettison every ninth person until the balloon no longer is falling. The user must provide the total weight to be ejected. Illustrate with suitable graphics.

Chapter 15

Moving on

15.1 Introduction

This book aims to develop the skills required by a professional programmer. Teaching these skills within the Delphi environment allows the programmer the fun of producing attractive Graphical User Interfaces (GUIs – gooeys), while learning the fundamentals of programming. We aimed to provide only a guide to Delphi and there are many more advanced or specialized topics that we have not covered. In this chapter we will indicate some of the ways in which you may wish to develop your programming skills.

15.2 Databases

Delphi provides the programmer with powerful and flexible facilities to access both local and remote databases. Describing the fundamentals of database design and the use of Delphi database tools is a specialist area. In this section we will give a brief overview.

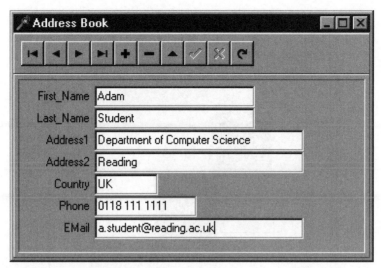

Figure 15.1   A sample database entry.

A simple database application may maintain an address book with the names of people, their addresses, telephone numbers and email accounts. The simplest database package will have facilities for entering and amending data records and deleting unwanted records. Any package would enable the user to run queries, such as extracting overseas addresses and to sort on date of birth.

More sophisticated packages allow for linking several database tables together, creating a relational database. A database of postal rates could be linked to the address database example to allow access to the current charge for sending post. Information can be stored locally or remotely. A local database is stored on the local machine or network and is in a known format. A remote database is stored elsewhere in an unknown format.

All versions of Delphi offer a number of data components that can be used to create and access databases. The Form Wizard available with the database options in later versions of Delphi facilitates the rapid adaptation of sample databases to personalized versions, in which we can enter, store and access data. An example is shown in Figure 15.1. With Delphi 1 the Form Expert (accessed via Options|Gallery) serves a similar purpose.

(15.3) MDI forms

MDI stands for Multiple Document Interface. This is the mechanism whereby word processors and spreadsheets allow one window (the MDI parent) to contain many other windows (the MDI children). The MDI parent acts as a container for multiple child windows. The child windows are restricted to the client area of the parent, within which they may be moved, resized, minimized and maximized.

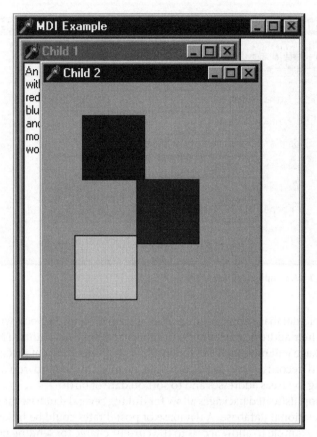

Figure 15.2 MDI example.

Delphi allows only one MDI form per project and this must be the main form: it is made MDI by setting the FormStyle property to fsMDIForm. As additional forms are created their FormStyle properties should be set to fsMDIChild. The child forms do not need to have the same functionality: one could be used for handling text, another images. As with all objects, if a number are created within a project, it is essential to destroy child windows when they are no longer required. Figure 15.2 shows an example of MDI.

(15.4) Help systems

Users expect professional Windows applications to offer a help system. Indeed users will often judge the quality of a system by the help provided. Drawing a map of the help topics to be offered and the links between them can aid the production of a friendly system. Ensure all the links exist, as users are not impressed by the message 'This topic does not exist' followed by suggestions that the user contact the vendor.

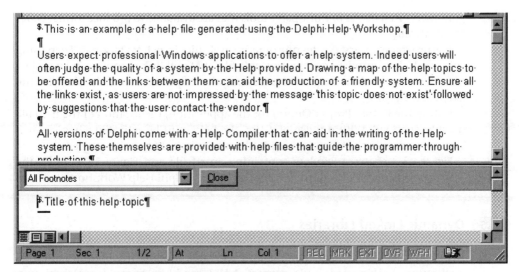

Figure 15.3   Rich text format file prepared in Microsoft Word.

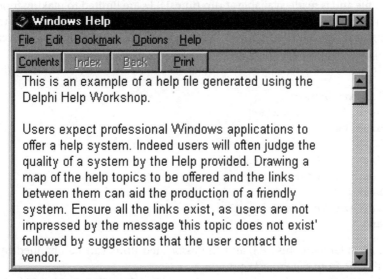

Figure 15.4   The help file generated.

All versions of Delphi come with a Help Compiler that can aid in the writing of the help system. These themselves are provided with help files that guide the programmer through production.

The approach used by Delphi requires the generation of a text file that is saved in rich text format (.rtf). Most word processors have an option that allows the user to save documents as rich text format. The programmer needs to add formatting codes, to indicate jumps, definitions and the like. Professional programmers often invest in third-party tools that are available to produce format codes automatically.

The programmer first creates one or more topic files in rich text format. Then using this, the Help Compiler creates a contents file, that will link to topics, and a project file. All elements of the help system are compiled to produce the help file (with the extension .hlp).

Within the Delphi Project|Option for the application, the location of the help file must be specified. Within the application the help must be activated when needed. There are a number of help commands that can be issued (including HelpJump).

Figure 15.3 shows a window containing an rtf file and Figure 15.4 shows the simple help file it produced when compiled by the Delphi Help Workshop.

(15.5) Dynamic Linked Libraries

A Dynamic Linked Library (DLL) is an executable module that permits multiple applications to share code and resources. A DLL can be compared to a Delphi unit, but a unit is linked into the executable at compile time, while a DLL resides in a separate file and is made available at run time. DLLs are limited to making functions and procedures available, whereas a unit can make data or objects available too. Delphi programs can use DLLs written in other languages, and programs written in other languages can use Delphi DLLs.

To create a DLL in Delphi the project file should be edited to the following format:

```
library name;
uses list of units;
exports
list of function and procedure definitions followed by an
index number, for example
testing index 1;
begin
any initialization code
end.
```

An executable of this DLL and the associated units can be obtained by selecting 'Build All' from the Project options.

To use a function from this in another project the following should be included in the implementation section:

```
function testing(const a: Integer): Integer;
external 'test.dll';
```

In Delphi 1 it will be necessary to indicate this is **far**. To avoid conflicts the index can also be specified.

Care is needed when strings are used by the DLL, because of the differences between the types of strings as highlighted in Chapter 7.

15.6 Component registering

Designing components can be likened to creating DLLs. A new component does not provide a complete application; it provides a component that an application writer will (hopefully) find useful. We have seen in Chapter 10 how to create new components based on existing components and from the generic type TObject, to use within the current application. Now we will discuss making such components more generally available.

A new component can be made available by putting it into the Component Palette. This is achieved by the following steps:

1. Write a Register procedure for the unit that contains the components you want to add.

2. Create a palette bitmap for each of the components.

3. Rebuild the Component Palette so as to include the new components.

The Register procedure must appear in the interface section of the unit. In the implementation section Register must include a call to RegisterComponents, for example:

```
RegisterComponents ('Samples',[TMyPanel]);
```

A suitable bitmap can be created using the image editor from the Tools menu and saved with the extension .dcr.

The component can then be installed using the Component|Install Component option with later versions of Delphi, or the Options| Install Component with Delphi 1.

15.7 Multimedia

The Delphi MediaPlayer component allows the incorporation of animation and sound into applications. Producing a professional quality display will need careful design and experimentation. However, getting a Delphi application to play music from a CD or a clip of a video is straightforward. On a form place a MediaPlayer component from the Systems page of the Component Palette. Setting the AutoOpen property to true and the FileName property to a file containing a video file (.avi) will create a simple video player. When executed, if the Play button is pressed a video window will open. The video can be made to play inside the form, by placing using a suitable component. In Figure 15.5 a panel has been placed on the form and the Display property of the MediaPlayer set to the panel. The video clip shown is from the Delphi distribution CD.

Figure 15.5 Multimedia.

(15.8) Communicating with other Windows applications

Windows allows several programs to run at once (multitask). We saw in Chapter 6 that it is possible to copy material from a word processing package and paste it into a running Delphi memo box. More sophisticated use of the clipboard can be made by including the ClipBrd unit in the **uses** statement of a unit. This allows exchange of data and images.

Dynamic Data Exchange (DDE) sends data to and receives data from other applications. With Delphi, text can be exchanged with other applications. It may also send commands and macros to other applications, so the Delphi application can control other applications.

The newer OLE (Object Linking and Embedding) goes beyond DDE, allowing the embedding of other applications within a Delphi application. There are many sophisticated ways of using this, but it is possible to create a simple example using the Paint package provided with Windows. Place on a form an OLEContainer (from the Systems page of the Component Palette), then double click on the container to bring up an Insert Object dialog box. In our example we chose a bitmap image, selecting to link one already in file. When this project is run, the bitmap is shown in the container. Double clicking on the image opens up our default bitmap editor (Paint). Changes made to the bitmap are reflected in the file and the Delphi form.

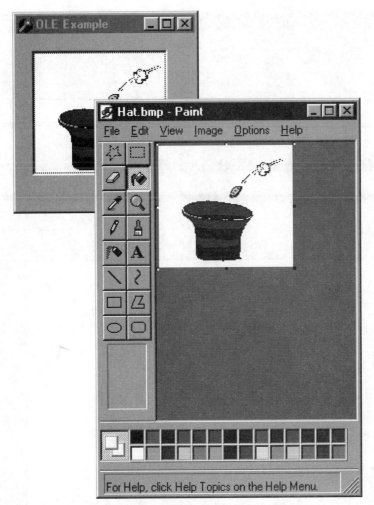

Figure 15.6 Using OLE to access another application.

(15.9) Internet and ActiveX

The Client-Server versions of Delphi provides a number of components that make building Internet and Intranet applications easy. The Internet refers to a generally accessible network, while the Intranet has limited access; for example, it is usually internal to a company. These facilitate interaction with the Web browser and allow the design of static and dynamic Web pages.

ActiveX is provided in newer versions of Delphi, allowing compatibility with other languages and systems, and encompassing the functionality of OLE. ActiveX facilitates communication between client and server objects. ActiveX is used extensively for the creation of dynamic Web pages, allowing the person reading the Web page to

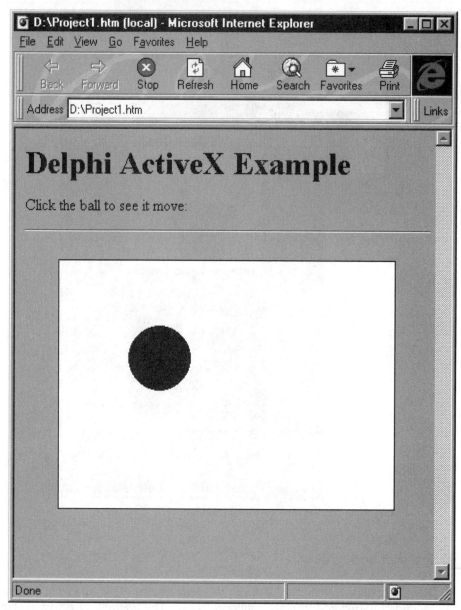

Figure 15.7   A Delphi program on an ActiveX form.

make choices and appropriate actions to be taken. The majority of the programs developed in this book could be placed on active forms and deployed in Web browsers. Figure 15.7 shows a Delphi program that has been adapted from the one developed in Chapter 5. The adapted program allows a ball to bounce across the Web page, here viewed via Microsoft Internet Explorer.

(15.10) Other programming languages

Having mastered Delphi it may be tempting to believe there will be no need to learn another programming language. For some people this may well be true. Others seeking employment in the computer industry will find that programmers are expected to know several programming languages. Our approach to introducing programming has covered general techniques as well as specifics, so learning the next language should be relatively easy.

If you choose to learn C++ using the Borland C++ Builder, this will enable you to work within an environment that is intrinsically the same as Delphi. Likewise using Borland's J Builder will offer the same advantages if you choose to learn Java.

(15.11) Summary

In this section we have offered a taste of the way in which you could develop your Delphi skills. There are many things you could do. We recommend you experiment with those that appeal to you.

Quiz

1. The easy way to create a database with Delphi is to use
   (a) the Form Expert
   (b) the Form Wizard
   (c) a relational database

2. MDI stands for
   (a) Media Device Interface
   (b) Multiple Device Interface
   (c) Multiple Document Interface

3. Rich text format (rtf) documents are best generated via
   (a) Delphi
   (b) a word processor
   (c) a drawing package

4. Generating help files should be done using
   (a) the Delphi help compiler
   (b) third-party tools
   (c) a map

5. The project file of a DLL (Dynamic Linked Library) should start with which of these keywords?
   (a) `program`
   (b) `unit`
   (c) `library`

6. Can Delphi programs use DLLs written in other programming languages?
    (a) yes
    (b) no
    (c) only those written in C++

7. What can an OLEContainer component access?
    (a) bitmap images
    (b) word processor documents
    (c) movie clips

8. The clipboard can be used to
    (a) exchange information between memo components
    (b) move objects from one Delphi form to another
    (c) exchange information between Delphi applications and other applications

9. Which versions of Delphi provide ActiveX?
    (a) Delphi 1
    (b) Delphi 2
    (c) Delphi 3 and 4

10. What other programming languages will it be useful to learn?
    (a) FORTRAN
    (b) Java
    (c) C++

Exercises

1. Create a CD player.

2. Develop a Delphi database for storing names and birthdays.

3. Create a multiple document form, where the user can enter text in one window and view bitmaps in another, add a Help option to the main menu and offer different advice depending on which window is active.

4. Link a spreadsheet into a Delphi application, use it for entering data and displaying graphs corresponding to rainfall over a period of weeks.

5. Create an active Web page.

Appendix A

Debugging aids and techniques

....

A.1 Introduction

A programmer writes source code, and then attempts to compile it. Usually, this is not too difficult to do within Delphi, because the Pascal compiler flags errors with a brief message. Pressing F1 shows further details if necessary. Pascal is strongly typed, so once the units compile, the project will usually start to execute. However, there are two further stages where problems can occur: at run time and in the logic.

A.2 Run time errors

These occur when the code is consistent, so it compiles, but obvious problems surface during the execution. Classic examples are an attempt to divide by zero, or to access a non-existent file. In either case, if the executable file is run outside Delphi, the operating system will stop execution, and display an error message such as that shown in Figure A.1; it will differ somewhat according to the operating system in use.

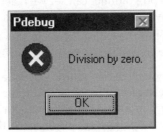

Figure A.1   Run time error division by zero in Windows 95.

If the project is run within Delphi, and if Break On Exception has been checked as in Figure A.4, then an exception will be raised indicating where the error occurred. For instance, if the code attempts to divide by zero, then the compiler will flag it, as illustrated in Figure A.2. We discussed the possibility of leaving Break On Exception unchecked, the programmer then providing code to deal with exceptions individually, in Chapter 11.

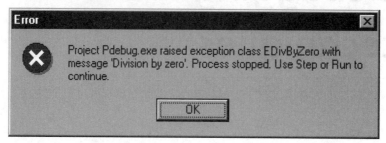

Figure A.2   Exception raised on division by zero.

A.3 Logical errors

These errors are apparent at an even later stage. Although the project runs to completion, the results are not as expected. In other words, the code appears perfect to the programming environment, but that code has not performed as the programmer intended. The source of such an error can be elusive, and the integrated debugger is an invaluable tool to track down logical errors.

A.4 Good programming practices to avoid errors

- Keep functions and procedures small, so they can be inspected and tested easily.
- Use meaningful identifiers, so inspection is easy.
- Test each function or procedure individually.
- Define variables and functions locally where possible.
- Indent your code, so that **begin end** pairs are aligned.
- Comment code, so a programmer can see what action is intended. This is particularly important if any obscure techniques are used.
- Check everything set in the Object Inspector; for this purpose the text listing of the * . dfm file can be viewed in the Code Editor window.

Even though all these guidelines are followed, subtle errors may still remain. This is where the integrated debugger helps. Note that there is another specialized product, the Turbo Debugger for Windows, which is useful for advanced programming, but is outside the scope of this text. If you do want to use the Turbo Debugger then check 'Include TD32 debug info' on the Linker tab of Project|Options in Delphi 2 or 3, but this is unnecessary for the integrated debugger. In Delphi 1 the equivalent is Options|Project, and the item to check is 'Include TDW debug info' in both Delphi 1 and 2. Checking Include TD32 Debug Info or equivalent makes the executable considerably bigger, so it is important to turn it off and recompile finally.

A.5 Using the integrated debugger

A.5.1 Compilation and preparation

In order to use a debugger the project must first be compiled with symbolic debug information, which connects the executable with the source code which created it. Suitable options are normally on by default, but if in doubt check that the debugging options are set as indicated in Figure A.3. Note that other versions of Delphi show a different layout and varying options.

If none of the debugging options in Figure A.3 is checked, then only globally declared variables will be available to Watches (see later), and they will only be available when outside procedures.

Checking Debug Information makes globally declared variables available to Watches within procedures also.

Checking Local Symbols makes all values in scope available within a procedure.

The extra information is stored in the appropriate Delphi Compiled Unit (.DCU) file.

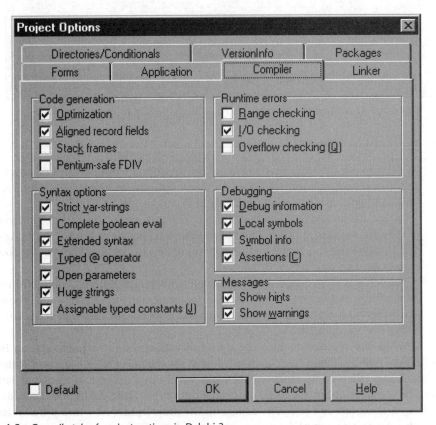

Figure A.3 Compile tab of project options in Delphi 3.

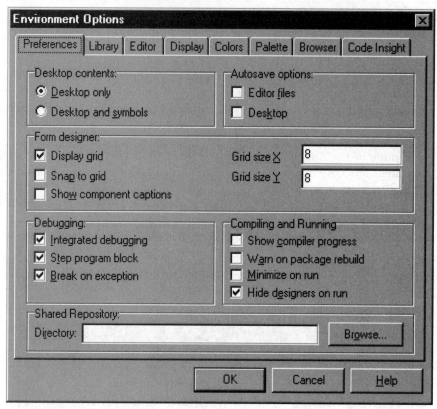

Figure A.4   Enabling the debugger.

A.5.2   Breakpoints and other facilities

In order to use the integrated debugger the appropriate option must be checked on the preferences tab for Tools|Environment options, as shown in Figure A.4 for Delphi 3 (Options|Environment in Delphi 1).

Within the debugger there are options to run the project line by line, and to pause at the current cursor position, and at pre-assigned positions known as breakpoints. The breakpoints can be viewed and manipulated in the Breakpoints window: see Figures A.5 and A.6.

The debugger is versatile, and hence there are several methods of doing things. It is also easy for the beginner to set breakpoints accidentally in Delphi 1 or 2. The easiest way to get rid of an unwanted breakpoint is to click the red stop sign at the left-hand end of the offending line.

While the application runs the values of variables or of expressions can be displayed continually in the Watch window as shown in Figure A.7, as long as they are in scope. This is complemented in Delphi 3 and 4 by a number of advanced features. The compiler optimizes code (unless the option in Figure A.3 is not checked). This can make it difficult to follow code, and the programmer may find it useful to turn off optimization whilst debugging.

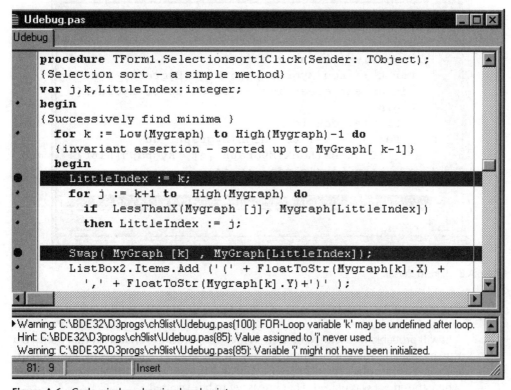

Figure A.5 Breakpoints window.

```
procedure TForm1.Selectionsort1Click(Sender: TObject);
{Selection sort - a simple method}
var j,k,LittleIndex:integer;
begin
{Successively find minima }
  for k := Low(Mygraph) to High(Mygraph)-1 do
  {invariant assertion - sorted up to MyGraph[ k-1]}
  begin
     LittleIndex := k;
    for j := k+1 to  High(Mygraph) do
      if LessThanX(Mygraph [j], Mygraph[LittleIndex])
      then LittleIndex := j;

     Swap( MyGraph [k] , MyGraph[LittleIndex]);
     ListBox2.Items.Add ('(' + FloatToStr(Mygraph[k].X) +
       ',' + FloatToStr(Mygraph[k].Y)+')' );
```

▶Warning: C:\BDE32\D3progs\ch9list\Udebug.pas(100): FOR-Loop variable 'k' may be undefined after loop.
Hint: C:\BDE32\D3progs\ch9list\Udebug.pas(85): Value assigned to 'j' never used.
Warning: C:\BDE32\D3progs\ch9list\Udebug.pas(85): Variable 'j' might not have been initialized.

81: 9   Insert

Figure A.6 Code window showing breakpoints.

A.5.3   Starting to use the debugger

Projects under development are best compiled with debug information, for use if required. If an unexplained run time or logical error appears, the offending code must be isolated. Usually the output from the project will give useful clues. At least

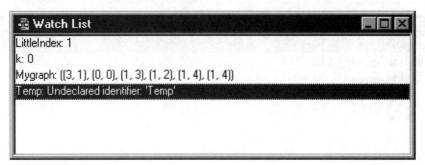

Figure A.7   Watch window during execution.

```
Udebug.pas                                        _ □ ✕

Udebug

    {Selection sort - a simple method}
    var j,k,LittleIndex:integer;
  •   begin
    {Successively find minima }
  •     for k := Low(Mygraph) to High(Mygraph)-1 do
        {invariant assertion - sorted up to MyGraph[
        begin
  •         LittleIndex := k;
  •         for j := k+1 to  High(Mygraph) do
  •             if  LessThanX(Mygraph [j], Mygraph[Littl
  •             then LittleIndex := j;

  • ⇨       Swap( MyGraph [k] , MyGraph[LittleIndex]);

    93: 1                      Insert
```

Figure A.8   Run To Cursor.

the programmer may be able to say that the code appears sound before a certain point.

It will probably be useful to find the values of significant variables at that point. Do this by placing the cursor appropriately in the code, then choosing Run|Run To Cursor. The result is shown in Figure A.8, and the arrow and highlighting indicate where the cursor was placed. That line is yet to be executed.

It is now possible to find the values of the variables in scope. Do this by adding variables to the Watch window (Figure A.10), by either

● placing the cursor in the code choosing Add Watch At Cursor from right mouse menu, or

● choosing View|Watches and the Add Watch from right mouse menu and typing a variable name.

Watch Properties   ✕

Expression: [   ] ▼

Repeat count: [0]   Digits: [18]   ☑ Enabled

○ Character   ○ Hex integer   ○ Record
○ String   ○ Ordinal   ◉ Default
○ Decimal integer ○ Pointer   ☐ Memory dump

[OK]   [Cancel]   [Help]

Figure A.9   Watch Properties.

Watch List   _ □ ✕

j: 6
k: 0
Mygraph: ((1, 1), (4, 1), (1, 4), (2, 4), (0, 2), (4, 1))

Figure A.10   Corresponding Watch window to Figure A.8.

In either case the Watch Properties window as seen in Figure A.9 will show. The variable name should be typed into the expression box, and, as the name suggests, expressions rather than simple variables can be inserted. In order to see values in the Watch window the program must be run; until it runs the variables will labelled 'process inaccessible'.

The bug will often be revealed by tracing from this point, that is, the programmer makes a row for each variable, then updates it as he or she considers the computer will, step by step, as shown:

j	?	0	1	2	3	4	5	6	6	6	
k	?	0	0	0	0	0	0	0	1	1	
i		?	?	?	?	?	?	?	?	?	
LittleIndex	?	0	0	0	2	2	2	2	2	1	

Such tracing can be compared with what indeed happens by choosing Run|TraceInto to step through the code line by line. The values in the Watch window will change, and more variables, or even expressions, can be added to the Watch window, as wanted. The right mouse button can be used to add, delete permanently or disable one or all Watch expressions.

Once the problem has been solved, Run|Program Reset can be used to return to the editing window. In Delphi 1 this gives rise to the rather alarming message shown in Figure A.11. Choosing OK is the normal option here for simple programs.

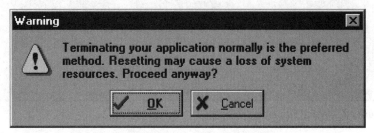

Figure A.11   Warning message after use of Program Reset in Delphi 1.

A5.4   More advanced use

Breakpoints allow the programmer to set, disable or delete a number of points where the project run halts. The programmer can set breakpoints either before running the code at all, or during a run. In any case the method is the same: clicking in the grey left-hand gutter in Delphi 3, or in a similar position in Delphi 1 and Delphi 2. As we have already mentioned, breakpoints can be removed by clicking on them. The programmer can then examine variables or expressions as has already been described, and run the project again from that point. A Breakpoints window, an example of which was shown in Figure A.5, can be manipulated within a window in much the same manner as the Watch window.

The Run menu has an option to show execution point, which is useful if that point is not obvious in an open window. Yet another advanced option is Run|Evaluate/Modify, which should be used with care: it enables the programmer to evaluate expressions, and to change the values of variables.

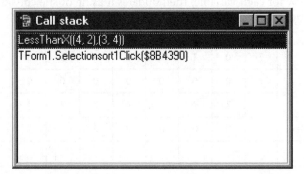

Figure A.12   Call Stack window.

The Call Stack window as shown in Figure A.12 shows a list of procedure and function calls and their parameters; the top one is the one last called. This is particularly useful for looking at recursive calls.

The Watch Properties window has options to change the display of expressions, although the default is sufficient for many purposes. It also has a repeat option, which shows the values in memory locations adjacent to a named variable.

Appendix B

Glossary

··

Actual parameters   The parameters used in a procedure call.

Ada   A high-level programming language developed for the American Department of Defense.

and   Boolean operator. X **and** Y evaluates to true only if both X and Y are true.

ANSI   American National Standards Institute. Extended ANSI refers to the 8-bit extension of the ASCII character code.

AnsiString   A long string available in later editions of Delphi.

API   The Windows Application Programming Interface.

Application   The executable file that is the sum of all the code the programmer has used or developed, sometimes called the program.

ASCII   American Standard Code for Information Interchange. The standard 7-bit code for representing characters; see also ANSI and UNICODE.

Assembler language   Computer language that uses mnemonics rather than 0 and 1 (machine language).

Assign   Place a value in a memory location, indicated in Object Pascal by := (note there is no space between the colon and the equals).

Assignment compatible   Two objects or variables sufficiently close in type for one to be assigned to the other.

BASIC   Beginners All-purpose Symbolic Instruction Code: a high-level programming language.

Binary   A number system to base 2; see bit.

Bit   A binary digit, either 0 or 1.

Bitmap   Type of file produced by typical painting applications, and stored as an array of pixels.

Boolean   Takes just two alternative values, true or false.

Breakpoint   A point in code marked for the debugger to pause execution at.

Bug   An error in code.

Byte   A data type capable of holding 8 bits (256 values).

C   A programming language that can be used in both a high-level and a low-level fashion.

C++   An object-oriented extension of C.

Canvas   The surface of an object that can be drawn on.

Cardinal   A non-negative whole number.

Case sensitive   Where the use of upper and lower case letters is significant. The Object Pascal compiler is not case sensitive.

Cast   Change the type an object is treated as belonging to.

Class   An object class declaration describes the constituent parts of the object. Formally it is a static description of an object that is used to create instances of objects.

Code Editor window   The window where code can be edited, initially hidden behind the Form Designer. Sometimes called the Code window. If more than one unit is open the project tabs can be used to switch between them.

Code window   See Code Editor window.

Colon
1. Used with types in declarations.
2. When placed immediately in front of the equals sign creates the *assigns to* symbol :=.

Column major   An array where the first index represents the column and the second the row, as with Delphi grid components; see also row major.

Comments   Information for the reader that is ignored by the compiler; see compiler directive.

Compile   To translate the whole of a unit's source code (Object Pascal) into machine code. See also interpret.

Compiler directive   Instruction to compiler software, enclosed in comment brackets.

Component   Object that can be used at design time. It can be a control or non-visual.

Component Palette   The tabbed list of component icons representing components that can be placed on a form at design time.

Compound statement   A group of statements, enclosed between a **begin** and an **end**. Can be treated as a statement.

Conditional   A branching statement.

Console   Window used for simple input/output, such as the DOS window.

Constant identifier   An identifier whose value cannot change, it is a literal.

Control   A visual component that can appear at run time.

Crash   A system failure, often resulting in the machine having to be rebooted.

C string   A null terminated string, provided in Delphi for compatibility with Windows API.

Database   A structured arrangement of data for user access.

DDE   Dynamic Data Exchange.

Debugging   The process of finding and fixing errors in programs.

Descendant   An object inheriting from another.

Design time   When a Delphi application is being designed using the Form Designer, Component Palette, Object Inspector and Code window. See also run time.

Deterministic loop   A loop in which the number of iterations is known before cycling starts.

Dialog box   Special window used to communicate with the application user.

Directory   The operating system's hierarchy for storing files is divided into directories and sub-directories, sometimes called folders.

DLLs   Dynamic Linked Libraries (DLLs) allow several programs to share code and resources.

DOS   Disc Operating System, the traditional PC operating system.

Dragging   Moving an object by pressing and holding down the left mouse button to drag the item to its new position.

Drawing package   A package that allows the user to create simple graphics, normally stored as bitmap files (e.g. Microsoft Paint). Advanced programmers can create one using Delphi.

Dropping   Releasing an object at the end of dragging.

Dynamic   Capable of altering as the program executes. For example, a dynamic data structure may be allocated memory and later in the program release it. Opposite of static.

Encapsulation   The grouping together of data and related operations into an object.

Event   A user action, such as a mouse click, or a system occurrence such as the end of a time interval.

Event handler   The code executed when an event occurs.

Exception   An object created by Delphi when it detects a run time error.

Exponent   Power, usually of base 10, indicated by superscript in mathematics.

Expression   Combination of operators and operands.

Field   One possible element of an object or record.

File   In general, a set of related records. A source file contains Object Pascal code; a data file can be of type text or binary.

Fixed format   Conventional representation of a floating-point number, in the form *whole.fraction.*

Focus   The component or window that will accept input from the keyboard. If a button has focus, pressing Enter will be the same as clicking it.

Folder   In newer versions of Windows, documents and programs are stored in folders; see also directory.

Form Designer   The prototype form used for designing the actual form, usually characterized by the grid of dots.

Formal parameters   The parameters used in a procedure definition.

FORTRAN   A high-level language designed for use by scientists.

Free format   Items need not appear in a particular position on a line and line breaks are not significant. Spaces can be used to improve readability, but they cannot be arbitrarily inserted in identifiers, strings or operators.

Fundamental   Independent of the platform.

Garbage collection   Releasing memory no longer required by an application for future use.

Generic   May vary across platforms. Usually generic types give more efficient code.

Gigabyte 10^9 bytes.

Global   In scope throughout the program, except when redeclared.

Graphic   General term covering pictorial representations from drawing, painting and other packages.

GUI   Graphical User Interface.

Hexadecimal   A number system to base 16, represented by digits 0 to 9 and letters A to F.

High-level language   A programming language allowing meaningful identifiers.

Icon   A pictorial representation, such as the Delphi temple, rather than text.

IDE   The Interactive Development Environment (IDE) consists of all the tools that facilitate the use of Delphi, including the Component Palette, Object Inspector and Form Designer.

Identifiers   A label or name in source code.

Image   In Delphi an image component is an area upon which a picture can be placed or drawings can be done.

Implementation section   The code following the keyword **implementation**. This is local to the unit and can only be accessed via the interface section.

Increment   Increase by a step, normally 1 by default.

Index   A variable used to access an element of an array.

Infinite loop   A loop that does not exit normally, often only stopped by rebooting the PC.

Inheritance   The ability to make descendant (child) classes descending from an ancestor (parent) or base class. A descendant inherits and can extend the fields, methods and properties of its ancestor object, except those that are private.

Input stream   Data obtained during execution, for example from the keyboard.

Instance   An object created from a class, sometimes referred to as an instantiation of an object.

Integer   Whole number.

Interface section   Specifies the objects, identifiers etc. that are available to other units. The corresponding code is in the implementation section.

Interpret   To translate source code line by line into machine code; thus produces less efficient code than the compilation approach used by Delphi. See also compile.

Iteration   Repeating code many times, as in a loop.

Keyword   A word or symbol having a special meaning (for example the word **begin**), see also reserved word.

Link   To join together the parts of a project, including the compiled files to create an executable file. See also linked lists.

Linked lists   A data structure built with pointers.

Literal   An actual number or character string.

Local   Only in scope within the current procedure or function.

Loop   See iteration.

Low-level language   A programming language reflecting the structure of the computer, usually with little resemblance to English.

Main menu   Menu bar across top of form, with drop down submenus.

MDI   Multiple Document Interface.

Megabyte 10^6 bytes.

Memory leakage   Memory that has been allocated to a program, which the program has lost access to but failed to release.

Memory location   Area of storage accessible via its address.

Menu bar   The list of menu options at the top of a form.

Metafile   Collection of commands to produce a graphic; requires less storage than a bitmap.

Method   A routine that performs operations on the fields of an object.

Modal   A form that must be closed before the remainder of the application can continue.

Modeless   A form that can remain open while the rest of the application continues.

Modula-2   A high-level programming language, part of the Pascal family.

Multimedia   The incorporation of animation and sound.

Nesting   Similar items inside each other.

Nil   A pointer value referencing nothing.

Non-deterministic loop   A loop in which the number of iterations is not known before cycling starts.

Null   Does nothing or represents the character #0.

Null terminated string   See C string.

Object   Data and related operations, encapsulated together.

Object Inspector   A design time window used to set design time properties of components and create event handlers.

Object oriented   A programming style based on objects.

Object Pascal   The underlying programming language of Delphi. See also Pascal.

OLE   Object Linking and Embedding.

Operand   Literal or value upon which an operator acts.

Operator   Symbol for an action, such as * for multiplication.

or   Boolean operator. X **or** Y evaluates to true only if either or both of X and Y are true.

Ordinal   A type with a specific number of elements in a definite order.

Overriding   A new method defined by a child object with the same name as an existing method in the parent.

Palette   Selection of alternatives, usually colours. Compare an artist's palette.

Parameter   Used to pass data to a procedure and receive data back.

Parsing   The process by which the compiler determines the meaning of each program statement.

Pascal   A high-level programming language.

PC   Personal computer.

Persistent variable   A variable that keeps its value even when it has been out of scope.

Pixel   One of the coloured dots that makes an image on the screen. The height and width of visual components are measured in pixels.

Platform   Computer type, such as IBM compatible PC, SUN workstation.

Pointer   A memory location containing the address of another location.

Polymorphism   Allows late-binding of methods, so the method to use with a particular object is not determined until run time. This allows the use of different methods depending on the class of object calling it.

Pop up menu   Alternative to a main menu which appears on an event, normally a right mouse click. Different pop up menus can be associated with parts of a form.

Precedence   Order in which operators are applied.

Precision   Accuracy of data either as stored or as displayed.

Program
  1. An executable file; see also application.
  2. A generic term for code that a programmer develops.
  3. The keyword that all projects start with.

Programmer   The person developing the program.

Project
  1. The collection of all the files that together make up a Delphi application.
  2. The main source code file that lists all the units the application depends on.

Property   An attribute of an object, which looks like a field of a record, but provides access to both fields and methods.

Prototype   First model, to be refined.

Pseudocode   An informal notation, representing a programming language with some natural language text.

Random   Usually means pseudo-random, an apparently random sequence produced by a formula. It depends on an initial 'seed'.

Real

1. A number with a decimal point.
2. Part of a complex number.

Rebooting   Stopping and restarting the PC; can be done by Ctrl+Alt+Delete, but work may be lost.

Recursion   A function or procedure that calls itself.

Reserved word   Identifier with predefined meaning, sometimes called keyword.

Rich text format (rtf)   A printable ASCII character set representation of text formatting. Used in the production of help files.

Row major   An array where the first index represents the rows and the second the columns.

Run time   The application as seen by the user when it is executed.

Scope   The visibility of an identifier within a program or unit.

Semantics   The rules defining the effect of an operation; see also syntax.

Semicolon   Separates Object Pascal statements; not to be confused with the colon.

Source code   The code written by the programmer which will be compiled. See compile.

Spreadsheet   Grid of rows and columns, facilitating calculations.

Speed bar   The speed bar provides shortcuts for frequently used menu commands.

Statement   A command or instruction. See also compound statement.

Static   Fixed at compile time, for example the memory allocation of a static variable is fixed at compile time. See also dynamic.

String   An array of characters.

Strongly typed   Every variable has a type which constrains its use. See also weakly typed.

Subrange   A contiguous range of an ordinal type.

Syntax   The rules defining the sequence of elements within a program; see also semantics.

Third-party components   Components written by other people. These can be purchased or are sometimes freely available via the Internet.

Turbo Pascal   Borland's PC-based Pascal.

Type checking   Verifying the type of an object.

Unary minus   A subtraction operator that negates a single operand, for example -3.

UNICODE   A 16-bit code for representing an extensive set of international characters; the first 256 characters match extended ANSI. See also ASCII.

Unit   The Object Pascal code for a project is stored in units. Each unit can be independently compiled thus facilitating modular programming.

Unit wide   In scope within the whole of the unit, unless redeclared.

UNIX™   An operating system.

User   The person running the program, usually distinct from the programmer who has written the code. Sometimes called the end user.

User-defined type   A type defined by the programmer.

Variable declaration   List of identifiers and their types.

Virtual method   The mechanism that allows polymorphism.

Watch expression   A value the programmer requests to be calculated by the debugger.

Weakly typed   Variables of different types can be mixed, which can lead to errors. See also strongly typed.

Word

1. A group of bits handled as a single item.
2. A popular word processor from Microsoft.

xor   Boolean operator. X **xor** Y evaluates to true if one and only one of X and Y is true.

Appendix C

References and suggested reading

On Delphi

These are the books on Delphi we have found most useful:

Cornell, G. (1996). *Delphi Nuts and Bolts for Experienced Programmers*, 2nd edition. McGraw-Hill, New York.

Duntemann, J., Mischel, J. and Taylor, D. (1996). *The New Delphi 2 Programming Explorer*. Coriolis Books, Scottsdale, AZ.

Gurewich, N. and Gurewich, O. (1995). *Teach Yourself Database Programming with Delphi*. SAMS Publishing, Indianapolis.

Miller, T., Powell, D. *et al.* (1997). *Special Edition using Delphi 3*. Que, Indianapolis.

Thorpe, D. (1997). *Delphi Component Design*. Addison-Wesley, New York.

On pointers and linked structures

Wirth, N. (1976). *Algorithms + Data Structures = Programs*. Prentice Hall, Englewood Cliffs, NJ.

On algorithms, including Quicksort

Sedgewick, R. (1988). *Algorithms*, 2nd edition. Addison-Wesley, New York.

General interest

Gleick, J. (1993). *Chaos*. Abacus, London.

Borland

Manuals and online help supplied with Delphi.

Web addresses

Borland site is currently at http://www.inprise.com/

Quiz answers

Chapter 1

1. (a)
2. (b)
3. (c)
4. (a) and (c)
5. (b)
6. (c)
7. (b)
8. (a)
9. (a)
10. (a), (b) and (c)

Chapter 2

1. (b)
2. (a)
3. (c)
4. (b)
5. (a)
6. (a)
7. (a)
8. (b)
9. (a)
10. (c)

Chapter 3

1. (a)
2. (b)
3. (a)
4. (b)
5. (a)

6. (b)
7. (a)
8. (b)
9. (c)
10. (a) and (c) in all versions, but also (b) in later versions

Chapter 4

1. (a)
2. (b)
3. (a)
4. (c)
5. (c)
6. (a) and (b)
7. (b)
8. (b) if `Number` is integer; it will be converted to a real type if `Number` is real.
9. (c)
10. (a) and (b)

Chapter 5

1. (b)
2. (a)
3. (b)
4. (b), though an in-built function might be useful too in some circumstances.
5. (c)
6. (c)

7. (a)
8. (b)
9. (b) Canvas itself has a pen property.
10. (b) More than one timer is allowed, but they are resource hungry.

Chapter 6

1. (b) or (c)
2. (a)
3. (c) However, several conditions may be combined into one Boolean expression, so (a) is true also.
4. All answers possible.
5. (b)
6. (c), but (b) is possible too, if the caption is changed.
7. (a)
8. (a)
9. (b) under Delphi 1, but (c) under later versions.
10. All answers possible.

Chapter 7

1. (a)
2. (a)
3. (c)
4. (b)
5. (c)
6. (c)
7. (c) AnsiString is the name of the type which represents long strings.
8. (b)
9. (a), though it can also be set via the Object Inspector.
10. (a); (b) is also valid for a one-dimensional array.

Chapter 8

1. (c), though strictly if there was anything else in scope with a field left it would change that.
2. (b), although (a) is also useful in

some situations, for example coordinates.
3. (a)
4. (a)
5. (c)
6. (a)
7. (b)
8. (a)
9. (a)
10. (c)

Chapter 9

1. (c)
2. (b)
3. (c)
4. (a)
5. (c)
6. (a)
7. (b)
8. (a), but (c) could be mutual recursion, where procedures or functions call each other.
9. (a) but also memos have a Lines property, and list boxes have an Items property, and both of these have an Add method.
10. (a)

Chapter 10

1. (c)
2. (c)
3. (a)
4. (c)
5. (a)
6. (b)
7. (c), that is in the interface or implementation section but not inside anything else.
8. (c)
9. (a)
10. (c)

Chapter 11

1. (c)

2. (a)
3. (c)
4. (a) or (b)
5. (c)
6. (a)
7. (a) or (b)
8. (c)
9. (b)
10. (b) or (c)

Chapter 12

1. (b)
2. (a)
3. (c) Compiler directives can be used to change the maximum number of elements.
4. (b)
5. (b) although initially none may be selected.
6. (c)
7. (c)
8. (c)
9. (a)
10. (a)

Chapter 13

1. (c)
2. (a) and (c)
3. (c)
4. (a)
5. (b) and (c)
6. (b)
7. (a)

8. (b)
9. (a), though it is also useful to agree on (c) or to follow organizational standards.
10. (b)

Chapter 14

1. (a) Pointers are useful but not essential for programming stacks and queues.
2. (c)
3. (a)
4. (c), but possibly (a) also, because space can be reused.
5. (b)
6. (a) and (b)
7. (a) and (c)
8. (c)
9. (b)
10. (b)

Chapter 15

1. (b) in later versions of Delphi, (a) in Delphi 1
2. (c)
3. (b)
4. (a) or (b)
5. (c)
6. (a)
7. (a), (b) or (c)
8. (a), (b) or (c)
9. (c)
10. That is for you to decide!

Summary of the main Object Pascal constructs

This appendix is provided as an aid to program design and writing, especially when away from the computer. It is not intended to replace the detailed syntax diagrams available within online help. In this appendix we use the term *action* to indicate that either a single statement or a compound statement can be used.

General

A compound statement is of the form:

```
begin statement 1; statement 2; ... statement n  end
```

For example

```
begin
  Number := -Number;
  NegativeTotal := NegativeTotal + Number;
  Inc(NumberOfNegativeNumbers);
end;
```

A **with** statement is of the form:

```
with record or class name do action
```

For example

```
with StartDate do
begin
  DayNo := 1;
  MonthNo := 10;
  Year := 1990;
end {with StartDate};
```

Commonly used types

```
Integer, Cardinal, Single, Double, Boolean, Char, string
```

For example
_____

```
var AInt, BInt: Integer; AChar: Char;
```

Conditional constructs

if _something is true_ **then** _action_

For example
_____

```
if Number < 0 then
   Number := -Number;
```

if _something is true_ **then** _action 1_ **else** _action 2_

For example
_____

```
if (Number >= 0) and (Number <= 100) then
   Inc(InRange)
else
   Inc(OutOfRange);

case selector of
ordinal list 1:
      action 1;
ordinal list 2:
      action 2;
...
ordinal list n:
      action n;
else
      other action;
end;
```

For example
_____

```
case Number of
   10: Inc(TenCount);
   20: Inc(TwentyCount);
   30: Inc(ThirtyCount);
```

```
else
    Inc(OutOfRangeCount)
end;
```

Looping constructs

for *control variable := initial value* **to** *final value* **do** *action*

```
for Count := 1 to 10 do
    ShowMessage('Here we are again');
```

for *control variable := initial value* **downto** *final value* **do**
    action;

```
for Count := -1 downto -10 do
    ShowMessage('Here we are again');
```

while *something is true* **do** *action*

```
while Cats+Kittens < MaxCat do
begin
  if (Months mod 3 = 0) and (Months > 0) then
  begin
    Cats := Cats+Kittens;
    Kittens := 2*OldCats;
  end; {if}
  Inc(Months);
end;
```

repeat *statements* **until** *something is true*

```
repeat
  Write('Enter initial number of cats: ');
  Read(Cats);
  Write('Enter initial number of kittens: ');
  Read(Kittens);
until (Cats >= 0) and (Kittens >= 0);
```

Procedure and function headers

procedure *procedure identifier(formal parameter list);*

function *function identifier(formal parameter list): result type;*

where

- *procedure identifier* and *function identifier* obey the usual rules for identifiers;
- *formal parameter list* is of the form

    var *or* **const** *or nothing identifier list 1 : type 1;*

    ...

    var *or* **const** *or nothing identifier list n : type n*

(For example)
_____

```
procedure SumA (const MyTen: array of Single; var Sum: Single);

function Growth(const x,Lambda: Double): Double;
```

Using procedures and functions

procedure identifier(actual parameter list);
my result := function identifier(actual parameter list);

where *actual parameter list* is of the form

        comma-separated identifier list

(For example)
_____

```
SumArray(TopTen, TopSum);

Edit1.Text := FloatToStr(Growth(0.03,2.5));
```

Defining user types

type *enumerated type name = (comma separated identifier list);*

(For example)
_____

```
type TDays = (Monday,Tuesday,Wednesday,Thursday,
              Friday,Saturday,Sunday);

type set type name = set of base ordinal type;
```

(For example) _____

```pascal
type TSetDays = set of TDays;

type array type name = array [ordinal subrange] of a type;
```

(For example) _____

```pascal
type TLetterCount = array ['A'..'Z'] of Integer;

type record type name = record
                          field name 1: type 1;
                          field name 2: type 2;
                          ...
                          field name n: type n;
                 end;
```

(For example) _____

```pascal
type
  TDate = record
            DayNo: 1..31;
            MonthNo: 1..12;
            Year: 1900..2100;
        end;

type class type name = class (ancestor type)
private
  ...
public
  ...
end;
```

(For example) _____

```pascal
type
  TComplex = class(TObject)
  private
    FRealPart: Integer;
    FImagPart: Integer;
  public
    procedure Add (const First,Second: TComplex);
    procedure Multiply (const First,Second: TComplex);
    function ToStr: string;
    procedure ToComplex (AString: string);
  end;
```

Using user types

```
set variable := [members of base ordinal type]
```

_____

```
OurFreeDays := [Saturday];
```

Within a suitable expression

```
enumerated variable
```

_____

```
Dec(Today,4);
```

```
array variable[index]
```

_____

```
TopTen[3] := TopTen[1] / 2;
```

```
record variable.field name
```

_____

```
StartDate.DayNo := 1;
```

```
class type name.method name
```

_____

```
AComplex.Add(BComplex,CComplex);
```

Exceptions

```
try
  statements A
  try
    statements B
  finally
    statements C
  end
except
  statements D
end
```

(**For example**) _____

```
try
  Reset(RainFile);
  Read(RainFile,RainGrid);
finally
  CloseFile(RainFile);
end;
```

Units

```
unit identifier;
interface
uses list of units;
public declarations
implementation
uses list of units used locally;
private declarations
implementation of procedures and functions
initialization
initialization code
end.
```

(**For example**) _____

```
unit Unit2;
interface
procedure test(var first: Integer; second: Single);
{this is a test procedure to illustrate the development
  process}
implementation
uses dialogs;
procedure test(var first: Integer; second: Single);
begin
  ShowMessage('procedure test not yet available');
end;
end.
```

List of operators

For integer types: + - * **div mod**

For example
_____

```
CoinCount := Rem div 50;
```

For real types: + - * /

For example
_____

```
Area := 2*Height*(Length+Width) + Ceiling;
```

For Boolean types: **and not or xor**

For example
_____

```
This and That
```

Relational operators: = <> < > <= >=

For example
_____

```
(Months mod 3 = 0) and (Months > 0)
```

in (for sets)

For example
_____

```
Monday in HisBusyDays
```

Commonly used functions

Mathematical functions

```
Abs, ArcTan, Cos, Sin, Exp, Ln, Pi, Sqr, Sqrt
```

For example
_____

```
AngleA := ArcTan(x/y)*180/Pi;
```

Conversion functions:

```
IntToStr, StrToInt, FloatToStr, StrToFloat
```

For example
_____

```
Edit4.Text := FloatToStr(AngleA);
```

Index